Rhythm & Blues

In New Orleans

Also by John Broven

**South to Louisiana, The Music of the Cajun Bayous
(Pelican, 1983)**

Rhythm & Blues

In New Orleans

John Broven

PELICAN PUBLISHING COMPANY

GRETNA 1988

Copyright © 1974
By John Broven
All rights reserved

First printing, April 1978
First paperback printing, October 1983
Second paperback printing, July 1988

Library of Congress Cataloging in Publication Data

Broven, John.
    Rhythm and Blues in New Orleans

    Includes discographies.
    Bibliography: p.
    Includes index.
    1. Blues (songs, etc.) Louisiana New Orleans
History and criticism. I. Title.
ML3561.B63B76   1978   784   77-13351
ISBN 0-88289-433-1

First published in Great Britain as *Walking to New Orleans: The
Story of New Orleans Rhythm and Blues* by Blues Unlimited,
38A Sackville Road, Bexhill-on-Sea, Sussex, England.

Manufactured in the United States of America
Published by Pelican Publishing Company, Inc.
1101 Monroe Street, Gretna, Louisiana, 70053

CONTENTS

To the memory of my father and Mike Leadbitter. And thanks to the musicians.

AUTHOR'S NOTE AND ACKNOWLEDGMENTS

Now Marcia's record shop in Bexhill really was a funky little place. It couldn't have been more than ten feet by ten with the sparsest of furnishing and decoration, but it didn't matter. Quite simply, Marcia's won hands down over her more glamorous competitors because she always had the latest American releases when the others didn't want to know. And in 1957 and 1958 that was something else, so we never missed out on the latest Fats Domino single on London-American or for that matter, Huey Smith's "Don't You Just Know It" on the maroon and gold Columbia label. Funny, really, but I never looked on those particular records at the time as anything other than great rock 'n' roll. Their New Orleans origin never really came into it, but I don't think I was alone in my ignorance. Somehow New Orleans has never received the wide recognition it deserves for its vast contribution to rhythm and blues and rock 'n' roll, or until recently that is. Those soaring sax breaks, those jazzy guitar licks, those pulsating piano patterns, those socking drum rhythms, that's New Orleans, that's rock 'n' roll.

Even when I started writing for *"Blues Unlimited"* in 1963 I still missed out on New Orleans, apart from a review of the Fats Domino London concerts in 1967. This blind spot in my musical appreciation was not really cured until I went to the United States in 1970 on a trip with Robin Gosden and Mike Leadbitter. New Orleans was our first port of call, and after meeting Huey Smith, Professor Longhair, Archibald, and Boogie Bill Webb in the space of two short days, it suddenly hit me, the famous New Orleans R & B artists were still alive, still capable of playing fine music and yet they'd been forgotten, forgotten. "Let's try and do something about this," I said to myself and it was this resolve that sparked off my research, fired with no little enthusiasm for the music itself.

This book is the result and in attempting to document the fluctuating fortunes of the New Orleans musical story, I have tried to detail the major events and pinpoint the important participants, and place them in the all-embracing context of the development of American popular music, both black and white. I have attempted to overcome my isolation from the scene of action—England is some 4,500 miles distant from New Orleans—and at the same time avoid any foibles of personal interpretation by relying much on the spoken word. My concentration on the record scene, as opposed to other aspects of the music business is intentional, since its influence was wider, more permanent. That said I make no apologies for underlining the importance of the hit record. "Commercial trash," some may say, but records are made to sell, to make money, and in doing so direct future trends in music. New Orleans certainly did just that.

I have quoted from the *"Billboard"* record charts throughout the text and I have referred to their R & B charts until November 1955, at which point in time the national "Hot 100" chart was introduced.

It would have been impossible for me to complete this book without the help of so many friends, collectors and enthusiasts. In England, my grateful thanks to Mike Leadbitter for his unselfish help and encouragement, Bill Millar for his constant interest and support, Tom Stagg for enlightening the early New Orleans music scene and writing the fine foreword, and Bob Trick for his enthusiasm for the project and the excellent drawings. In their own way, the following have readily come to my assistance whenever asked, whether in opening their files, supplying photographs or playing rare records: Bruce Bastin, Robin Gosden, Bill Greensmith, Simon Napier, Pete Preston, Steve Richards, Clive Richardson, Mike Rowe, Dave Sax, Roy Simonds, Ray Topping, Mike Vernon, Dave Williams and Valerie Wilmer. In Europe, Karl Gert zur Heide has never stopped sending information, and thanks are also due to Hans Andreasson, Jacques Demetre and indirectly Jonas Bernholm, Bertrand Demeusy and Kurt Mohr. In the United States, I am indebted to the complete generosity of James La Rocca and his whole family who housed and fed me with such lavishness in 1970 and 1973, and the help offered by Barret Hansen, Pete Lowry, Frank Oddo, Terry Pattison, Steve La Vere and Chris Strachwitz of Arhoolie Records.

I am deeply grateful to the following for the use of extracts from their own taped interviews: John Abbey (Harold Battiste,

Johnny Vincent), Richard Allen of Tulane University Jazz Archives (the late Harrison Verrett), Charlie Gillett (Lee Allen, Shirley Goodman), Mike Leadbitter (James Booker), Jim Santella (Dave Bartholomew), Art Turco (Bobby Robinson) and Ian Whitcomb (Art Rupe).

And then those wonderful, beautiful people in New Orleans who took such an interest in my project and offered so much help in broadening my knowledge and understanding of their own scene, past and present. Words are not enough to express my gratitude to Gerri Hall, Justin Adams, the late Archibald, Chuck Badie, Joe Banashak, Dave Bartholomew, Milton Batiste, Erving Charles, Jr., Lawrence Cotton, Frank Fields, Henry "Hawk" Hawkins, Clarence "Frogman" Henry, Chris Kenner, Earl King, Cosimo Matassa, Deacon John Moore, Warren Myles, Art Neville, Professor Longhair, Mac Rebennack, Al Reed, Tommy Ridgley, Marshall Sehorn, Huey Smith, Jim Stewart, Willie Tee, Allen Toussaint, Earl Turbinton, Alvin "Red" Tyler and Boogie Bill Webb. Thanks are also due to Candy Green, Jay Miller, Floyd Soileau, Johnny Vincent and the Musicians' Union. Everyone spoke so freely and with an expression and artistry, natural to all Southerners, that had to be marvelled at. However, ultimate responsibility in publication must be entirely my own.

My eternal thanks must go to my mother and late father who tolerated so much that was intolerable on my part. I have to admit that the great music which blasted from my record player did not gain anything as it travelled from one end of the house to the other, disappearing as it did in a mass of distorted bass notes in the family lounge.

And, last of all, I must hope that this book, "Walking To New Orleans," will justify all the helpfulness shown towards me during my research.

Polegate, Sussex, 1973   JOHN BROVEN

FOREWORD BY TOM STAGG

The Early Days

Although in the past thousands of words have been written on the origins of New Orleans music the task today is really just as difficult as it was at the beginning. The modern historian has without doubt more background material to work from, and from the 1950's onwards many of the older musicians have been interviewed, but with this greater knowledge has come conflicting reports, dates and occurrences. The project was started far too late, and so this foreword will just try and pinpoint known facts and steer away from some of the fantasy which has grown with the music up to the present day.

New Orleans music was founded in a cosmopolitan atmosphere which absorbed the influences of many indigenous cultures. As a major American seaport in the nineteenth century the City was inhabited by people of many colours and customs. The American had already taken his roots, coming from British, French, Spanish, Italian and even Chinese stock, and on the other hand the newly freed Negro of African and West Indian descent had already begun to mix with the poorer Cuban and Haitian immigrants and the American Indian. With this already split environment the City found itself divided, an American city west of Canal Street—"uptown," and east of Canal Street a French city—"downtown." In the heart of downtown New Orleans was the Vieux Carre, later to be known as Storyville, the Red Light District and today the tourist stricken French Quarter, but in the early days the district was populated with French families, their Negro servants and the families of mixed descent, the Creoles of Color. New Orleans always having been a city of strict social upbringing, classes and barriers, sometimes found it difficult to accept the Creoles, but many of them became successful, especially in popular social events such as the French Opera. The musicians of the French Opera were in the main trained in Europe; the young Creoles found an outlet in this environment, an acceptance which brought with it great prestige. There was an abundance of symphony orchestras, many of them using Creoles, especially in the reed and string sections, and it was these musicians who got together the dance bands, large trained units who played the social events in the Vieux Carre and uptown for the white American families. Brass bands were popular amongst the Creoles and the standards of music were high, they played from written arrangements, popular classical pieces and military numbers, but as early as 1885 there was a report of the Excelsior Cornet Band playing their standard arrangements followed by a waltz. These bands got their work from the many social clubs, masonic lodges and the like. They played for parties, exhibitions, social gatherings, outdoor and indoor dances and for funerals, the people following these bands often numbering up to three thousand. One of the earliest reports of a brass band in New Orleans is in fact about 100 years before 1885 when a marching band met a party of immigrant Carmelite nuns, but nothing further is known about this occurrence.

The Vieux Carre was already a lucrative spot for musicians, the atmosphere and environment were just right, and in the section there was an abundance of musically untrained entertainers, hurdy gurdy men, piano and guitar players, some strangers to the City, some from uptown. They played popular and love songs, in 1890 "After The Ball Is Over" was all the rage. The uptown musicians were in the main poor and uneducated, they felt musically inferior to their Creole counterparts, and although the same outlet through music was open to them they found it difficult to assimilate European culture. To them the problem became worse after the 1894 enactment of legislative code No. 111 which included Creoles in restrictions of racial segregation. The Creoles made the most of this set-back; although proud people with a high status, they took advantage of getting the best jobs working for white families. There was a natural resentment by the uptown musicians, who themselves had brass and dance bands, but they were unschooled in comparison to the Creole orchestras. Their only outlet was to play for their own people, and so from a struggle to mimic and copy the Creole music an improvised and hot style of music gradually emerged. By 1899 when the Spanish-American War ended the musicians returning found the Creole status declining, they just could not survive in the new society. The old Vieux Carre had been small in comparison to the rest of the City, some of the wealthier families had already left and the coloured community liked this new hot music which satisfied their needs. The brass bands became noisier, the Creoles found it hard to survive against the uptown bands without playing in a hotter alien style and the scenes on the streets became rough with bands trying to "cut" each other, the noisiest bands taking the "second line" with them.

Three years previous to 1899 a hard blow hit the Vieux Carre area. Sidney Story, a New Orleans alderman, forced a city ordinance which restricted prostitution to a thirty-eight block red light district adjoining Canal Street, known then and to this day as Storyville. The toughest characters in town moved in, and in this rough tough district there was money to be made for the hot bands and solo entertainers. Outside the district there was still work for musicians at society dances, wearing military jackets and reading the music. Many younger musicians were moving into town from outlying locations, and they continued to play in the city the new rags which had become popular, these three or four strain tunes which the musicians had adapted from orchestral ragtime then being played by the remainder of the Creole dance orchestras.

Although this book is primarily concerned with the Negro musicians of New Orleans it must be remembered that the white musicians were also developing the music, and as early as 1901 Jack Laine was leading what he called a ragtime band in the city.

The Red Light became notorious; prostitutes, hustlers, pimps, gamblers and thieves plied the streets. Saloons, bawdy houses and high-class brothels lined the streets block by block, and then in 1913 following a killing in the Tuxedo Dance Hall the dance halls were closed down in the district. This hit many of the musicians hard, and small groups sprung up in the new cabarets which blossomed, the standard of music taking a step backward as with lesser men any arrangements suffered and hot improvisations as fill-ins were the order of the day. This new popular music spread to the brass bands and the new Tuxedo Brass Band began to take work from the older reading bands like the Excelsior.

After rumours and speculation Storyville was closed down on November 12, 1917, following War and Navy Department orders—it was too great a hazard to national interest. The result was that many of the houses of ill-repute were closed down completely while others moved quietly away to the uptown honky tonks. The musicians were hit hard, and many of them found themselves out of work; it was especially hard for the abundance of piano players who had made a good living in the multitude of cheap brothel establishments. The better musicians took the call and went North and West to New York, Chicago and California, following in the footsteps of musicians who had already established themselves there. The lesser trained musicians stayed behind and made a living where they could, many took day jobs while others went into the Army and Navy as the U.S.A. was now involved in the First World War. The migration out of New Orleans brought the Southern music to the World, but that is another story. Now we must go back briefly to 1908—to date there has been no mention of jazz music.

Jack Laine, born in 1873, formed his first band in 1891. He trained many fine white musicians including the members of a group known as the Dixieland Band. This band was formed in 1908, and playing hot ragtime and fast improvised blues achieved a certain amount of local success before being booked as the Original Dixieland Band in Chicago's Hotel Sherman in 1914. Whilst there a local "straight" musician using an obscene term referred to this strange music as "jass" or "jazz," and the term caught on. It was this white band which brought the word jazz, as referred to a hot band, back to New Orleans in 1920.

By 1919 when the last of the musicians had returned home after the war they found the music was changing, ragtime was out of fashion and the old tunes were back, only they were being played slower with swing. The violin and brass bass had lost popularity and instead the bands were boasting saxophones, banjos and the string bass. The brass bands were smaller and played in a much freer style, there were still good reading bands on the riverboats and the dance bands played hot, there was no noticeable split in the city as there had been twenty-five years previously. During the twenties work got less and less, this was the beginning of the Depression and times were hard. Few could afford to hire a brass band and small units got the advertising jobs playing on wagons riding up and down Canal Street. There were still lodge meeting parades and funerals but many of the older men were dying and the younger ones were using modern adaptations. The trumpet player Bunk Johnson was finding it difficult getting work, Punch Miller left town, Chris Kelly died in 1927, Buddy Petit in 1931. The A. J. Piron Orchestra, an old society band, found fame in New York, but Papa Celestin stayed at home and so did Sam Morgan and Kid Rena. John Handy was in town and beginning to make a name for himself, and so was Kid Howard, Thomas Valentine and so many others.

The Depression hit New Orleans hard in the thirties, there was little or no music around Canal Street and only a few neighbourhood dance halls survived, but there was no money to be made. To keep musicians together societies such as the W.P.A. and E.R.A. were formed but these depended upon people contacting the offices and the W.P.A. starting with 183 men was down to six by 1937. The brass bands died one after the other, and the few who survived played pop songs and hymns instead of the written marches of a few years earlier. There were no more bands on the river, solo piano players got any work that was going and a band rarely sported more than four pieces.

By the end of the 1930's jazz had developed into swing in the North, and the music had spread into the Midwest states. These territory bands used many New Orleans musicians and one in particular, the Don Albert Orchestra, used almost a complete New Orleans personnel out of San Antonio, Texas. Musicians away from home talked freely about the old days, and enough interest was aroused for enthusiasts to visit the city and begin to document the history of this musical city.

New Orleans has always had a musical heritage, this fore-word has only tried to pinpoint the salient features. This music came from Black Africa, Europe, from the rural blues, ragtime, church music and from the classics. It developed into jazz, dance and brass band music and on to rhythm and blues, rock 'n' roll and soul. The music has grown with the city so today's sound is black soul. Dixieland or jazz bands, white and coloured, are still there for the tourists, there is even a band back on the river again. The brass bands play the occasional funeral and if you are very lucky you can still find the odd neighbourhood dance. This has been the story of the beginnings, this book continues the saga of one of the natural environmental changes to New Orleans music, the story of rhythm and blues.

Purley, Surrey, 1973   TOM STAGG

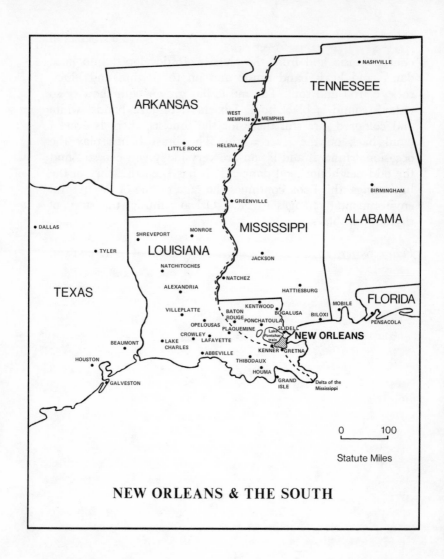

NEW ORLEANS & THE SOUTH

INTRODUCTION

"This time I'm walking to New Orleans,
I'm gonna need two pairs of shoes,
When I get through walking these blues,
When I get back to New Orleans."

So sings Fats Domino. He's got to get back to his home town even if he has to take the long way. The place has that sort of attraction.

Far better, though, to come in by aeroplane. And as you fly into the International Airport at Kenner in the dark on a regular Jumbo jet flight, and look down at the neon mass below, you can see how New Orleans got called "The Crescent City"—the bright lights of the big city literally hug the banks of the Mississippi in one huge half-moon shape. And could it be down there that Fats Domino, Professor Longhair, Huey Smiht, Allen Toussaint, Earl King, Ernie K-Doe, Lee Dorsey and a whole hos of talented musicians made their names and *actually* live?

New Orleans! A city of colour, gaiety and intrigue, bathed in its semi-tropical climate, colonial background, Catholic and Baptist religions. Standing on the banks of the mighty Mississippi River, it's known as "America's International Gateway," and because of its port is the focal point of the South which has attracted so many different races and cultures. It's a true melting-pot in which its population of just over one million has managed to retain its humour and *joie de vivre* to this day despite all sorts of social and political pressures.

New Orleans and the French Quarter, a hundred blocks of the Old World transferred into the New, with hustlers disdainfully grabbing the dollar bills from the gullible tourist and giving little in return. Oh yes, there are the alluring enticements of the strippers, the synthetic dixieland music blaring from the clubs on Bourbon Street, and, of course, the souvenir gift shops, antique stores and restaurants liberally spread throughout the Vieux Carre. New Orleans and the Mardi Gras with its colourful parades and drunken orgies. New Orleans and the wild Saturday night parties and fish fries, followed on Sunday by confession at church. New Orleans and memories of Marie Laveau and all that Voodoo and Gris-Gris. New Orleans and its High Society still clinging dutifully to its luxurious ballroom dances, operas and ballets. All magical ingredients to the exotic gumbo that is New Orleans.

New Orleans is for living and enjoyment all right, whether you are from the Garden District or the Projects, have a few oil wells tucked away or are supported by Welfare.

And the music, the real live music, goes with New Orleans just like red beans and rice. Its story since the War revolves around rhythm and blues music and it tells how New Orleans became an important musical centre in the 1950's and early 1960's and then lost its way, so much so that today thoughts have to be given towards a possible revival.

The freewheeling, happy-go-lucky music is known as the New Orleans Sound, which has its roots in the original beat of the old parade bands of the nineteenth century. Whether it's rhythm and blues, rock 'n' roll, soul, or modern jazz, the parade beat is the ubiquitous common factor, the foundation if you like. The music has changed, it's progressed, it's still moving. Whatever ephemeral sounds there have been, they have represented a kind of dressing up process which has mirrored the general fashions of the mercurial American music trends at any one time. New Orleans has followed the overriding patterns to keep up with the crowd, yet in doing so has managed to keep much of its own identity.

What is the New Orleans Sound?

"As long as there's a Mardi Gras or a second line funeral, you're gonna have the New Orleans beat," said Marshall Sehorn, the joint head of Sansu Enterprises, the leading record producers in New Orleans right now. "This is the home of the second line, that extra syncopated beat that has been in existence ever since the first black man picked up a tambourine."

The Second Line. Pianist Jelly Roll Morton told Alan Lomax how it was: "Those parades were really tremendous things, the drums would start off, the trumpets and trombones rolling into something like 'Stars and Stripes' or 'The National

Anthem' and everybody would strut off down the street, the
bass drum player twirling his beater in the air, the snare
drummer throwing his sticks up and bouncing them off the
ground, the kids jumping and hollering, the grand marshall
and his aides in their expensive uniforms moving along dignified,
women on top of women strutting along back of the aides and
out in front of everybody—the second line, armed with sticks
and bottles and baseball bats and all forms of ammunition to
fight the foe when they reached the dividing line. It's a funny
thing that the *second line* marched at the head of the parade
but that's the way it had to be in New Orleans."

The present musicians still have much awareness of their
heritage and the New Orleans Sound.

"I find that here in New Orleans," said Earl King, a highly
respected local artist and songwriter, "that people talk about
our sound, but I think in New Orleans the thing is the rhythm
in the tune. The individuals, the bands who never rehearse,
can perform together because they have adjusted themselves to
a certain mental tune, rhythmically. People may think of New
Orleans just being a mass of sound but we have general
rhythm attitudes that the people can play. It's an attitude,
they feel like that when they're fixing to play the riff, it's the
second line or something like that. And this thing that the
people adjust to, it just falls into place.

"The root of funk was created in the studios, Earl Palmer
the drummer was really responsible for that word 'funk.' He
would say all the time, like, if them guys like Lee Allen were
playing at the recording sessions, he would say, 'Look, man,
let's play a little funkier,' and the word would start going
around. So a guy like Jerry Wexler of Atlantic Records would
come down and say, 'Look, man, you're playing it, but you
ain't funky enough,' so you started saying it in the studio with
different people. Then it emanated right on out until everyday
people just say it. It implies a concentrated rhythm and
stiffness and more concentration. Sometimes Charles Williams,
'Hungry,' they called him, a drummer that intensified everything, like you thought you had a rhythm going and he would
slide in and start playing. He would tighten everything up and
this would be funky because everything would get stiff, man.

And real there, it was like magic when he would sit behind the drums.

"The funky thing is really an extension of the dixieland, it was just that early dixie we had here, it was somewhat sophisticated and less syncopated to have any definite abruptness. Then as the years went they started syncopating dixie here and there, now when it got syncopated some of the drummers started listening and what we call 'funk' today goes back into the dixie and when you hear where they first started syncopating, you say 'Uh huh, that's where it came from, man.' Because today it's nothing to hear drummers accent the syncopated things and one time it was hard to get outside drummers play. If he was from here he could play anywhere in the world."

Alvin Tyler is a well-known and respected New Orleans musician, everyone calls him "Red." He is a very talented tenor and baritone saxophone player who was present on countless recording sessions. He's been right through the New Orleans post-war scene as a sideman, bandleader, artist, writer, arranger, producer and label owner. Today he leads a swinging modern jazz quartet in New Orleans. Red has not forgotten his early influences:

"Really I had no one in the family who played music, none. We had an old piano and I fooled around on that. But it wasn't until 1939 that I first became interested in music. Going back to the second line at the burials, remember, when the jazz musicians would die, after they went to the cemetery they went into the real groovy second line music and all. Well, I stayed on Bienville about five blocks from St Louis Cemetery, so all these things passed in my neighbourhood and I was quite familiar with the second line beat and all that.

"I don't think the true New Orleans Sound has really been captured yet. There are certain little things that the rest of this country, in the world, there are certain little things they still don't know, a certain little groove that they haven't really heard. Actually all the older musicians, the musicians I came up with, in the back of their minds they constantly hear the second line beat and it's all from the bass drum, '*bom . . . bom-bom . . . de-dom . . . dom-dom*,' and this is where the groove is. You see, there is a certain group of guys and when they say, 'Let's get funky!' that is what they hear in the back of their minds, they hear this bass drum. You see the guys going around with their umbrellas and shakin', this is where the groove really is!"

PART I

Rhythm and Blues, 1946-55

Hit Singles by New Orleans R & B Artists

Note: This Graph reflects the *number* of chart entries, not the relative sales volumes.

Allowance must be made for the period 1946–1955 when the hits only appeared in the more restrictive R & B charts; from November 1955 the "Top 100" lists were used, thus giving a far wider range.

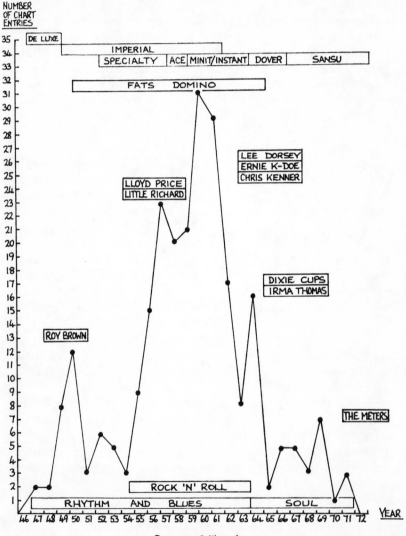

Source: Billboard

JOHN BROVEN
BOB TRICK

Background

The War years gave the break which led to the relaxation of the grip the handful of major record companies had over the music business, the loosening of the hold of the New York—Hollywood "Tin Pan Alley" axis, if you like. Musically the big, dazzling dance and swing bands continued unabated, spreading joy and happiness, veneer-like, through a nation in times of distress.

The destruction of the old order began when the radio networks disagreed over licensing terms with ASCAP, the cartel of a small and select membership of writers and composers who had a monopoly in the field of performance licensing. If you were a budding writer and couldn't get entry into ASCAP you might as well have forgotten about it. Following the disagreement, ASCAP songs were banned from the air on January 1, 1941. As a result a new licensing organisation, Broadcast Music Inc. (BMI) was formed, and by the time the ban was lifted in October 1941, BMI was firmly established and growing rapidly. As BMI stated in their own publicity handouts, "BMI has dropped the bars and now the new men, the young men, the men you have not known, can bring you their songs."

Just as significant for the record industry was the ban on all recording announced by J. C. Petrillo, President of the American Federation of Musicians, in July 1942 which was prompted by the anxiety over the effects of radio airplay and jukeboxes on live music. Coupled with the rationing of shellac for the 78 rpm records, this ban effectively put the record industry in cold storage for two years. Not only the record companies, but the radio stations and jukebox operators were hit. And the public, with their hands full of wartime dollars, were desperate for new records.

The Negro market was ready for exploitation, the whole field was wide open. There were no records, no radio broadcasts, no distribution set-ups for independents, few pressing plants. Problems had to be overcome, of course, like the matrix system was patented by the major record companies, so you had to go to them to start with to get masters made. The lack of shellac for pressing records presented obvious headaches. If you were lucky you could get enough to manufacture 500 records, and it had to be cash on the nail, otherwise the guy in the queue behind would have it. But it was worth persevering. After all, it was impossible not to make money when you knew that the record stores were selling only old 78's, and the Victor salesmen wouldn't bother to set foot in the ghettoes to supply them with new releases.

As for the music itself, the solid rhythm foundations of swing bands like Jimmie Lunceford, Cab Calloway, Lionel Hampton, and Count Basie had great appeal to the dance loving black community, and it was these bands which started playing the early rhythm and blues form. Booting saxes, increased use of electrical amplification and the subtle influence of gospel music all played their part in moulding the eventual shape of R & B, and after the end of the War, it was all systems go.

New Orleans Jazz

"New Orleans was another scene in the 1940's, it was all jazz," said Ralph Bass, a famous record producer with Chess. "New Orleans blues came later." It was pretty accurate as far as generalisations go, and the dixieland bands were still getting plenty of jobs at dances and other functions, besides becoming an important tourist attraction.

Traditional bands like Kid Thomas, Capt. John Handy, Billie and De De Pierce, George Lewis, were still playing the old dixieland sounds, although by the early 1950's they were including occasional R & B based tunes like "Boogie Woogie," "Shake Rattle And Roll," and "Caldonia" in their acts. There are no stop-start phases in the history of music, and with this overlap it is understandable how the traditional dixieland and R & B musicians mingled and played together, as they still do today. Most of the R & B musicians were young men, a third strain of New Orleans musicians who were as sympathetic and adaptable in their approach as their fathers and grandfathers before them. R & B was a new music, but the roots were not lost.

Clarence Ford, a saxophone player who was the cornerstone of Fats Domino's band for many years, came from a musical family where six uncles played in different bands. He got his first job with the famed Eureka Brass Band in 1945. "I only knew four numbers," he said, "but that was all we played on Mardi Gras day." In 1948 Ford joined a band led by Wallace Davenport, a trumpeter who had started with the dixieland bands of Sidney Desvigne and Papa Celestin. This band was called the Be-Bop Jockeys, whose very name gave acknow-ledgment to its mentors, Dizzy Gillespie and Charlie Parker, who were terribly influential amongst the young New Orleans horn men. "In fact I had two bands then," said Davenport, "one for playing dixieland and the other for modern jazz." Later on, Davenport played with Lionel Hampton, Lloyd Price, Ray Charles and Fats Domino, further emphasising the all-round nature of his musical abilities. Ford and Davenport, in their eclecticism, were not untypical of their generation of musicians in New Orleans.

The Pianists

Like the dixieland players, the pianists spanned the War years. In their heyday in the 1920's, the pianists were featured at small clubs, brothels and dives, and their musical repertoire was expected to be broad and wide to cater for every request. They were particularly popular at parties and Saturday night fish fries where they used to play for moonshine whisky and homebrew. In their playing, it seemed that every source of New Orleans cosmopolitan culture had been absorbed, and the older piano styles are still extant in the works of Jack Dupree and Cousin Joe. Fats Pichon and Archibald, who were both active in the early post-war years, have since died, but of all these men it is Professor Longhair who is the most important.

PROFESSOR LONGHAIR

"The first time I saw 'Fess, there was this guy in a tuxedo, he was real real bald like Yul Brynner. I said, 'Wow, man, where's Professor Longhair?' And that's him with tails on." Earl King was rapping with Al Reed, a local songwriter and artist. "The first time I saw 'Fess," replied Reed, "I saw him below the Canal, a little joint on Derbigny Street at the end

of the nightwalk. They had mud out there about 8 feet deep
and they had cows and pigs over the fence. And him, him and
Jessie Hill. Jessie had a little snare drum on a little chair, had
that guitar, and believe me while 'Fess was playing and kicking
on the piano, the wall was shaking. It was the littlest, tiniest
joint I've ever been in. Oh man, first time I saw 'Fess, it was
an experience."

The musicians in New Orleans have a special respect for
Professor Longhair, as indeed have most people who've come
in contact with New Orleans music. Yes, 'Fess is a great and
original pianist, and when somebody like Allen Toussaint
describes him as "The Bach of Rock 'n' Roll" then you have
to sit up and take notice. His innovatory style is universally
recognised, laden as it is with Spanish and rhumba accents,
which has influenced every modern New Orleans pianist.

Alvin Tyler knows it too: "The first guy to come along was
Professor Longhair, but 'Fess was not as equipped as Huey
Smith was. Now Huey Smith heard 'Fess and he liked what he
heard and tried to copy him but he couldn't, because it was
so unorthodox so he came up with another kind of thing.
Allen Toussaint was influenced by Huey Smith, who was
therefore influenced by Professor Longhair. So it was a line."

Regrettably, Professor Longhair has not benefitted from his
unique talent. Most of the hard luck stories which come out
of New Orleans seem to revolve around him and to see him
living poorly in a decaying wooden home on South Rampart
Street makes you realise that here is somebody who's seen hard
times. It can't all be explained away by bad record deals,
managers running off with money, or even his card playing
habits.

Longhair's real name is Henry Roeland Byrd and he was born
in 1918 in the Klan dominated town of Bogalusa which is
situated on the Pearl River near the Louisiana/Mississippi
border. His family moved to New Orleans when he was young,
and Longhair soon found that he was able to reproduce the
styles of pianists he heard like Sullivan Rock, Kid Stormy
Weather and Bertrand, and turn them into his own thing. It's
what you'd call natural talent.

He tells how he got started in 1949 when he was in the old

The French Quarter. PHOTOGRAPH BY MIKE ROWE

Old Lady on Rampart Street. PHOTOGRAPH BY MIKE ROWE

The Fairview Baptist Church Band. PHOTOGRAPH BY CHRIS STRACHWITZ

J. & M. Studio Building.
PHOTOGRAPH BY JOHN BROVEN

Cosimo's Studio Building.
PHOTOGRAPH BY JOHN BROVEN

Jazz City Studio Building. PHOTOGRAPH BY JAMES LA ROCCA

Champion Jack Dupree, c. 1958. PHOTOGRAPH COURTESY MIKE LEADBITTER

Cousin Joe, 1968.
PHOTOGRAPH BY
PETER LOWRY

Archibald, 1970. PHOTOGRAPH BY JOHN
BROVEN

Professor Longhair, 1972. PHOTOGRAPH BY CHRIS STRACHWITZ

Roy Brown, 1949. PHOTOGRAPH COURTESY BILL GREENSMITH

Paul Gayten, 1949. PHOTOGRAPH
COURTESY MIKE LEADBITTER

Annie Laurie, 1949. PHOTOGRAPH
COURTESY MIKE LEADBITTER

Larry Darnell, 1949. PHOTOGRAPH
COURTESY MIKE LEADBITTER

Eddie Gorman, 1949. PHOTOGRAPH
COURTESY MIKE LEADBITTER

Fats Domino and Harrison Verrett, c. 1955.

PHOTOGRAPH COURTESY MIKE LEADBITTER

Fats Domino and Dave Bartholomew, c. 1956.

PHOTOGRAPH COURTESY MELODY MAKER

Tommy Ridgley, 1950.

PHOTOGRAPH COURTESY TOMMY RIDGLEY

Caldonia Inn listening to Dave Bartholomew's band and asked if he could sit in for Bartholomew's pianist, Salvador Doucette, when he took a break. With Longhair playing his original piano sounds, the crowds started coming in from the streets and Longhair was hired on the spot. That's history according to the Professor.

After this Byrd formed his own group which was called the Four Hairs combo, and he got the name of Professor Longhair. His first record session was held later in 1949 when he was waxed by Jesse Erikson, the owner of the Dallas-based Star Talent label. Four titles were cut, his famous "She Ain't Got No Hair," "Mardi Gras In New Orleans," "Professor Long-hair's Boogie" and "Bye Bye Baby," and all were released with credits to "Professor Longhair and his Shuffling Hungarians." The session was made at the Hi-Hat club.

Soon after, Longhair was introduced to Mercury Records by William B. Allen who ran a radio and instrument shop. A session was held in makeshift studios on Canal Street and one of the songs, "Baldhead," a remake of "She Ain't Got No Hair," reached No. 5 in *"Billboard's"* R & B Chart in August 1950. Although a follow-up was released, there were financial disagreements and so the link with Mercury was severed.

A meeting with Ahmet Ertegun in New Orleans led to Longhair recording for Atlantic in 1950, but the Mercury success was not repeated. He recorded for Federal in 1951 and "Gone So Long" was a moderate R & B seller, but he did not record again until November 1953 when Atlantic took up his contract once more. From these sessions came "Tipitina" which is one of Longhair's best records and a classic example of early New Orleans R & B. It made the local New Orleans sales charts briefly in March 1954.

Atlantic issued an album in 1972 compiled of the recordings made by Longhair in 1950 and 1953 and this release gives a good insight into the originality of Longhair's music. They have also promised royalties of 5 per cent.

Around about 1953, Wasco Records, of Memphis, put out a crude 78 which Longhair cannot recall making; it could have been a pirate record of a club performance. Leola Rupe's West Coast-based Ebb Records came to town in 1957 and

B

released three singles from the long session they had, and in 1959 Longhair had two records out on Joe Ruffino's Ron label. Another version of "Mardi Gras In New Orleans" retitled "Go To The Mardi Gras" (he had already cut this song for Star Talent and Atlantic) was the highlight of the Ron session and is still played every year in New Orleans at Mardi Gras time. The All South distributors reckon that they move 15,000 copies annually, but it's no use worrying about royalties because he was probably given a straight session fee in the first place. He hasn't received any, of course.

In 1962 he had one session for Rip Records and then he was recorded by Watch in 1963 and 1964. "Big Chief" is the best known of the Watch records, mainly because Dr John recorded it on his "Gumbo" album and gave the tune a lot of publicity. The Longhair credit is a bit of a misnomer on this typical Indian chant since Earl King handles the vocal and whistling chores. It was Earl King who also shared the vocal with Longhair on "Third House From the Corner," a travesty for Longhair as King exhorts him to moan out his vocal trademark *"Tra La La"* (that's all, nothing else) like some mindless machine. Musically, the third Watch, "There Is Something On Your Mind," is one of the best things Longhair has put down on record, with a superb Fats Domino-inspired arrangement by Wardell Quezergue.

And that's Professor Longhair's record career to date. A lot of good, interesting records but very few which are outstanding. The instrumental accompaniment, led by his piano, is where he scores since his vocals lack range and in a way fail to communicate with his audience. But this does not explain why he was out of work for most of the 1960's.

Happily, things are taking a better turn in more recent times following successful appearances at the Louisiana Heritage Festival in 1972 and 1973 and the Montreux Festival, in Switzerland, in June 1973. A decent album now would do him the world of good.

Alvin Tyler seems to say it all, in summing up the real importance of Professor Longhair to New Orleans and the outside world: "Now the thing about Professor Longhair is that his piano playing is unorthodox. Now to a trained musician, what he was doing was so unorthodox that you had to listen because it was something different. You know, usually with a trained musician we have a certain pattern we are going to play, follow a certain normal chord progression, rhythms and things. He would throw them all out the window and we'd go and listen at this guy when we got off of our gigs because it was so different.

"It was a gas to play with him. I have on occasions played with him on gigs and recording sessions and it was so unorthodox. It was funny to you at all times, because the things he did were so unorthodox until when he'd do some of these things it would just amuse you. You understood what he was doing but it was really unorthodox and it was a gas. But he had a group, none of the musicians he used were of the calibre that could sit in with us, because their musical knowledge was limited. But they worked together hand in glove, they understood each other, but when that ended, it's never been the same since. I recall going into a recording studio with 'Fess, and you take a trained musician and he'd play his thing, he found it was quite awkward, some guys couldn't get it. There was no sense in telling 'Fess, 'No, what we're gonna do is four bars here, two bars here,' it didn't mean anything to him. So you had to have the right people with him.

"He's never been big, he's never made any money and to me he's the most unique musician in rock or R & B to come out of New Orleans, personally, that's my belief. And he's never really made it. He had a hit in 1950 with 'Baldhead' but how much of a hit was it? It was never the kind of hit that would put him in the status symbol of a Cadillac. He never had enough money to buy a Cadillac. In other words, the success of a guy was judged in terms of how soon he could get his first Cadillac. He was never in that category.

"I think he was abused and misled by a lot of local people that handled him. You see, with 'Fess not being well educated, he'd make a record and nine out of ten times it would be his own material. Now the monies that he should have got as the writer, the artist, was handled by some of the people that was smarter than he was. So not being a smart guy, saying, 'Here's my contract, I'm gonna get my lawyer check on how many sales of this,' he would go up to the guys if he was up against it and say, 'Look, man, I'm in trouble, they're gonna turn my lights off, my rent is due.' So they would give him 150 bucks, then $50, then $25, so even if the tune was a hit he never knew it because at the end of the year, when it came to settling up, they would say, 'You remember when you borrowed $150, you borrowed $75.' So really he was had.

"He's never had the recognition, he'll probably die and then somebody will say, 'Hey, man, listen to this guy.' It's too late. Things are getting better now but it's still small time. Maybe they would appreciate him more in England. I would like to see him get in the position where he can make some money before he passes. I think maybe he's a little sick now and he's had a stroke. I see him now and then but he doesn't look well."

Marshall Sehorn mentions with obvious delight that 'Fess was captured on film "for posterity" at the Montreux Festival. That's how they feel about him in New Orleans.

CHAMPION JACK DUPREE

Jack Dupree was raised in New Orleans and although he had moved away from the city by 1940 he had been there long enough to pick up his own style which is still recognisable today as New Orleans. "I spent a lot of time in the streets and in the clubs," he said, "and one man took me under his wing. His name was Drive 'Em Down and he played piano in a barrelhouse where all the rough cats hung out. Drive 'Em Down would let me sit near him and watch him play. After a while . . . he began to teach me his style." After a prolific recording career in Chicago and New York stretching through from 1940 to 1960, Dupree moved to Europe and now lives in Halifax, England. He has managed to retain his zestful show-manship, and his impish, rib-tickling humour which all reflect his New Orleans background.

COUSIN JOE

Cousin Joe is a pianist and guitarist well known on Bourbon Street. He is a fine entertainer who somehow has been unable to equate his entertaining abilities with recordings of real merit.

Much of his work has been done outside the Crescent City and of his many recordings the De Luxe, Imperial and Flip cuts show most connection with the New Orleans R & B scene. He lives now in New Orleans and still plays; his deep growling voice, huge infectious laugh and a sly sense of humour are aided by a knocked-out piano style which harks back to a previous age.

WALTER "FATS" PICHON

Now deceased, Walter "Fats" Pichon was a popular club pianist, who spent many years playing on the riverboats. According to Dave Bartholomew he was a fine musician and a very fine arranger. He specialised in a sophisticated repertoire of popular standard melodies which was well received by the audiences at the Old Absinthe House on Bourbon Street where he was resident for a long time in the 1940's and early 1950's. He also had a nice line in refined boogie numbers. He recorded just for Raymac and De Luxe in the forties and an album for Decca in 1956.

ARCHIBALD

Archibald was one of the last in the long line of traditional New Orleans pianist entertainers. It had seemed that he had a promising future ahead of him when his first record, "Stack-A-Lee," sold well enough on Imperial to enter the R & B charts in October 1950. The record was in two parts and Archibald had plenty of scope to perform this old folk song as he must have done many times before in the bars and clubs of New Orleans, including a healthy ration of his delightful piano work.

A tour of the West Coast was organised but this was cancelled when Archibald fell sick with ulcer trouble. Although he had further records on Imperial and Colony, he never had the chance again and was not recorded after 1952. Johnny Vincent tried to record him for his Ace label in the late 1950's but said Archibald's voice had gone; Archibald himself said Vincent did not offer enough money.

Archibald was born Leon T. Gross in 1912 on September 14 at 12.16 a.m., just off Plum and Hillary in New Orleans, as he used to delight in telling. When he started playing the fraternity houses and the wild parties in the early days he was known as "Archie Boy" and he was mainly influenced by Burnell Santiago, the self-styled "King of Boogie" as well as other pianists like Eileen Dufeau, Miss Isobel and Stack-O-Lee. He was drafted into the Army in the War years and on his return continued playing in New Orleans before he was signed by Al Young, the talent scout, for Imperial in 1950. "Stack-A-Lee" was his first record.

He was resident at the Poodle Patio Club on Bourbon Street for many years, but when a small party visited him in 1970 at his small wooden one-storey home on 4th Street, it was clear times were not exactly good. He was suspicious, but after passing a bottle of whisky his confidence improved and he sat down at his battered piano and proceeded to give as good a show as one could wish for in an informal session on a wet Saturday April morning. He sang in a Kansas City shouting style, fond of scat improvisation, and among the songs he played were "Stack-A-Lee," "Blueberry Hill," "Swanee River Hop," "Early Morning Blues," "Pinetop's Boogie," "Muskrat Ramble" and an amazing "Hungarian Rhapsody Boogie." Even singing and playing in his own living room, he had tremendous presence, and it was easy to imagine his popularity in the bar clubs of New Orleans.

Somehow, Archibald's importance as one of the last links of the old New Orleans piano style has been overlooked, and now it's too late because he died of a heart attack in 1973. So, sadly, his music must remain a relic of the past, a magnificent pianist whose boogieing New Orleans style never came to grips with the rock 'n' roll age. One album might have made all the difference.

Cosimo Matassa and His Recording Studios

Said Mac Rebennack, the white New Orleans artist who is better known as Dr John, "Cosimo was the type of engineer who believed in one type of scene. He would set the knobs for the session and very rarely moved anything. If the piano was mixed too low at the beginning it would stay mixed too low until the end of the session, unless the producer came and changed it. But this was how record sessions were conducted for a long time. He developed what is known as the 'Cosimo Sound' which was strong drums, heavy bass, light piano, heavy guitar and light horn sound and a strong vocal lead.

"That was the start of what eventually became known as the New Orleans Sound with the guitar doubling the bass line, the baritone and tenor doubling the bass line, making it a real strong sound and playing around it. It got to be known as 'Cosimo's Sound' but it was the musicians' sound because they were playing the music. But it was his little mix job which got the credit, and the record companies used to say, 'Cos has got a good sound, so we'll cut a record in New Orleans.' There were so many hits coming out of New Orleans and this was why the record companies were interested in coming there."

The whole New Orleans R & B record scene was centred around the recording studios of Cosimo Matassa. Apart from isolated sessions in radio stations or on "field" locations, almost every R & B record made in New Orleans from the 1940's until the late 1960's was cut in his studios. Cosimo is mystified when asked why others did not try to establish another studio. "Beats the hell out of me, I don't know," he said. "It could be New Orleans is just like a big small town, and now it's only just growing out of that."

The first recording studio was the J & M Studio and located on North Rampart and Dumaine. "The studio started in 1945, as early as that," said Cosimo Matassa. "I was in the jukebox, the coin operating business, and we graduated to selling the records off phonographs, used things that we brought in. The customers then asked us for new ones. And then going into the new record business, going from an old record shop to a new record shop, we decided, well, let's put a studio in the back. And then I just gravitated on to the studio business out of the jukebox in time. I guess by the early 1950's I was out of the jukebox business, just doing the studio.

"The first thing we had was a Duo-Presto disc recorder, it was called a 28N, two Presto 8N recorders, and we used to do wild cuts on 33⅓ and 16-inch discs. That means everything had to be transferred just once generally, that 16-inch to what was originally the 78 masters. We cut two simultaneously and we didn't play the one that hopefully was going to be transferred to the master disc. You made a master and a safety, and you played back the safety to see what you got. So that meant all of the performances, there was no intercutting, no tape editing, in fact those were the good performances, probably some of the best. Because they were really performances as opposed to the synthesised record you make today, when you lay down the rhythm and start putting things on it, three months and 12 sessions later nobody knows what the original thing was really going to be like."

Tommy Ridgley could recall the old disc-cutting machine. "They had a man catch the wax as the needle was playing," he said, "the quality of mixing was poor. Nobody really knew what they were doing, we were all learning at the same time."

Cosimo continues: "I wasn't that market conscious (about rock 'n' roll) really, regrettably. Probably the biggest splurge of things was when all the first independent record companies were doing things that the majors weren't doing—or if they did they weren't bothering to promote them or sell them. This was about the time when Specialty Records, Aladdin Records, companies like that were running around the country recording R & B artists and selling, doing good business. Then Chess.

"The guys would come into town and say, 'New Orleans got some good records coming out, I want to record some.' So you take them to all the places and let them hear whoever is, in my opinion, worth a hearing and that sort of stuff. I was still a kinda general direction pusher, but obviously these guys decided on their own who they wanted. I never did really get into the thing of being a producer as such. I regret it now of course! I just enjoyed doing it.

"We didn't have any financial interest in these companies. Most of them came in, did whatever they had to, just pay their studio time. Most of the musicians either got nominal royalties and questionable accounting—you can quote me there, 'questionable accounting'—or they got nothing. A flat fee. I think the Union scale was $18.75 for a leader right at the beginning. We used to charge $15 an hour. Of course the bill would be for quite a few hours, because they would start from scratch. Like Fats Domino, he would usually start at 8, 9, 10 o'clock in the morning and run through to at least 5, and on, and this was doing things, boom, right on the disc or tape. No overdubbing.

"J & M Studio was on Rampart and Dumaine, and we moved from there to Governor Nicholls Street in 1956, changed the name to Cosimo's then. Everybody knew me by my first name, and mainly because they would say, 'What's your name?' and I would say 'Cosimo,' and they'd say, 'What's your first name?', you know (laugh). So that was enough to struggle with.

"Before we had used Cosimo's we had already gotten into tape. I bought one of the Ampex models 300's which was a $\frac{1}{4}$ inch single-channel tape machine before I moved over to Gov. Nicholls Street. I guess that opened up the first editing and intercutting possibilities, although there wasn't a lot of it done. Probably the biggest single thing that happened with those first tape things was that we sent a lot of the Fats Domino things out to the West Coast and Lew Chudd who owned Imperial Records used to have his engineers speed them up slightly in the transfers because, you know, whenever there is a popular record artist, all of the kids' bands emulate them. And the kids would come into the studio to make little records of their own, and they could never play in the keys of those things because they were never in a key! You know, they were in some speeded up thing, and all your harmonic relationships get distorted when you speed up the tape because you get an unharmonic type of, the intervals get distorted, spaced away from the tonic, the keys didn't sound right because they weren't. This happened a lot, it was fun really.

"I would say the first overdubbing as such was probably a

year or so after we moved to the second studio on Gov. Nicholls Street, we had a couple of three-track machines and it was a sweetening kind of overdub. Everything was done and then they decided to add something, and did an overdub on to the second tape, not in the sense of laying tracks and adding lead parts, and then adding the fill type things which grew into this final thing we've got now with everything synthetic, a brick at a time, you know. Which produces some great things but I don't particularly care for it. That interplay of musicians, the emotions you might say, doesn't prosper, although obviously now some guys can groove to the track, but it's not a jazz thing which is simultaneous.

"It's hard to say which sessions went best. There are two kinds of best. Best in the sense of those that work nice and those others that may not be easy to work with but what they did was good. Fats Domino was in that latter category. To tell you the truth, he was a pain in the ass to record. Not because he was a nasty guy about anything, but right in the middle of a take he'd say, 'How do I sound?', you know. Pretty bad, especially if it's the first good take of the thing you had."

The third studio, Jazz City, was opened up at 748, Camp Street in 1969. "I dug that name out for 'em," he said, "because I think if ever a city deserved a second name that fits, it's New Orleans and Jazz City. I had a penchant for locating places and deserted old buildings, but that was only because that's the cheapest place to find a lot of space. Actually Gov. Nicholls was two locations in a sense. When I first went there I went to 523 Gov. Nicholls and put in a small studio, about 17 feet × 28 feet, and then got the place next door, 525, Gov. Nicholls which is where we had the big studio, 35 feet × 75 feet. Well that building was sold to a real estate entrepreneur, who was going to do a thing in the French Quarter there. So that's why we got up on 748 Camp again because there was space to put in a studio. That one is 31 feet × 72 feet, something like that, and with the advent of amplified things and bigger groups you need a little room to let it get out.

"But we never had any trouble getting our sound or separation. People would walk in and say the place sounds 'live', but maybe it was 'live' in the sense that they heard something ringing around the room for a little while, but it wasn't live in the sense of being muddied. I always was careful of damping down the bottom end a lot so that most of the bottom end you heard was instruments.

"I would always pride myself in being able to walk out into a studio, stick a mike, the right microphone in the right place, and set up a group and record them. I think I can still do that. That comes from a guy who lays a lot of bricks, just the way that he knows how to grab a brick and trowel, you know. I've had my share.

"I don't know if you could call the 'Cosimo Sound' that distinctive. I tend to feel less about that than other people seem to. I'm not impressed with myself."

De Luxe Records

David and Julian Braun, the owners of De Luxe Records, came down to New Orleans from New Jersey looking for material for their new label in 1947. They were the first of many independent record company owners to realise that New Orleans had an abundance of talent that was ready for exploitation. Their enterprise was typical of the spirit of opportunity which gripped these independent companies, willing and eager as they were to step into markets that the major companies had chosen to ignore.

"The Braun Brothers were the first people to come out of town," said Cosimo Matassa. "People had been coming in and out of New Orleans, a few of the jazz type people before that. But a few of the guys made expeditions with portable disc machines and did some location blues and jazz things, at the time I didn't even know about." Cosimo was referring to the pre-war field trips of Victor, Decca, Okeh and others.

DAVE BARTHOLOMEW (I)

According to Dave Bartholomew, the Braun Brothers just walked around the clubs looking for talent. They told him they would like to record his band, and they recorded just about everybody else too. "Country Boy" was Bartholomew's biggest record for De Luxe, selling around 100,000 copies in 1949. It's still his best seller.

Dave Bartholomew had formed his own band in 1946 immediately after his return from the Army and had quickly established himself as the top bandleader in the town, with a reputation second to none. Red Tyler joined the band a little later as tenor player. "It was shortly after I was playing professionally that I joined Dave Bartholomew's band," he said, "and in this band were guys like Earl Palmer, drummer, Frank Fields, bassman, Ernest McLean, guitarist, Salvador Doucette was on piano, several other guys but Dave Bartholomew was one of the first local bands to record artists, Roy Brown, Fats Domino, people like this. To show you how far I'm going back, some of the first recordings on Roy Brown and some of the other artists were done at a local high school on the stage, they didn't have a studio here. The Dave Bartholomew Band was the band in the city as far as rhythm and blues was concerned. We played all the big dances, we played quite a few of the shows. At that time the Dew Drop was going, with the shows and everything. They used to have stage shows and we used to play those things.

"I think it was all good experience to work with Dave's band because he was truly a professional. He has a very firm hand. For a musician who is not capable he can put a lot of pressure on you, because he didn't permit goofing around, we didn't smoke or we didn't drink on the bandstand, except on rare occasions (laugh). But you came on time, you played the music the way it was, you started to tune the way it was supposed to be started, and if you didn't he called you down then. Very firm, but I think it was a good school for young musicians."

Bartholomew was soaked in the dixieland tradition, which still shows through in his red hot, driving trumpet playing and strong blues shouting voice. Born in the small town of Edgard, Louisiana some 30 miles from New Orleans, his father was Louis Bartholomew, a noted New Orleans tuba player. "My father had a fine band in New Orleans with Wilbert Tillman on brass and Willie Humphrey on clarinet. Later he played with the Kid Harrison band, this was dixieland and really a dance band. They had no radio stations to advertise so they used to get back on the back of trucks and I used to haul them all over. That's how I got started."

He was then contracted to play with Fats Pichon on the S.S. Capitol riverboat which used to leave New Orleans and go up to St Paul, Minnesota, and stay a week or two at St Louis which was the headquarters of the Strecfus family who owned the boats. Trips were then made up the Ohio and back to Cairo, Illinois, before returning to St Paul and then down to New Orleans. When Pichon left to be a single act at the Old Absinthe House in 1941, Dave Bartholomew took charge of the band until he was drafted in the Army in 1942. He went to France first and it was in the Army that he learnt to arrange whilst playing with the 196 AGF band.

With this sort of background, Dave Bartholomew had no difficulty in leading his band to the top of the New Orleans music scene. It was through recording, however, that he became recognised as a national name by writing and arranging for Fats Domino.

PAUL GAYTEN (1)

The Braun Brothers had immediate success when they recorded Paul Gayten who was the leader of another popular band at the time. His hit tune, "True," was a romantic ballad which was reminiscent of the cool sounds coming out of the West Coast from Nat King Cole, Charles Brown and Ivory Joe Hunter. Along with Dave Bartholomew, Paul Gayten was to become an influential figure in the early New Orleans music scene.

Paul Gayten came from Kentwood, Louisiana, a small sawmill town some 40 miles north of Lake Pontchartrain, smack in the middle of the "redneck" district of Louisiana. His mother, Aris Montgomery, was a sister of Little Brother Montgomery, the Chicago-based blues pianist. In the mid-1930's the young Gayten worked as pianist with the Don Dunbar Orchestra which was based in Jackson, Mississippi, before coming down to New Orleans. "Paul Gayten was the only local artist that stood out at the time," said Al Reed, "he had one of the better known and best bands. Of course there were other good bands around New Orleans that mostly teenagers would go to and listen to at the local high schools."

ANNIE LAURIE

"Since I Fell For You" was a bigger record than "True" and featured Annie Laurie as vocalist with Paul Gayten's band. "Annie Laurie did the first really good record that I liked, that I always think of," said Cosimo Matassa. " 'Since I Fell For You,' that was done earlier by Buddy Johnson and Sister Ella Johnson, a real good record. But this Annie Laurie was just fantastic, I mean nobody will ever make another version like that." Annie Laurie, an attractive woman with a big voice similar to LaVern Baker, was the acknowledged star performer as she toured with Paul Gayten through Louisiana and Texas.

Still recalling this period in New Orleans, Cosimo Matassa continued, "I did the things for the De Luxe record company, and then we had a dead period, you know there were a couple of times when the Musicians' Union went on strike and no phonograph records were made. We had a real heyday of recording there for a while, with everybody rushing to get material done. And I guess the first one we did was Cousin Joe, you know Pleasant Joe, Roy Brown and Paul Gayten."

The "dead period" was the second ban on recording by James Petrillo which started from midnight, December 31, 1947. Remembering the last standstill, the independent companies took a calculated risk when they decided to record as much as possible before the ban became effective so they would have enough material to see them through this period, which they anticipated correctly would last for several months. If it had not, many of them would have been in trouble, having spent their capital and being left with stockpiles of material which would date quickly in a fast moving, competitive market. At any rate the gamble paid off, so much so that independent companies like De Luxe, Specialty, Aladdin, Savoy and King came out of it far stronger and better established than before.

ROY BROWN

It was in 1947 before the ban came into operation that Roy Brown recorded "Good Rockin' Tonight" for De Luxe. Brown's version didn't make the R & B charts until June 1948 and by then Wynonie Harris had covered the record on King and helped himself to a big hit; the song has since acquired "classic" status as a result of being remade by Elvis Presley for his second record on Sun. But more than any other single factor, it was this record by Roy Brown which turned the national spotlight on to New Orleans.

"As I recall, prior to this there were no big rock 'n' roll artists in the stature of Roy Brown at the time," said Red Tyler. "You had other artists who were pretty good but Roy Brown really took the country on fire with 'Good Rockin' Tonight.' This was recorded at J & M Studio on Rampart Street with the Bob Ogden band, and it was done on an acetate record. In other words, at that time when you got into recording you could do the whole thing perfect and get to the last few seconds of it and then made a boober, that destroyed it. You had to start all over again. But unfortunately I didn't play on this record but he was a pretty hot artist. Good Rockin' Roy Brown."

Al Reed has good memories, too: "As a teenager I listened to guys like Roy Brown and his Mighty Men. I never knew that when I grew up to be a man I would be part of his organisation, eventually play piano with Roy Brown and be a Mighty Man! I also became friendly with Paul Gayten who introduced Roy into the field of rhythm and blues at a club called The Robin Hood down on Saxon Avenue and Loyola, this was in the 1940's. Actually Roy was introduced on the stage of the Lincoln Theatre which was a movie house, that had vaudeville shows and bands, that's where I first heard Roy. There was also this chick that also sang with Paul Gayten, Annie Laurie. We were friends."

Although born in New Orleans in 1925, Roy Brown cut his musical teeth in Texas, and in 1946 he obtained a long club residency in Galveston, the port where sailors lost their inhibitions (and more) after serving on the high seas during the War years. It was wide open and earned itself the name of

"Playground of the South"; vice and music flourished hand in hand. It was in this exciting environment that Roy Brown was making a name for himself, singing in the local bars and clubs. "Roy was doing ballads, he was a popular entertainer," said Candy Green, a Texas pianist. "He was a very good singer and had a good personality. He was a big guy, over 6 feet tall."

During this period, artists like Louis Jordan, Roy Milton, Joe Turner, Wynonie Harris, Bullmoose Jackson and Texas's own T-Bone Walker were exerting a huge influence over the Negro market. Local Texas artists who reflected these sounds were Goree Carter, Clarence Samuels, Clarence Garlow and Little Willie Littlefield, and with roaring riffs and honking saxes from the band, a singer just *had* to be a shouter. The impact of this school of singers, and more particularly the band backings, was later felt in New Orleans.

Roy Brown's musical career had actually started in 1945 when he won prizes in amateur singing contests in Los Angeles, where he had sought a career in boxing. After returning to Houston and failing an Army medical, he obtained an engagement at Billy Riley's Palace Park in Shreveport before getting the residency of the Club Grenada in Galveston. He then went back to New Orleans, his home town, where he recorded "Good Rockin' Tonight," a song that is claimed to be written by Joel Harris, a Galveston school teacher, although Roy strongly denies this.

His records, for De Luxe, started to sell big, and his popularity at the time is illustrated vividly by Bill "Hoss" Allen, a former disc jockey with WLAC Radio, Nashville: "In my early days in radio, I ran a listeners' contest, trying to find my listeners' favourite blues singer. This was in 1948, and Roy was far and away the 'write in' winner. Shortly thereafter, I presented him in concert at the old Ryman Auditorium in Nashville, Tennessee, better known as the Grand Ole Opry House. I remember it so well, Roy strolls into the spotlight so casually that he might have been just passing through. He moans . . . the band answers, he moans again, again the band answers. So easily he pulls the audience all the way into himself as the initial number begins . . . it builds . . . some urge him on 'Yeah, Roy' . . . 'Come on, Roy' . . . and then seeming to sense that they are truly with him, he leans back, closes his eyes and moves into 'Trouble At Midnight' and he is instantly transformed from a performer on stage into a downhearted pouring out his pain to a woman who has walked all over his heart."

Roy Brown with his crying, pleading, swooping gospel-based style, always had a story to tell his expectant audience, whether in an exuberant fast boogie or a slow sad blues. He was the first singer of soul, and B. B. King and Bobby Bland have headed this popular urban blues style through to this day.

At the start of 1949, the Braun Brothers still had New Orleans to themselves, and were literally cleaning up on the blues and R & B side. Material they already had in the can included recordings by Smiley Lewis, Oscar "Papa" Celestin, Paul Gayten vocalists Eddie Gorman and Earl Williams, female singers Chubby Newsom and Jewel King, as well as the other best selling De Luxe artists.

But it was Roy Brown who was making the real action, and as a result King Records, of Cincinnati, bought up the entire De Luxe catalogue and also Roy Brown's contract from the Braun Brothers. The Brauns continued in the record business by starting a new label, Regal, which was centred around Paul Gayten, Annie Laurie and new vocalist, Larry Darnell.

For a while Roy Brown was lost to New Orleans but King's investment in him soon paid off when "Good Rockin' Tonight" made a reappearance in the charts in April 1949. "We were restricted with our possibilities of promoting this song," said Henry Glover, the King A & R man, "into realms beyond where we had it (i.e. the R & B market) because it was considered filth. They had a definition in those days of the word 'rock' meaning the sex act, rather than having it known as 'a good time' as they did later." Brown had another big hit in late 1950 with "Hard Luck Blues" which stayed in the R & B charts for eighteen weeks and made the No. 1 position. "He had one very soulful record titled 'Hard Luck Blues' that had a tremendous lyric on it," said Glover. "I can't see why maybe some of the rock groups today who have gone back that far didn't pick up such a copyright and re-do it, because it was so great. Some of the lines in it are fantastic."

And so throughout 1949 and 1950, every Roy Brown record

was "gold," "Boogie At Midnight," "Hard Luck Blues," "Love Don't Love Nobody," "Long About Sundown" and "Cadillac Baby." Sessions were held in Cincinnati, Dallas, Los Angeles, as well as New Orleans, but by 1951 Roy Brown was finished as a hit record maker, at least for a few years. Henry Glover put it down to the fact that Roy did not play guitar, like B. B. King, but in truth his records were all beginning to sound the same.

Even so, the speed of his demise was breathtaking. King kept on trying until 1956 when Dave Bartholomew offered him a recording contract with Imperial. At the time Dave Bartholomew was on the crest of a wave with Fats Domino and with the best session men in New Orleans, Bartholomew was able to inject new life into Roy Brown's records. An unlikely cover version of Buddy Knox's "Party Doll" crept into the charts first of all, and then in the summer of 1957, "Let The Four Winds Blow," with its typical New Orleans shuffle beat, climbed to a respectable No. 38 position on "*Billboard's*" charts. Perhaps best of all was a rip-roaring performance on "Saturday Night" which fully captured the Saturday night party atmosphere in New Orleans when "everyone goes ballin'."

But the rock 'n' roll craze was at its peak and Roy Brown's renewed success couldn't last. King took him back in 1959 for a couple more unproductive sessions and then he was signed to Reuben Cherry's and Celia Camp's Home of the Blues label of Memphis. Again no hits, but some great records with Willie Mitchell's band making some storming backings.

Apart from an album for Bluesway in 1968 and a few singles releases on the West Coast the 1960's have been a blank for Roy Brown. Johnny Otis brought him back for the nostalgic Monterey festival of 1970 but on that evidence Roy's voice is not what it was. For all this, one can't help recalling Johnny Otis's own words when talking not only about Roy Brown but his contemporaries, Charles Brown, Roy Milton, Eddie Vinson and Joe Turner, "These men are national treasures and the way they've been treated is a national disgrace."

LARRY DARNELL

When Roy Brown went to King in the De Luxe deal, Paul

Gayten tried to replace him with two big-voiced balladeers, Eddie Gorman and Larry Darnell. It was Darnell who made it with "For You My Love," which turned out to be the second biggest R & B record of 1950, and stayed in the charts for a full twenty-two weeks. Other hits by "Mr Heart and Soul," as he became known, were "I'll Get Along Somehow," "I Love My Baby" and "Oh Babe." The records appeared on Regal, the Braun Brothers' new label, but then Darnell faded out as completely as Roy Brown by the end of 1951. He returned to New Orleans briefly in 1969 when he cut an impressive soul record on Instant called "Son Of A Son Of A Slave," but it didn't happen, and he has since returned to Philadelphia.

De Luxe Records had helped put New Orleans on the musical map. In the absence of any home based record company, it was inevitable that more independent labels would become interested in recording other local talent in New Orleans. The Golden Age of Rhythm and Blues was just around the corner, and the lucky man who stumbled upon this El Dorado was Lew Chudd of Imperial Records.

Imperial Records, 1947–52

"Lew Chudd had a remarkable knack of filling distributors' warehouses with the wrong sounding records," said Johnny Vincent, President of Ace Records and a former distributor himself. It's true Lew Chudd was a businessman first, and as a record man he came a poor second. On the other hand professional jealousy, and perhaps sneaking admiration, may lie behind Vincent's remarks, since in Fats Domino, Slim Whitman and Ricky Nelson, Lew Chudd had three of the hottest stars in the 1950's and their records did not impose too much on the distributors' valuable floor space.

Lew Chudd was a university graduate who came into the record business through his interest in electronics. He set up Imperial in the autumn of 1947, just before the impending

Petrillo Ban. This meant he had to rush several sessions through before the deadline, and as a result of this there are a long string of initial releases by the West Coast jump bands of Charlie Davis, Poison Gardner, Lloyd Glenn and King Porter. Although interest in this type of music, inspired by Lionel Hampton and Count Basie, had peaked in the War years, there was now a distinct trend away from this big band sound. Imperial had got off to an inauspicious start.

Activity cooled for a while, and in the early part of 1949 Chudd was in Texas peddling Mexican records. "That's all he was selling," said Dave Bartholomew, "there were a lot of Mexicans in Houston and San Antonio."

Lew Chudd's long and friendly association with Dave Bartholomew began when they met whilst Bartholomew's band was playing at the Bronze Peacock club in Houston, which was owned by Don Robey along with Peacock Records and the Buffalo Booking Agency. Bartholomew's New Orleans outfit impressed Chudd. "He asked me about the material I was playing, the band was doing a lot of original material," said Dave Bartholomew. "He told me he was thinking he might go into the rhythm and blues field, you could call it rock 'n' roll, all types of things, but when you boil it down it's rhythm and blues. I said I was very interested. Six months later he knocked on my door and said, 'I'm ready to go into the record business.'"

Also working closely with Chudd and Bartholomew was Al Young, who had a record shop called The Bop Shop on North Rampart Street and Dumaine near Cosimo's J & M Studio. "Anyhow, about the first local guy, and he wasn't really local because he had moved here from somewhere else was Al Young, who sought and did Fats Domino," said Cosimo Matassa. "He was the first guy in town who was a producer as such. Of course he worked with Paul Gayten, who exerted a fair amount of influence, and Dave Bartholomew. Dave was really the musical director, generally the head type thing, it was generally Dave Bartholomew who put them together, with whoever the sidemen were at the time. Al Young could be called the entrepreneur."

The first sessions which Dave Bartholomew cut at J & M

Studio for Lew Chudd and Imperial were by the woman blues singer Jewel King and blues balladeer Tommy Ridgley.

JEWEL KING

"We had a split session," recalled Red Tyler, "and the hit out of that was '3 × 7 = 21' by Jewel King. She was the hot artist. I think it was the solo I played on that, that everybody, that all the musicians started copying. It was a kinda catchy solo that I played, I played tenor on that. What happened after it was a hit, there was a guitarist that was playing with Paul Gayten, his name was Jack Scott, a pretty good arranger, and they got together, and I think with her having this hit record they got their heads together and she went with him. And you never heard of her again . . . Great plans but it didn't happen!"

TOMMY RIDGLEY (1)

"The first band I started singing with was a dixieland band over here," said Tommy Ridgley, "we used to play at Sam Genera's place. I remember the type of singing, it was strictly heavy blues because Roy Brown, Big Joe Turner, T-Bone Walker, you know those type of things and that's what I started singing. Well, I always could sing ballads pretty well, so I had a good variety. In fact even today they like to label me as a ballad singer, but I'm a blues singer.

"After this band, I left and then went with another band in the city, Earl Anderson's band, in 1949. And we got the Greystone, no, the Starlight, and Dave Bartholomew heard me and he came over to listen. And so I made my first recording and that was 'Shrewsbury Blues,' Shrewsbury is the district in New Orleans that I come from. It was a successful tune, I don't know how far it went because back in those days you didn't get paid. No recording artist, well I know I didn't. Dave Bartholomew and Mr Al Young signed me to a contract, they took me to the music lawyer in town, I think he's there to the present time, Mr Charles Levy. I must have signed fifty papers, I didn't know what in the world I was signing, I just signed. Because you know, it's an honour for people to think enough of you to want to record you. I signed all the papers and I had a real succession of recordings. It was Dave Bartholomew's band backing."

DAVE BARTHOLOMEW'S PRODUCTIONS

The early Imperial sessions had a muzzy jazz-based jump blues sound, with the dixieland-type alto saxophone of Joe Harris well to the fore. It took a little time for the clean-cut rhythmic sound and fat unison horn riffs which were to become the hallmarks of Dave Bartholomew's productions to filter through. Cosimo's early primitive studio did not really help, even if it was typical of the time. Said Dave Bartholomew, "When I was working with Lew Chudd he said, 'The studios are no good down there, you'll have to go where you can get a good sound.' We never had a board in New Orleans. You don't have to have a big, beautiful studio, you can have one room, but if you've got the right equipment you can go ahead and do anything you want. Cosimo has never, we've never had the right equipment in New Orleans."

About his own recording philosophy, Bartholomew said, "I always tried to keep things as simple as possible, and we always wanted something the kids could sing. I always kept a commercial mind and kept abreast of the market."

Mac Rebennack saw it in a similar light: "Dave was very good with putting together small arrangements like two or three horns which were basically head arrangements, but he influenced to a degree from his own knowledge and trumpet playing ability. He was able to write melodies that were very easy to remember. As a result he had so many successful records between him and Fats with those chord-type melodies, almost children's melodies. Dave's real thing was he kept all kind of talent around him, writers, arrangers and the people he needed to make good records."

Another recognisable trait in his productions was the shortness of the records. A maximum of two and a half minutes, more often nearer two minutes, sometimes less. A record had to be short in length in the 1950's, otherwise it would be ignored by the disc jockeys and jukebox operators. As a result all the energy and creativity of the producer, artist and musicians had to be squeezed into this short space of time. Self discipline, in effect, and it worked.

FATS DOMINO (I)

However, it was through the discovery of Fats Domino that the fame and fortune of Dave Bartholomew, Lew Chudd and indeed Domino himself were made. This partnership was destined to project Domino into a well-respected world-wide star during the rock 'n' roll era, and influence a whole lot of popular music. "Domino, he was creative," said Cosimo Matassa. "What he did, like fooling with some of the standard tunes for instance, he put his stamp on them. Boy, they were Domino versions, without question, and that is what makes an artist with me. No matter what he does comes through. He could be singing the National Anthem, which everybody until recently did straight, no fooling around or anything, you'd still know by the time he said two words it was him, obviously, unmistakeably, and pleasurably him. Domino fits that, just opens his mouth . . . in fact he just hits an opening chord on his piano and you know it. I'd like to have that. I think anybody would."

Antoine "Fats" Domino was born in New Orleans in 1928 and although his father was a violinist, he was the only one of nine children to take up music. He was taught to play piano by the late Harrison Verrett, a talented musician who had played guitar and banjo with Papa Celestin, Kid Ory and many other dixieland musicians. Verrett had married Domino's sister when Fats was 4½ years old and Fats followed him around town on music jobs. When teaching him the piano Verrett used to write the names of the notes on the white keys in ink and the names of the notes on the black keys on white tape. He then showed him how to form chords and how to run the scales. According to Harrison Verrett, at first Domino would sing in one key while playing different time, and when that problem was solved, he booked him into various clubs and got him into the Union.

In between playing the honky tonks, the young Fats Domino earned extra cash by mowing some of the palatial lawns in New Orleans for $1.50 a day; later, he worked in a local factory and suffered an industrial injury that nearly resulted in several fingers being amputated. He married his childhood sweetheart, Rose Mary, at 20, and soon after he took up a job as pianist with bassist Billy Diamond's combo at The Hideaway Club.

When Lew Chudd told Dave Bartholomew he was ready to start up Imperial again, he asked Bartholomew if he knew anybody they could record. "I said, 'Well, I don't really know but I'd heard about a guy named Fats Domino who was playing at The Hideaway Club. They tell me he's terrific.' It was a Friday night and I wasn't working. So we went down and Fats was singing a song the prisoners used to sing, 'Junkers Blues,' you know a song about the junkie. In December 1949 most people didn't know what the word meant. We went down and we heard Fats and we really liked it. So I told Fats would he like to record and introduced him to Lew and we went on from there."

It was Harrison Verrett who advised Fats to get a contract for royalties rather than sell his numbers outright. According to Verrett, a man named Melvin Cade had a contract with Domino before he made his first recording which guaranteed Domino $103 a night; sometimes the gross for a dance would be a few thousand dollars. Cade was killed in an automobile accident when he was driving Domino to an engagement in Bunkie, Louisiana. His death released Domino from the contract.

The first session was set up and Dave Bartholomew brought in his own musicians as accompanists. Eight titles were recorded and from these "The Fat Man" was chosen as the first release. It was a R & B hit, entering the "*Billboard*" charts on April 1, 1950, and making No. 6 during its three week stay in the Top 10. Only three weeks in the charts, but records lasted longer in those days, and by 1953 sales had accumulated to earn Fats a gold record for a million sales.

The main attractions of "The Fat Man" were the dominant piano, the swinging band, and Domino's use of his voice as an additional instrument, almost like a muted trumpet. And, of course, the song was readily identifiable with him, he was "The Fat Man," all 224 pounds and five feet five of him.

Dave Bartholomew's account of the session neatly pinpoints

early recording problems. "The sax sound was too harsh," he said, "and I really was responsible for it because I couldn't play trumpet as I was in the control room. So what happened, Fats played loud at the piano, we made a mistake and sent the record out. The piano was much higher than everything else, we didn't really want it that way but at the time we couldn't do anything about it. Today with eight tracks or so you could bury the piano, but Lew Chudd put the record out and they liked it."

Following "The Fat Man," Fats went on tour with Dave Bartholomew's band and Jewel King, who was hotter because she had a bigger record with "3 × 7 = 21." "Well, when the tour was over," said Red Tyler, "it was obvious that Fats Domino was going to be a star. At the time he wasn't a hit, he was playing locally, around the city but nothing fantastic. I was quite surprised and loads of people were quite surprised when he got to be as popular as he was, because we thought there were far better artists, you know, that knocked us out more. Like Professor Longhair."

Harrison Verrett then got a band together for Domino, and at first Fats wouldn't play without him in the band. As more pieces were added, Harrison Verrett got another guitar player, and left himself out of the band. But Fats still insisted that Verrett travelled with the band to help him gain courage.

Domino's rise to fame was not astronomic. In fact, the next three 78 rpm releases, all taken from that first session, were flops and this losing run was ended when the slow bluesy ballad, "Every Night About This Time," sold through the fall of 1950 into 1951. More so than "The Fat Man," "Every Night About This Time" was to have far greater significance on Fats' future style for this is the first example of his triplet piano style on record. "Fats always did the triplet piano himself," said Dave Bartholomew, "he got this from a guy called Little Willie Littlefield. He had a record out years ago ('It's Midnight' on Modern in 1948) and that was where Fats got the triplet piano. That was a '68' piano on that. Fats did not originate this but he made it popular. Once he made it popular, naturally, he couldn't leave it. He toned down his adventurous piano because the distributors wanted it that way. That's how we were able to sell Fats with a triplet piano."

This is another indication of the Texas influence on New Orleans for Littlefield was a pianist who came from Houston before going to the West Coast. In Domino's case, though, the line can be drawn further back to include the boogie pianists, Albert Ammons, Pete Johnson and Meade Lux Lewis.

Fats Domino's vocals were equally unique, with their warm, rich French Creole intonations. "We all thought of him as a country and western singer," said Dave Bartholomew. "Not real downhearted, but he always had that flavour, not the gutbucket sound. By gutbucket I mean a blues singer sings from the bottom of the stomach and it comes up and it comes out. So we always considered Fats more C & W."

Harrison Verrett made similar comments when asked to explain Fats' popularity. "Alan Freed coined the name 'rock 'n' roll' but that music was just blues and rhythm," he said. "The music is just old two-beat, like dixieland but with rhythm and blues. But if he attempted to change his style of singing or his pronounciation, which is 'country,' then he would flop."

"Careless Love," the traditional tune used by so many dixieland bands, was recorded at the same second session as "Every Night About This Time." Besides establishing a fruitful source of material which Bartholomew and Domino were to draw on frequently over the years, it was also an early example of the guitar sound which Ernest McLean, Justin Adams and Walter Nelson were to use on so many New Orleans recording sessions. "The guitarists were more or less rhythm but played a figure arrangement," said Dave Bartholomew, "just like a bassist would use a guitar. I would have them doing something different from the bass, and at that time we would have nothing but an upright bass. So what I would do if I wanted something strong from the bass, I would double the guitar on the lower register with the bass so I would get more of a bottom."

Already Fats Domino's style was beginning to take shape.

His stardom was really established when "Goin' Home" made No. 1 on the R & B charts in the summer of 1952. The melody line had a lot going for it, but it was the lyrics which sold the song; *"Goin' home tomorrow, can't stand your evil ways"* must have meant much to the disillusioned Negro slaving away in the factories of the Northern cities. But the recording balance was terrible, and for once the sax solo a mess, so unlike the lilting melodic solos which Herb Hardesty perfected over the years. Nevertheless, the record sold and gained another gold record.

Fats Domino and Dave Bartholomew were on their way. "Things began to look up in the early 1950's for Dave and Fats, you see the rest of us didn't get in on that," said Red Tyler, "the gravy went right to Fats and Dave Bartholomew. During this time Dave Bartholomew's band was still the hottest small group in town and we worked, played maybe three or four or five times a week in the city and surroundings, the small towns, you know. But Dave at the time had got into the other end of the thing as arranger and songwriter for Fats Domino. So whereas he was making a lot more money at the time, we were still playing in his band and he liked it enough to continue to play. The big money was really made by Fats and Dave locally."

DAVE BARTHOLOMEW (2)

Dave Bartholomew has made a whole bunch of records, far more than he's given credit for—his productions for other artists have tended to obscure his own efforts. Most were on Imperial and they cover a wide range of material from the free-blowing jazz of "Shrimps And Gumbo," excellent R & B with "The Monkey" and "Another Mule" to the novelties "My Ding A Ling" (the same number which Chuck Berry made famous in 1972) and "Yeah Yeah." But apart from "Country Boy" for De Luxe in 1949, the commercial touch which he found for others eluded himself.

SMILEY LEWIS

If Bartholomew's own records had something of an escapist element about them, then his productions for Smiley Lewis were far more serious affairs. Imperial tried like hell to break him big but they met with only moderate success with "The Bells Are Ringing" in 1952 and the more famous "I Hear

You Knocking" in 1955 with Huey Smith providing the classic piano introduction. "I Hear You Knocking" was a natural hit but the gilt was taken off by Gale Storm's cover version which attained No. 2 spot in *"Billboard's"* Hot 100 charts. Elvis Presley did the same thing in 1958 when he made an expurgated version of Smiley's "One Night (of sin)" and took it into the charts—everything he did then was a hit anyway—and called it "One Night (of love)."

"Poor Smiley, God bless the dead, just could not get started," said Dave Bartholomew. "He always seemed to have the best material. By this I'm trying to say that after Smiley would record a tune, and even after a tune in New Orleans and surrounding places for about 200 miles was popular, we just couldn't break it nationally like everyone else."

Smiley Lewis's real name was Overton Amos Lemons, and if anybody wanted to tease him they just called him by his full name. He hated it. He came from the small town of Union, Louisiana but was raised in New Orleans and had a strong blues voice like Joe Turner's. "Smiley was the closest New Orleans artist playing early blues but he graduated," observed Dave Bartholomew."

He had recorded first of all with De Luxe in 1947 and was billed as "Smiling" Lewis. He was then signed by Imperial in 1950 and stayed with them until 1960. In this time he put down some really great records which included "Tee Nah Nah" (1950), "Blue Monday," "Real Gone Lover" and "Lost Weekend" (with the immortal line, *"Hand me another drink, bartender, on the house"*) (1954), "Down Yonder We Go Ballin'," "Someday" and "Please Listen To Me" (1956) and "I Shall Not Be Moved" (1958), with vocal support from the great Gerri Hall and a superb guitar solo from Edgar Blanchard. The standard throughout was of the highest and it is small wonder that Dave Bartholomew was disappointed at the lack of commercial success. Perhaps Smiley's voice was just too strong, again like Joe Turner's to be accepted by the rock' n' roll audiences, although ironically, his record of "Shame Shame Shame" is now a rock 'n' roll classic.

After Smiley left Imperial, he had records released on Okeh, Dot and a nice remake of "The Bells Are Ringing" on Loma which was produced by Allen Toussaint. None of these got noticed in any way, and just as he was trying to make a comeback he died of stomach cancer in 1966.

Although the "big one" eluded Smiley Lewis, he must be considered as a major New Orleans artist. "Smiley used to work around New Orleans, he played guitar in the troubador tradition," said Mac Rebennack. "He used to walk from table to table to sing and serenade people at the clubs. He was never a great guitar player but could play enough to accompany himself. He could sing so loud and strong, he could sing without a microphone. Smiley was one of those cats who could sing his own songs, scat sing, do solos, improvise, sing horn parts and stuff like this. He was really talented. He had dixieland tradition and be-bop tradition. He was not only a blues singer but he was a pop singer. In fact, he was an all-round guy with a totally distinctive voice, just like Percy Mayfield there's only one Smiley Lewis. Smiley was very clean cut and, y'know, a real good person, and I don't think anybody said anything bad about Smiley. But he was never as big as he could have been."

Winds Of Change

By 1952, the Winds of Change were blowing. Until this time R & B records had been bought almost exclusively by the Negro market, but no longer. Ahmet Ertegun and Jerry Wexler, of Atlantic Records, wrote an important article on the whole subject in *"Cash Box"* in 1954:

> "As far as we can determine, the first area where the blues stepped out in the current renaissance was the South. Distributors there about two years ago began to report that white high school and college kids were picking up on the rhythm and blues records, primarily to dance to. From all accounts, the movement was initiated by youthful hillbilly fans rather than the pop bobby-soxers, and the later group followed right along. A few alert pop disc jockeys observed the current, switched to rhythm and blues formats, and soon were deluged with greater audiences, both white and Negro, and more and more sponsors. Conservative old line Victor franchised record stores in Southern cities, who not long ago regarded Decca and Mercury as offbrand upstarts, found themselves compelled to stock, display, and push rhythm and blues recordings, and are happily wailing up a lot of volume to the pop audience that their Northern counterparts are now beginning to suspect may be there."

Specialty Records, 1952

Art Rupe was another man who knew what was happening. He had formed his Specialty label in Hollywood in 1944, and had enjoyed considerable success with the records of Roy Milton, Joe Liggins and Percy Mayfield, along with a best-selling gospel line. Hitherto his activities had been confined entirely to the West Coast, with its predominant big city sound, but in 1952 he made his first field trip South. "Well, I had never gone South until this field trip," said Art Rupe, "I had never been South until I went to New Orleans. Because all my friends, my black friends, said 'Man, it's out, there's nowhere to go. You end up in a hokey, you know, in the jug.' So I stayed away from the South. The only reason I went South was because I was very impressed with Fats Domino. I really dug Fats Domino, I liked his sound. There was something pristine about it. Remember this was in 1952 when I went to New Orleans, our musicians (in Los Angeles) were getting a little bit glib, doing the same thing. I didn't feel the spontaneity that I felt originally. Either I needed a change or they needed a change, so I felt maybe it was me, because I responded to Fats Domino, he had something.

LLOYD PRICE

"I went down there to find some talent in New Orleans and I made an announcement on a black radio show called 'The Okey Dokey Radio Show' that I was looking for talent. I had no way of getting this talent to come to this recording studio, Cosimo Matassa's. It was one little recording studio in the black section, right off the French Quarter there, where the black people went to.

"And I was having my auditions and I was getting ready to come back. I felt I had failed, they all sounded very amateurish and quite poor, and I feel funny when I tell you this but it's true. The last one to audition was Lloyd Price and he was just 17-years-old, he was rehearsing and rehearsing and chewing up the clock, and I finally said to him, 'Look, kid, if you don't get yourself together I'm splitting.' The kid literally began to cry and so I said 'O.K., I'll listen to it', and he sang 'Lawdy Miss Clawdy,' I should say cried 'Lawdy Miss Clawdy.' And the kid got to me the way he did, it was very emotional, and I cancelled my plane trip and I spent four or five days there. He had no band or anything and I got Fats Domino to play the piano and Bartholomew, who was Fats' manager and arranger, to get the musicians together. And that's what introduced me to New Orleans and that was a very, very fertile ground to find talent.

"The record was very, very successful, to my knowledge that was the first black record that wasn't intended to be a white record, it became a white record, it became a white record versus the previous black records which were designed for the white market.

"I heard this from the distributors, you get an amazing feedback in the independent record business. You know, you're talking to distributors regularly in all the key areas of the country, and they will be reordering and I asked them why the record was selling way out in proportion to the ordinary black records. So when you see an anomaly like this you investigate what's caused this. The reason why, I can't tell you what happened, but white people, white kids began to buy this record. They had heard it on black stations and I think it started in the South oddly enough where we felt there was the most prejudice. I think that's where the cultures overlap, musically there was less prejudice in the South. Politically there was prejudice but not musically.

"By this time there were more and more stations playing black music. As a matter of fact, certain stations which were very poor commercially became ethnic stations. They either became, er, Spanish stations in Spanish communities or they became black stations, farming, and that's the way our records began to have a wider audience. I think it was that spillover that was material to helping 'Lawdy Miss Clawdy' happen, and incidentally 'Lawdy Miss Clawdy' became the No. 1 record on all the *Billboard* charts, that was the first award that we got. It actually nearly sold a million, publicity-wise, five or six. . . ."

"Lawdy Miss Clawdy," in fact, became No. 1 R & B "Record of the Year" on the *"Billboard"* and *"Cash Box"* charts. It also earned Lloyd Price the *"Cash Box"* award for the "Best New R & B Singer of 1952," and a gold record.

"Lloyd and I grew up together," recalled Tommy Ridgley. "When Lloyd made his first record I tell you, there's a real story to that. Well, I'd been singing, I had been making records in those days and Lloyd had been coming up under me because I'm older, you see. But Lloyd was doing auditions for all these record companies including Specialty and they all turned him down. Well, he said, 'Man, I'm gonna give you that tune, let you record it.' So this was maybe like Thursday or Friday. Well, anyway, we fixed a date for Monday, and on Monday, over the weekend Lloyd got a telegram from Specialty at the last minute telling him they was going to record the tune. But I almost got 'Lawdy Miss Clawdy' and I was going to do it exactly like he did.

Lloyd Price, c. 1958. PHOTOGRAPH COURTESY MIKE LEADBITTER

SHIRLEY & LEE
THE SWEETHEARTS OF THE BLUES
RECORDING STARS

GALE AGENCY Inc
48 West 48th St.
New York, N.Y.

Shirley & Lee, c. 1955. PHOTOGRAPH COURTESY
MIKE LEADBITTER

Papa Lightfoot, c. 1954. PHOTOGRAPH COURTESY
STEVE LA VERE

Sugar Boy Review, 'Cash Box', 1954.

PHOTOGRAPH COURTESY MIKE VERNON

Ray Charles, c. 1953. PHOTOGRAPH
COURTESY BLUES UNLIMITED

Guitar Slim, 1957. PHOTOGRAPH COURTESY MIKE LEADBITTER

'*The Things That I Used To Do.*' PHOTOGRAPH BY BILL GREENSMITH

Guitar Slim Review, 'Cash Box', 1954. PHOTOGRAPH COURTESY MIKE VERNON

THE CASH BOX

Rhythm 'N Blues SLEEPER OF THE WEEK

"THE THINGS THAT I USED TO DO" (2:57)
[Venice BMI—E. Jones]

"WELL, I DONE GOT OVER IT" (2:22)
[Venice BMI—E. Jones]

GUITAR SLIM
(Specialty 482)

● Guitar Slim comes up with a pair that look like sure shots for hitdom. The upper deck, "The Things that I Used To Do," is a a slow southern blues rhythmically chanted by the blues shouter. Slim chants "he's gonna send her back to her mother and go back to his family too." The artist does a great vocal with the proper blues styling and this side is headed for sales. The lower end, "Well, I Done Got Over it," is a middle tempo jump blues and Slim handles his chore with excellent results. He sings, "he was so in love he was miserable, but he done got over it." Two top notch efforts. A two for the price of one disk.

The Spiders, 1954. PHOTOGRAPH COURTESY BLUES UNLIMITED

Fats Domino, c. 1956. PHOTOGRAPH COURTESY BLUES UNLIMITED

Smiley Lewis Trio, 1949. Left to right: Smiley Lewis, Herman Seale, Isidore 'Tuts' Washington. PHOTOGRAPH COURTESY ISIDORE WASHINGTON AND KARL GURT ZUR HEIDE

'Mighty, Mighty Man'.

PHOTOGRAPH BY BILL GREENSMITH

'She Ain't Got No Hair'.

PHOTOGRAPH BY BILL GREENSMITH

'3 × 7 = 21'.

PHOTOGRAPH BY BILL GREENSMITH

'I'm Gone'.

PHOTOGRAPH BY BILL GREENSMITH

"But now after he made the hit, when he got to go out, he was due to open in Houston, he didn't have a band so he came to my house and said 'I don't know what to do.'

"So I knew all the musicians so I helped him form a band, in fact the saxophone player was Larry Marinot. We got together, it took about a day or two. We formed a band, I went with him, bought uniforms for the band, and during this time Lloyd had to be emancipated 21 because he was only 19, by law. But he was afraid to go by himself so he asked me to go to Houston with him. And I said, 'Well, man, I have some jobs of my own, I can't leave. But I'll meet you when you come back.' I met him in Crowville and I played a date with him. But anyway we got back here and I said, 'Man, you can take care of yourself,' and he went on from there. Even right now Lloyd has offered me some things to come to New York, anyway, he says, 'You come up here, you don't have to worry, you can stay at my place, I see you straight until you get situated.' "

The success of "Lawdy Miss Clawdy" can be attributed as much to the beautiful band accompaniment on this rolling 8 bar blues, and to Fats Domino's piano in particular, as much as to Price's expressive, wailing vocal.

Its influence was tremendous, and in New Orleans itself, it seemed that every record made over the next eighteen months or so was loosely based on the song.

The rest of Lloyd Price's Specialty recordings, not surprisingly, could not match "Lawdy Miss Clawdy" in terms of originality, musical quality or indeed sales returns. The follow-up, "Restless Heart," reached No. 5 on the "*Billboard*" R & B charts riding in the wake of the hit, "Ain't That A Shame" was No. 7 in February 1953 and the remainder were just local hits. All his records from this period were recorded in New Orleans and they show the strong bluesy Fats Domino influence of the time.

Price was unable to capitalise on his good start in music mainly because he was drafted into the Army in 1953 when he was assigned to the Special Services in the Far East, serving in Korea and Japan. Despite this set-back, Art Rupe tried to keep his man in the spotlight and every so often brief news items appeared in "*Cash Box*," like "Lloyd Price says he does

C

not like the Army" and "Please get me out" to Art Rupe. By the time he was discharged Art Rupe had found a new star in Little Richard.

After leaving Specialty Lloyd Price had an immediate hit with "Just Because" on ABC Paramount and then he formed a record company, KRC, with Harold Logan and Bill Boskent which was distributed first by Atlantic and then Ace. The label was not a commercial success but records like "Down By The River" and "Georgianna" by Price and "Yeah Baby" by Stella Johnson had a good New Orleans sound. He returned to ABC Paramount and had the nation's No. 1 hit record with "Stagger Lee" early in 1959.

"Stagger Lee," of course, was an adaption of the traditional folk song "Stagolee," which Archibald had turned into a hit as "Stack-A-Lee" in 1950. The band had a New Orleans sound but the selling point was the horrible female chorus with their machine-gun like overdubbed shouts of "*da da dada*" and "*Go Stagger Lee.*" Specialty even tried to cash in by re-releasing "Lawdy Miss Clawdy" with similar horrendous female overdubs, but failed. And so "Stagger Lee" earned Lloyd Price his second gold record. It effectively marked the end of his connections with New Orleans, and he was now a pop star, notching up further gold records with "I'm Gonna Get Married" and "Personality" in 1959. During the 1960's, he tried his hand as a singer of sophisticated night club material and got involved in several business ventures including his own record companies, night clubs and discotheques in New York.

Lloyd Price has made it in terms of show business success, but he had to leave New Orleans to do it. "New Orleans has so many singers and entertainers," said Mac Rebennack, "that until a guy is known away from New Orleans and comes back, he is never respected." Unfortunately, it's a recurring theme.

Aladdin Records

The Mesner Brothers, Eddie and Leo, arrived in New Orleans a little before Art Rupe, in the fall of 1951 to be more exact when they recorded the Texas-styled blues shouter, Jesse Allen.

Word was getting around about the prolific New Orleans music scene. Aladdin Records had been founded in Hollywood in 1945 and had sold a lot of records by Amos Milburn, Charles Brown, Peppermint Harris, the Five Keys, Floyd Dixon and Lightnin' Hopkins. Just like other independent record company owners of the time, the Mesners were continually on the road, peddling their records to radio stations, distributors and the jukebox trade, as well as seeking out new talent.

SHIRLEY & LEE

Although the Jesse Allen record did nothing, and he had no better luck with good records on Imperial, Vin and Duplex, Eddie Mesner came back and recorded Shirley & Lee in June 1952. By the end of the year, "I'm Gone," their first release, had hit the R & B charts, making No. 2 spot. This session was produced by Dave Bartholomew. "They were on Aladdin," he said, "at the time I was freelancing and they came into the studio and I recorded them. But that was the only one because after that I had two or three hits at one time and Lew Chudd gave me the best offer and it was best for me to stay with one company rather than freelance. That was the reason I had to leave them."

"Well, it all started when we were the home neighbourhood kids," said Shirley Goodman. "We had about thirty kids that went to the studio in New Orleans, Cosimo's, the only one, and we had to put 5 cents each or the pennies, whatever we had. He charged us $2 to cut a demo. So we all sang, and Lee and I sang lead on the demo and Cosimo gave us the tape and ran us off. Well, about a month later Eddie Mesner came to town and he was getting ready to record Lloyd Price. But at the time when he was making a tape Cosimo was erasing tapes, and when he got to the one we had cut he said, 'Man, these are some kids that just blew my mind, like they bugged me. Listen to this, the whole neighbourhood.' Like $2, the cheapest tape he ever cut. He said, 'I just let them cut this record, they wrote it and everything. And listen.' It was 'I'm Gone.' And he heard it, like it had fifteen verses, it went on and on . . . Eddie Mesner heard it, and heard my voice, and to our luck, really, he picked it out. He said, 'Get the boy and girl for me.'

And he did and a week later we were in the studio singing
for him. Earl Palmer, which is a very good drummer and in
Los Angeles now, Lee Allen who played tenor sax and travelled
with people like Fats, also Justin Adams who played guitar,
Ernest McLean who played guitar, Dave Bartholomew was
trumpet on that, Dude Fields who was a very good upright
bassman and Edward Frank who played piano."

Shirley Goodman was only 14 and Leonard Lee 15 when they
made their first record. As the "Sweethearts of the Blues,"
they really laid on the boy-meets-girl love story situation. Every
record was a never-ending saga in a teen magazine. "Continuing the story of the Shirley-Lee romance" was how "Cash
Box" started their review of "Lee's Goofed" in February 1954.
"Lee leaves Shirley this time and in answer to her pleas he
reminds her of the humiliation when she left him." Strong stuff,
but it sold records and in 1956 Shirley & Lee gave Aladdin
their first million seller with the rollicking "Let The Good
Times Roll," which was a No. 27 hit on "Billboard's" Hot 100.
"I Feel Good," also in 1956, reached No. 38, and they had
three minor hits for Warwick in 1960 and 1961, including a
remake of "Let The Good Times Roll." After some good sides
for Imperial, the couple split in 1963. Shirley moved out to the
West Coast, made a couple of things with Jessie Hill as "Shirley
& Jessie" and did a lot of session work with Harold Battiste
and Dr John. Leonard Lee recorded for Imperial and Broadmoor in his own name.

However, they did get together in 1972, caught up in "The
9th Rock 'n' Roll Revival Show" in New York. "Shirley &
Lee looked as though they were held together with girdles,
surgical trusses and a fair amount of sellotape," wrote Roy
Hollingworth in his hip "Melody Maker" review. "Lee was all
decked out in an outsize blazer and dicky, while big mama
Shirley was wearing enough turquoise lurex to make a double
bed, and still have enough left to run up a pair of curtains.
They stood on stage, awkwardly swaying from side to side
like a shot from Waltz of the Hippos, swooning out sickly love
tunes. But when they sizzled into 'Let The Good Times Roll'
they brought the house down, and started to hop around like a
couple of 5-year-olds. 'Right on,' yelled a brace of rightonners."

It is not easy to evaluate the music of Shirley & Lee, and perhaps it's not meant to be placed on an intellectual pedestal. Certainly, their music is often considered to be as ephemeral as the love affairs their songs portrayed, a joke if you like. Shirley's theatrical, shrill, child-like voice does not really help the case for the defence, but Leonard's remarkable blues voice is another matter. There was more to the lyrical content, of course, than met the eye and when they sang "Rock All Night" or "Rockin' With The Clock" they weren't just singing about dancing down at the local palais. But it is the musical side which has been grossly overlooked. Shirley & Lee's records were nothing but good, socking New Orleans rock 'n' roll with the great session men blasting away in their own inimitable rocking way. And whilst on the road they used both Huey Smith and Allen Toussaint as pianists. Yes, Shirley & Lee do have an important place in New Orleans' musical heritage, and with their man-woman singing team their influence stretched out much further than New Orleans.

PAPA LIGHTFOOT

In November 1952, Aladdin came back to New Orleans and recorded harmonica bluesman Papa Lightfoot and the vocal group, the Cha-Paka-Shaweez, in addition to Shirley & Lee.

Papa Lightfoot had previously recorded with Edgar Blanchard's Gondoliers in Houston for Peacock in 1949, and was one of the few hard bluesmen to play regularly in New Orleans. Somehow with its long musical history, with many musicians able to read music and do arrangements, New Orleans was altogether too sophisticated to tolerate the rawness and crudity of rural bluesmen. In fact, the New Orleans definition of a blues artist differs greatly from the European and white American concept. Get into conversation with any native Orleanian about the local bluesmen and he will mention Guitar Slim, Smiley Lewis and Fats Domino. It's a case of different interpretation but it's hard to argue against.

A rare recollection of the older type blues in New Orleans came from the late J. B. Lenoir when he recalled how he met famous bluesmen, Sonny Boy Williamson and Elmore James, in New Orleans in 1944 and played on their bandstand on

Rampart Street at the New York Inn. Sonny Boy Williamson later had a local hit in 1954 with a rhumba-type blues, "Gettin' Out Of Town" on Trumpet.

Men like Polka Dot Slim and Harmonica Al were restricted to working mainly in the rough ghettoes and places like the project bars in the 9th Ward with just a couple of guitars in accompaniment. "It was nothing unusual for there to be two or three murders on a gig, especially Saturday night," said Mac Rebennack. "You could get killed for stepping on another guy's foot, or looking at his girl. For the poor people, the biggest kick was to have a fight."

The late Alexander Lightfoot came down the river from Natchez, Mississippi, to New Orleans in the late 1940's and among the artists he sat in with were Fats Domino, Tommy Ridgley and Shirley & Lee. He did a tour with Smiley Lewis as a fake Little Walter, "Little Papa Walter", driving in a '55 station wagon between Nashville and Cincinnatti. His claim to fame, though, will always be the famous 1954 Imperial session when he put down two of the most stomping, rocking amplified harmonica blues and boogies you could ever wish to hear with "When The Saints Go Marching In" and "Wine, Women, Whiskey."

THE CHA-PAKA-SHAWEEZ

The Cha-Paka-Shaweez' session on November 23, 1952, was their first and last. "No One To Love Me" is one of those records which did not sell, and yet has since been accorded legendary status by record collectors. More important than any tag subsequently stuck on the song, are the individual members who made up the Shaweez (as they were also known), lead vocalist Edgar "Big Boy" Myles, James "Sugar Boy" Crawford, Edgar's brother Warren "Jake" Myles, and blues guitarist Irving Banister. All were destined to establish a good local reputation in the years ahead.

The Aladdin files for this session reveal the stranglehold placed upon artists by their record contracts, and help explain why they rarely got the royalties they expected. The royalties were simply too small and besides were offset by the several deductions listed in the contract. The files read as follows:

"*Edgar Myles session:*

Recording contracts, songwriter's agreements, etc., sent to Vern Winslow, 1956 Pleasure Street, New Orleans, Louisiana, on December 18, 1952.

Edgar Myles (artist's) contract, 4 sides, 6 months from November 23, 1952, 3 years options, royalty, 1c, 1¼c, 2c, 2¼c. Advance scale on options, 8 sides per year. Payments for arrangements or for side musicians are advance royalties chargeable to artist. Vernon gets royalty of ½c, 90 per cent clause. No royalties owing until after advance royalties to Edgar Myles have been exceeded. Liquidated damages in case Edgar breaches contract. On all tunes, ½c per song per record manufactured and sold to be divided among writers. No performance payments to writers.

Also sent to Edgar Myles mech. lic. agreement with rec. artist at ½c, and assignment of original music by rec. artist."

You see, you had to have a big hit to make money.

Aladdin continued to hold sessions in New Orleans until the label folded in 1959. Quite naturally, they concentrated on Shirley & Lee, but they also brought in some of their other stars to record. "I did 'Merry Christmas Baby' and all that with Charles Brown," said regular session guitarist Justin Adams, "I did 'Chicken Shack' with Amos Milburn. On that record was Red Tyler, Charles Williams, Frank Fields, tenor player named Nat Perrilliat, he's dead, Amos on piano. It was a split thing, a couple on Charles a couple on him. They was always together." Other outside artists like Lowell Fulson and Clarence Garlow were also recorded, along with local men Bobby Marchan, Alvin Johnson and Lee Allen, plus the Monitors and the Charmers vocal groups.

Savoy Records

In 1953, Savoy joined the swelling ranks of the "indies," as the record industry called the independent labels, who came to record in New Orleans.

Savoy was based in Newark, New Jersey, and was founded by Herman Lubinsky in 1942. Over the years they had built up an impressive jazz, blues and gospel catalogue, without ever hitting upon the magical formula for a steady flow of good selling records. Maybe New Orleans would work its good luck charm as it had for others, but it was not to be. Two sorties were made in 1953 and 1954. On the first trip they put down the first sides by Earl King, who recorded under another assumed name, Earl Johnson, and Huey Smith. Both records were pretty good, Earl King sounding very young on the jump blues "Have You Gone Crazy" and Huey Smith vocalising on a raunchy, lowdown blues, "You Made Me Cry." Earl still has his old Savoy contract which gave him $10 per side, with promises of increased royalties if he had a national hit. He didn't, of course.

The second trip was mentioned in *"Cash Box"* on March 6, 1954: "Fred Mendelsohn, Savoy Records, was in New Orleans cutting and signing new singers, Dave Dixon and Aletra Hampton and the Hampton Singers." Dixon had a local hit with "My Plea," a slow blues ballad, on Savoy. Later he was a founder member of Huey Smith's Clowns when they started with Ace in 1956. He made more records for Home of the Blues in Memphis in 1961 along with Roy Brown, and is now living in Los Angeles.

Earl Williams, a blues ballad singer, the Blue Diamonds with a young Ernie K-Doe and George "Blazer Boy" Stevenson were also recorded by Savoy, but none of the records sold well and Savoy retreated to their East Coast home, vainly trying to defend themselves from the coming onslaught of rock 'n' roll.

Chess Records, 1953–54

The Chess label is rightly associated with the hard blues of Chicago and began to grab attention in the early 1950's with hit records by Muddy Waters, Little Walter and Howlin' Wolf. The Jewish brothers, Len and Phil Chess, however, were not content to remain inward looking and were always willing to take in material from outside the blues-drenched environment of Chicago. Leasing served a possible twofold purpose. It could be a licence to print instant money with a "cert" hit bought cheaply or else it was a useful method to wipe out local competition—the idea was to buy up the opposition record, quietly lose it in your catalogue, and leave the way clear for your own hot record to take all the action. Sounds absurd but it happened that way, and often too.

SUGAR BOY CRAWFORD

"I Don't Know What I'll Do" was the first record Chess released which was made in New Orleans, and it was the first record cut by James "Sugar Boy" Crawford, formerly of the Shaweez, in his own name. It was a moderate local hit in New Orleans in 1953 and so was the follow-up "Jock-A-Mo" which was the same song recorded later by the Dixie Cups and then Dr John as "Iko Iko."

Sugar Boy's recording career was hardly prolific, and after he left Checker he had just four singles on Imperial in 1956 and 1957 which veered from the explosive rhythms of "She's Got A Wobble When She Walks" to C & W type ballads on "You Gave Me Love." Solitary singles on Ace, Peacock and Jin completed the sum total of his contributions on record.

Such a small output does not do the man justice, and it comes nowhere near to explaining that Sugar Boy and his band, the Cane Cutters, were one of the most popular groups in New Orleans and district during the late fifties.

"My favourite band of the rock era?" veteran bassist Frank Fields asked, "I would have to say Sugar Boy, because we had some records and the records made little hits. He turned down a lot of dates in New York simply because he wanted to play around here. He was kind of a homely boy. I would say that was my favourite rock band."

Sugar Boy's career came to a premature end when he got roughed up a few years back by a bunch of "rednecks" when he was playing a date around the Louisiana/Mississippi borders near Bogalusa. "It was a very bad scene because Sugar Boy had contributed so much," Mac Rebennack said. A couple of benefit concerts have been held but his previous good health has not been restored. In 1973 he was trying to get a gospel group together.

THE HAWKETTS

Then in 1954, Chess released the New Orleans recording of "Mardi Gras Mambo" by the Hawketts. A hypnotic rhythmic record it's still played on the radio every year at Mardi Gras time, and like Professor Longhair's "Go To The Mardi Gras" drives everybody mad as it is broadcast faithfully every half-hour or so. And like Longhair's record, it's re-pressed every year and still sells.

"We were really the No. 1 group around the city for a long while," said founder member Art Neville, who's now part of the Meters group. "All of the guys were still at school, and we recorded a thing which has been released every year since, a thing called 'Mardi Gras Mambo' on the Chess label. All of the guys wrote the tune, the producer is dead, so we don't know who has it now but it's still being released every year.

"The producer was a disc jockey here in New Orleans, WWEZ; it's been off the air a long time now, a disc jockey by the name of Ken Elliott. Well, we recorded it in the radio studios, you know, we had about a nine-piece group. We were foolish, we had never recorded anything, everybody was eager to do it, you know, so we did it and it happened. But as far as moneywise we didn't reap any benefits but it did do a lot for us. We did make money by getting personal appearances but as far as the royalties and things like that, we didn't get any. George Davis was on guitar and John Boudreaux was the drummer, he's in California now.

"The jock, Ken Elliott, he was known as 'Jack The Cat.' Him and two other guys wrote the tune and he called us and wanted us to do it. He had a melody and the thing just happened, must have sold over a million records.

"We played a lot of clubs at that particular time, most of the guys weren't even playing then, my brother Aaron hadn't even started then. Most of the clubs were what you'd call a discotheque joint now, just weekend jobs, three nights a week at one particular club. Like we'd travel up to Baton Rouge and around the country parts, up into Mississippi and these type of places. The good old days! Really was. Then there was the high school things, a whole lot of proms and high school dances. At the time we were just about the No. 1 group around here, if you had to rate it like that, because we had most of the work. I was playing piano and singing at the time."

Despite their success with the record the Hawketts never went into a studio again. Chess did not follow up further talent in New Orleans immediately until they contracted Paul Gayten as producer and promotion man. That was a couple of years later.

Atlantic Records

Atlantic Records has achieved phenomenal success over the years in the R & B field, then soul music, and more latterly white progressive music. Keeping in line with their far-sighted and profitable policies, Ahmet Ertegun and Jerry Wexler were not the types to miss out on a good thing, and New Orleans was no exception.

After the sessions with Professor Longhair in 1950, Atlantic returned to New Orleans in a big way in the latter part of 1953 and recorded Professor Longhair again, Tommy Ridgley, the mighty Joe Turner who had also recorded in New Orleans for Imperial, and most important of all, one R. C. Robinson, Ray Charles. Gospel sessions were also held with the Fountain of Life Singers, the Jackson Gospel Singers and the Booker Singers.

Tommy Ridgley scored big locally with "I'm Gonna Cross That River," "Ooh Lawdy My Baby" which had Ray Charles on piano, and "Jam Up," a wild instrumental which still brings in royalties as a result of being placed on several of Atlantic's compilation albums.

RAY CHARLES

Ray Charles was the biggest catch of all, and you couldn't ask for anything bigger. After a spell on the West Coast imitating the cool blues of Charles Brown and Nat King Cole, it was in New Orleans that he really found his new style, and in turn he has influenced many New Orleans artists since.

"I can remember when we were playing the high schools,"

said Art Neville, "and that's when the biggest hall you had was the Labour Union Hall, and like the only people that would pack this place would be the Hawketts and Ray Charles, that was when Ray Charles had just started that church thing. We played some gigs with him, he was around New Orleans a long time. I remember playing jobs with him, that was before he got into his band thing. Like the money these people were making out of it at the time, we didn't even know what was happening. All we wanted to do was play, we wanted a chick and $100 to play!!"

"Ray Charles was the greatest influence on me," said Al Reed, "as a teenager and a young man. As I learned to play the piano more efficiently and effectively in the service, I started music school under the G. I. Bill in 1952 and during that time Ray Charles was recording here in New Orleans and he was playing here quite often, and he rehearsed his band here. And we could go sit in on his rehearsals, we'd go to all his dances and everything, and eventually he just became my idol. So I started playing Ray Charles-type piano and then I found myself imitating Ray Charles. And every time a new record would hit the jukebox, well, to hell, I learned that, man, and I had to do that on my gig that night, you know."

By 1955, Atlantic was doing very nicely, thank you, with their incredibly talented crop of artists in New York, the Drifters, Ruth Brown, the Clovers, plus Joe Turner and Ray Charles. There was no need for them to make the long journey to New Orleans once Tommy Ridgley stopped selling.

Specialty Records, 1954

When Lloyd Price was drafted into the Army in 1953 it looked as if Specialty had lost its rising star without the prospect of an understudy waiting in the wings. It didn't stay that way long once they had signed Guitar Slim.

GUITAR SLIM

It was Johnny Vincent, who was acting as promotion man and distributor for Specialty at the time, who discovered Guitar Slim. Art Rupe was unable to get down to New Orleans, so he gave Vincent instructions over the telephone as to how he wanted the session conducted.

The result was "The Things That I Used To Do," another seminal record in New Orleans history, following on "The Fat Man" and "Lawdy Miss Clawdy". It was a monster smash and sold a million. "*Cash Box,*" in the January 16, 1954 issue, summed up the general surprise: "Guitar Slim has clicked so big all over with 'The Things That I Used To Do,' he was originally considered to be mostly a Southern artist but fooled everyone."

It was one of those records which had everything. The opening line, "*The things I used to do, I ain't gonna do no more,*" was a universal emotional experience, the instantly memorable melodic line ebbed and flowed with the now familar New Orleans riff set up by the band, Slim's crying, gospel-tinged vocal effectively interpreted the anguished lyrics and, if anything else was needed—and it was the clincher—there was Slim's incredibly majestic and powerful guitar break.

It's impact was such that it inspired a succession of records with the same melodic and lyrical base, including "Sho' Nuff I Do" by Elmore James and "The Way You Treat Me" by Ike Turner. There have been many versions of the song recorded over the years.

Art Rupe wanted details of his career to pass on to the disc jockeys, and Guitar Slim replied, "Concerning my biography, I was born Eddie Jones in Greenwood, Mississippi, December 10, 1926. I started my career as a vocalist singing with a choir in church. Later I joined a trio as a blues vocalist and after a nationally known tour I became interested in playing the guitar. I first became known to the public as a blues vocalist and guitar player in New Orleans, at Mr Frank Painia's Club, Dew Drop Inn, in 1950."

When Slim started in 1949, the great Texas blues guitarist, Clarence "Gatemouth" Brown, had a hit record out with "Boogie Rambler," and Slim adopted this as his theme tune. The trio mentioned by Slim consisted of the 15-year-old Huey Smith, drummer Willie Nettles and himself.

In 1951, Guitar Slim was recorded for the first time by Imperial. He was taken to J & M Studio by Al Young, but the session was a lack lustre affair. The next record was far better, "Feelin' Sad," which was cut whilst on tour in Nashville for Jim Bulleit's J-B label using Percy Stovall's band. "It had the real church feel," said Mac Rebennack, "the first church music to be employed on R & B records before Ray Charles."

"The Things That I Used To Do" brought him into the big time in 1954. "One of the most exciting personalities in today's long list of stellar headliners," wrote the incredibly hip *"Cash Box"* writers, "he's a pretty tall fellow who wields one of the grooviest guitars around, which is why he's called Guitar Slim."

Slim was much in demand for public performances, and he used Lloyd Lambert's group as accompanists. Pianist Lawrence Cotton, who was playing with Dave Bartholomew in 1973, was in the band at the time: "They had all sorts of music then, music was very popular, we used to play a lot of dance music. At that one time we had rhythm and blues, the other people had rock 'n' roll. These people were trying to do the dancing we've always done. We used to play across the river and from there Lloyd went on the road with Good Rockin' Brown, Lloyd went out as bass player. Then I was playing in Lloyd's band here in New Orleans, well at least at various night clubs across the river, over at Harvey, Westwego, and I forgot the other place. And he came back off the road and he decided he could do just as well as some of the bands the places that he had gone, the bands that he had heard, and he felt the group he had could do just as well. And this is how we went on the road.

"And at the time Slim had his hit, Guitar Slim, that was around '54 I think it was. We went all over the States, everywhere that he was wanted, everywhere that his record was heard, his office did the arrangements for him to get there. We travelled that way. Everywhere he went he was just a smashing hit. You know, people enjoyed seeing him because to a lot of people it appeared as if he had rubber legs, he'd rock on his legs and you'd be looking for him to fall. He'd close his eyes you know, and he had a long chord on his guitar, and he had a heavy guy and he'd get on his shoulder, walk on out, he had a long chord that would extend all the way out of the corridor.

And this guy would carry him out on his shoulder through the crowd, and the people would go wild for this sort of thing. And everywhere he went he was a hit.

"It was very enjoyable. Lloyd's band stayed with Slim all the time, all the time, in fact I stayed with him until December 1958."

Guitar Slim had a strong follow-up to "The Things That I Used To Do" with "The Story Of My Life," which was cut at the same session. After this, Art Rupe took him out to the West Coast to record for the rest of his time with Specialty which ended in 1956. It has often been said that New Orleans music does not travel, and it was true in Slim's case. That sound just did not come again. Specialty have issued an album of his work, and ignoring the irritating and unnecessary overdubs, the four New Orleans cuts (that's all he did there) are a class above the West Coast songs.

He was then signed by Atco and four rather despairing singles were released in 1957 and 1958. The spectre of "The Things That I Used To Do" seemed to hang over everything he was doing and the harder he tried to re-create it the more miserable the failure seemed to be. What even the bright boys at Atco had overlooked was that nobody ever recorded Slim's guitar as high and loud as Johnny Vincent had done on that first Specialty session.

Slim died in 1959 at the early age of 32 and was buried in his adopted home town of Thibodaux, Louisiana. "Drink killed him," said Huey Smith.

Guitar Slim was a major influence on the New Orleans scene, and apart from "The Things That I Used To Do," it's something that his records don't really show. Memories are as long as they are fond, and Al Reed's feelings about him are by no means isolated:

"Course we played a lot on the road and we played behind guys like Earl King, Smiley Lewis, Guitar Slim and most of the guys who were real swingers. Real heavy blues, man. And rock was just coming into its own at the time. I would think that a lot of the electric rock sound has been attributed to Chuck Berry but many people aren't aware of the type of guitar that Guitar Slim played. Guitar Slim was I would think a most profound musician, in that we played behind this guy and this guy had cords on his guitar that was something like 200 feet long. This guy would play on stage with his band, he would get off the stage, walk out of the door at the club, go out into the middle of the street and go across on the other side of the street, still playing his guitar, and never drop a beat, *never* drop a beat. And he could not hear what the band were doing inside the club. But he never dropped a beat and we would be playing inside the club and hear him outside, and this guy was still playing along with the band. He had an electric sound like you never heard and they would open the club doors wide so that the sound could just go in and out of the club, and he would draw people off the street. Big passing automobiles would stop and just listen to this guy play and watch him walk. And he wore these loud clothes, like red suits, cherry red, and snow white, and the loudest greens.

"I think he had a greater impact on the electric sound than any other guitarist. Because he used the electric sound very much as it is used today. And Chuck Berry was not using that sound at the time. I hear them speak of Jimi Hendrix. Jimi Hendrix was a late-comer with his electric sound. The man who had a hell of a lot to do with the electric sound was Guitar Slim, because his was the finest and his was about the first. No one else had done it before.

"He was a backwoods country boy, he came to New Orleans with just what he had on his back, didn't even have an instrument to play. People who heard him considered him a clown, but they didn't know about his musicianship. He was a clown because that was the appearance he gave. And of course, man, he made the worst faces and grimaces while he was playing and he had an accent so thick you couldn't understand more than one out of ten words. But he was a lot of fun, he was a great guy to be around, he was a man you could learn from, not what you heard but what you saw, because he could exhilarate you, man, he would lift you above and beyond clouds as he played, he would create sensations within your body that really played tricks with your mind. He was the first man to do this."

Lloyd Price and now Guitar Slim had justified Art Rupe's interest in New Orleans, but Specialty's involvement was still small, especially when compared to Imperial. They had a local hit with Earl King's "A Mother's Love," which despite the mawkishness hinted by the title, was a strong Guitar Slim-styled blues with another scintillating guitar break. Alonzo Stewart, who had previously recorded for Imperial and was a long-time member of Edgar Blanchard's Gondoliers, was also recorded. Matters were not helped when Rupe's local man, Johnny Vincent, started his own label, Ace Records, taking much of the best Specialty talent with him, notably Earl King and Huey Smith. But there was still Little Richard to come a year or so later.

Imperial Records, 1953–54

The years 1953 and 1954 were a period of intense activity for Imperial in New Orleans, which was inspired by the increasing recognition of Fats Domino. His records, however, were still classified as R & B at this stage.

FATS DOMINO (2)

After "Goin' Home" in 1952, Fats Domino consolidated this success with two blockbusters in 1953, "Goin' To The River," which reached No. 2 in a stay of fourteen weeks on the "*Billboard*" R & B chart, and "Please Don't Leave Me," a' No. 5 hit. But 1954 was a comparatively barren year. His records were still selling but not in sufficient quantities to register a single hit record. Maybe Fats was saving it up for the grand slam the following year, but even "*Cash Box*" was showing concern when in their review of "Don't You Hear Me Calling You" they stated that "the chanter has been in a bit of a slump but this platter could be the one to start things moving strong again." It did not, but personal appearances were going well, and during the year he played at Laurel Garden, New York, in February, embarked on a tour of the West Coast and North West during late summer and ended up the year with a "Midwestern junket," hitting Chicago over the Christmas holidays.

THE SPIDERS

New Orleans has never been strong on vocal groups. "In New Orleans, guys couldn't get together as a vocal group," said Dave Bartholomew, "everybody who was successful was single. There was only the Spiders who were the greatest group we've ever had out of New Orleans."

The Spiders, led by Chuck Carbo, were a curious throwback in time, for their sounds were firmly rooted in the old style vocal groups like the Dominoes and the Ravens, even with the lively backing of Dave Bartholomew's band. They were discovered at the Pelican Club in New Orleans and registered strongly with their first record in 1954, "I Didn't Want To Do It," which turned out to be their biggest hit. "You're The One" and "Witchcraft" were other popular records in their mellow ballad style.

"The Spiders, there were two brothers," said Cosimo Matassa, "one of them had a great baritone voice and his brother did the bass things. Chick and Chuck Carbo. They were originally a gospel group and I was partly instrumental in deconverting them, you might say. But they were really good and the guy who wrote some of the best things they ever did, Adolph Smith, he wrote a thing called 'You're The One.' I can hear that record now and get goose pimples. That record for me is just an emotional experience, just beautiful, and we did a couple of gospel things. Hayward used to have a great voice but he came down with tuberculosis and he was in hospital a long time. He was never able to get it together again. While he was out of the group, Leonard Carbo did some things with the Spiders and then as a single. Good voice, big, deep, that was Chuck. He had some moderate success and did some nice things."

Dave Bartholomew also recorded the Hawks and the Bees but they never matched the popularity of the Spiders.

BILLY TATE

One of the best Imperial releases from this pre-rock 'n' roll period was the almost unknown "Single Life" by Billy Tate, a blind guitarist and bass player. The Imperial files note that Tate sings "sharp" and they're right, but what they don't say is that

he approaches the song with a gay abandon, rejoicing in his
bachelor freedom,

> *"I'm a single man, and I love my single life,*   (× 2)
> *I know you want to marry, but I don't want no wife"*

Enthusiastic as Tate's vocal is, it's the magnificent piano solo
which must commute this record to an exalted status. It's not
original by any means, for it's a straight take-off of Fats Domino's
playing on "The Fat Man," but it's a sound which creates
excitement every time it's heard, rather like the "Dust My
Broom" guitar licks of Elmore James. The musicians backed
Tate with a "Fannie Mae" type riff (in 1954, remember), and
another feature was the heavy backbeat drumming, not common
in New Orleans where 2/4 time prevails, which set up an
irresistible foot-tapping beat. A whole lot of good things cooking,
then, in the record's two minutes twelve seconds time span. But
it did not sell. Tate cut other records including "Don't Call My
Name" in 1956 for Peacock, which again was done in exciting
style. He also did session and club work.

BOBBY MITCHELL

Bobby Mitchell, in contrast to Billy Tate, did sell records even if
only locally. His first releases were made with the Toppers
vocal group and "Baby's Gone" scored in New Orleans in 1954.
He recorded irregularly for Imperial right up to 1963, with a
couple of records issued on Ron in 1962. With a high-pitched
voice similar to Bobby Marchan his records did have a distinctive flavour, and among his better numbers are "4–11=44"
(the washwoman's gig in policy), "Try Rock 'n' Roll,"
"You Always Hurt The One You Love" and the definitive
version of "I'm Gonna Be A Wheel Someday." The last two
were turned into hit records later by Clarence Henry and Fats
Domino.

At this time Imperial cut Fat Man Matthews, Little Sonny
Jones and Boo Breeding, but they were really no more than

front-line vocalists for Dave Bartholomew's band and if the "Bartholomew Sound" worked for Fats Domino, its uniformity did tend to cloak these singers in a certain anonymity. More distinctive productions were made with Jesse Allen, Papa Lightfoot, Boogie Bill Webb and Roosevelt Sykes, all of whom had a harder, more blues-based style of their own. In 1954, Bartholomew also cut James Booker, a young and gifted pianist who became very much involved in the New Orleans recording scene in the next few years. "Thinkin' 'Bout My Baby" and "Doing The Hambone" are both heavy rhythmic numbers, and if the vocal chords of the 14-year-old boy weren't quite up to it, there was enough good piano to confirm his stature in years ahead.

It was also in this period of high activity that Imperial brought Pee Wee Crayton, and later, Johnny Fuller, two West Coast artists, to record under Dave Bartholomew. The sound was 100 per cent New Orleans.

PART II

Rock 'n' Roll, 1955-59

Rock 'n' Roll Music

1955 was an exciting year in the record industry, and the heat was turned on by a new craze, rock 'n' roll music. Well, not quite new, for it was nothing but a fusion of the existing blues, rhythm and blues, country and western and popular music cultures. Up until then, the markets had been quite separate, although the trend of "crossing over" had first been spotted in 1952. It took Elvis Presley and his musical hybrid style, in an unconscious way, to breakdown the existing barriers which had already been weakened by the events of the preceding three years. Presley just gave the final push.

What rock 'n' roll really stood for was a final rejection of the old orders which had been perpetuated by the major record companies like Columbia, Decca, RCA Victor and Capitol and the conveyor-belt-like "easy listening" music which their quality artists churned out. Predictably there were emotional outbursts against rock 'n' roll from the prim establishment of the time, which even went as far as Congress in Washington. Accusations like "crude and primitive," "improper enunciation," "poor grammar," "lyrical nonsense," "deafening noise" and worse, "nigger music" were bandied about freely; and from the host of the American "Juke Box Jury" programme, "All rhythm and blues records are dirty and as bad for the kids as dope." Emotional words, but rock 'n' roll had arrived.

Immediate offshoots of the rock 'n' roll craze were seen in the increasing use of electronics and advanced recording techniques, and the era's own invention, the echo chamber.

Suddenly record charts assumed an importance which had not been fully realised until now, and *"Billboard"* and *"Cash Box"* acknowledged this by extending their charts to cover the Top 100 best selling records in the country which included R & B and C & W records for the first time. Way down the ladder, local newspapers, radio stations and teen magazines were all doing the same thing. Unconsciously these charts were to have a far wider importance than the ephemera they purported to list one week, only to be replaced the next. They are now seen as valuable research documents for plotting the course of popular music in general, and individual records in particular. Besides publishing their own charts (and it is here that the roots of payola and corruption lie), the radio stations had bigger audience and advertiser response thanks to rock 'n' roll; local hops were more prominent, personal appearances by artists more frequent—in fact, more all-round interest, much more. The music business had received a welcome shot in the arm.

The music itself was real, the music of now which had no truck with the past. An invention, if you like, of the younger generation, the teenagers. "The Big Beat," for that is what it was, was the honking of saxophones, the hot licks of the electric guitar, the pounding of the piano, the slapping of the string bass and the crashing of the drums.

The rebellion was summed up vocally by the insult of "*You ain't nothin' but a hound dog, you ain't no friend of mine,*" the threat of "*Whatever you do, don't you step on my blue suede shoes,*" and of course the wild nonsense of "*Tutti frutti, au rutti.*"

LITTLE RICHARD

Little Richard's "Tutti Frutti" was one of the original rock 'n' roll records. It also happened to be recorded in New Orleans, backed by New Orleans musicians and was written by a New Orleans writer. Above all its sound was New Orleans, and it was this same sound that established Little Richard as an international artist. From the beginning, New Orleans had made an almighty contribution to rock 'n' roll.

Little Richard, coming after Lloyd Price and Guitar Slim, completed a notable hat-trick for Art Rupe in New Orleans. "Art Rupe was a lucky cat, being at the right place at the right time," commented Mac Rebennack.

Richard Penniman came from Macon, Georgia, and had an uninspiring record career until "Tutti Frutti." He had recorded a series of Roy Brown-type blues for RCA Victor in 1951 and then was signed by Don Robey for his Peacock label. At Peacock Little Richard recorded bluesy material with Johnny Otis's band and also the Tempo Toppers.

"The first place I saw Little Richard was at the Club Tijuana," said Earl King. "As a matter of fact, that's where Little Richard kicked off his imagery thing. He had a group called the Tempo Toppers and they had just made a recording and anyway Little Richard used to pack the place, man. Every night of the week, you couldn't get in there. And it was another style of singing, he was doing some Dinah Washington things, some standards, different things he was getting over, then he'd go into his own routines. With the Tempo Toppers, that's where I first met Baby Face, everybody calls him Baby Face, a hell of a piano player; Richard had this guy named Billy Brooks in his group who later cut some things on his own. That was a bad group he had, the Tempo Toppers. They were doing pretty things, Richard was in that other thing, man."

According to Bumps Blackwell, Little Richard's producer and manager, Specialty bought out his Peacock contract for a mere $600. Blackwell was sent down to New Orleans to record him, and "Tutti Frutti" came from this first session. It may be rather hard to believe but "Tutti Frutti" was the only rocker, and the other songs, which included "He's My Star," "I'm Wondering," "Directly From My Heart," "Baby," "Kansas City" and "I'm Just A Lonely Guy" were in a more sophisticated R & B style. In fact "Tutti Frutti" was only recorded at the tail-end of the session, when Blackwell had sensed it was a potential hit after Little Richard started singing an obscene song called "Wop Bop Aloo Bop" during a session break. He called in Dorothy La Bostrie, a local songwriter who wrote great lyrics but tended to use the same melody for each song, to clean up the tune. When she had finished writing "Tutti Frutti," there was only fifteen minutes' studio time left. Bumps Blackwell felt there was not enough time to teach Huey Smith, the session pianist, the piano arrangement, so he rearranged the microphone system, including one in the piano, so that Richard could sing and play at the same time. "Tutti Frutti" was cut in three takes and went on to sell 500,000 copies and make No. 21 on "*Billboard*." It was still the age of cover versions, though, and Pat Boone took the song and sold a million copies in the process. Elvis Presley also recorded this classic rock 'n' roll song.

"Little Richard had things before but he was not successful until Lee Allen and Red Tyler put that sound on him and put that good hard rock feel on him," said Mac Rebennack. "It was the New Orleans Sound that got Little Richard across and since he's left that sound behind he's never been successful."

Little Richard was later recorded by Art Rupe on the West Coast, although further sessions were held in New Orleans. " 'Long Tall Sally' I produced out here in Los Angeles," said Art Rupe, "the version that came out. What they had done in New Orleans wasn't acceptable and the title of it then was called 'The Thing.' There was a horror movie out at the time, and Richard called it 'The Thing.' When I told them I didn't like that, they came up with 'Bald Head Sally' and then we came up with 'Long Tall Sally.' 'The Girl Can't Help It' was an unusual song for Little Richard and this was recorded in New Orleans."

Unfortunately, Richard's camp antics on and off stage seem to have completely overshadowed the music he is putting down these days. However, he still returns to his New Orleans background on occasions, as when he sang lead with the Upsetters on Fats Domino's tunes, "I'm In Love Again" and "Every Night About This Time" on Little Star, and making records like "Dew Drop Inn" and "Second Line" on Reprise with a distinct New Orleans flavour.

FATS DOMINO (3)

Quite how Fats Domino fitted into the new world of rock 'n' roll does not figure at first. Warm, chubby, cuddly Fats, R & B singer. And yet there he was on a lofty pedestal along-side Elvis Presley, Bill Haley and Little Richard.

Somehow he was rock 'n' roll's safety valve, and all he was putting down was good time New Orleans music. It is as well, perhaps, to emphasise that Fats' music had not changed in any way to meet his increased popularity. He was still a rhythm and blues singer whose music just happened to be the roots of rock 'n' roll. What he had in abundance was a natural, mellow infectiousness which was instantly recognisable whether the songs were happy frolics or merely plaintive ballads. Relaxed good humour permeated his records, everything was so simple and danceable. He had no need to change.

His band helped a lot, of course. Almost every record had a tenor saxophone solo, usually from Herb Hardesty or Lee

Allen, and it so happened that the saxophone was the first musical symbol of rock 'n' roll. The band also supplied the compulsive rhythmic beat which was far more subtle than the heavy backbeat of commercial rock 'n' roll. And they could play, too.

The turning point for Fats came in 1955 when he had a strong line of releases. "Thinking Of You," "Don't You Know," "All By Myself," "Poor Me" and "Don't Blame It On Me" were still only R & B chart material, although this was some improvement on the previous lean year. "Ain't That A Shame" was something different, however, and it became his first record to hit the newly formed national charts, if only for one week in November 1955. Musically, it was still the same old Fats although the staccato breaks must have appealed to the upcoming rock 'n' rollers weaned on the stop-go of "Rock Around The Clock." However, it was the era of cover versions by white artists and family favourite, Pat Boone, took the song and made it into his first hit record and million seller.

"Bo Weevil" was also covered, this time by Teresa Brewer of the wavery voice, but the traditional song was a natural for Fats anyway and his own record went to No. 35 on *"Billboard."* Fats was now a national chart name and things were to stay that way right through until 1964.

His next record, "I'm In Love Again," was a terrific hit and went to No. 5 spot on *"Billboard's"* Hot 100. The song had a great tune that was instantly memorable, and the drive of Lee Allen's tenor stood out as he echoed Fats' vocals in call-and-response fashion. Nothing was immaterial, nothing wasted. And it was just this high all-round musical quality of Fats Domino's records which has prevented them, in general, from being stylistically dated. The sound is as fresh today as it was in the 1950's. And, in digression, the same can be said about many other New Orleans R & B records.

"My Blue Heaven" was the flip of "I'm In Love Again," and the appearance of this old favourite seemed to antagonise the detractors of rock 'n' roll, rather than appease them. "How could they do that to *our* song" seemed to be the cry of the establishment. There was a good reason behind the increased use of standard tunes. "The booking agencies," said Harrison

Verrett, "were asking all their rock 'n' roll clients to learn and use standards because they thought rock 'n' roll was on the way out and standards were coming back in. The agents couldn't book rock 'n' roll groups into some places, such as Boston."

Another standard, "Blueberry Hill," was the song that confirmed Fats Domino as a leader in his field. It was tuneful, it was rhythmic, it was simply Fats." "'Blueberry Hill' was the biggest hit," said Dave Bartholomew, "it had been done a million times before and I wasn't too interested in Fats doing it. But he insisted he wanted to do 'Blueberry Hill.' We were in Los Angeles at the time and we set out to get the music but we couldn't find it. Fats' brother-in-law, Harrison Verrett, told us most of the words so we got it together bit by bit. So what happened, Fats forgot the words in the middle of the song and this time the guy in the studio was very good and he said do the bits you know and he put all the pieces together. That was unheard of then."

So "Blueberry Hill," rather like another R & B classic, "Keep A Knockin' " by Little Richard, was made by pasting together a couple of verses on tape.

"When I first heard the record," continued Bartholomew, "Lew Chudd asked me what did I think and I said it was horrible, pull it off the streets fast, you're gonna ruin Fats. He said, 'What do you mean, we just sold two million records,' and that was in two weeks."

The quality of Fats Domino's recordings during 1956 and 1957 was uniformly high. "So Long," with its alto saxophone solo followed by the rolling piano break, is rightly considered a classic record, and coupled with the romping "When My Dreamboat Comes Home" was a double-sided hit in the summer of 1956. "Blueberry Hill" came next and then "Blue Monday," which was a No. 9 hit in the early months of 1957.

Not only was Fats reaping artists' royalties on the sales of these records, but he was also getting writers' royalties, in most cases along with Dave Bartholomew. "They'd give us so much material to pick from and I'd send him fifteen to twenty songs," admitted Dave Bartholomew. "Fats would pick the best and besides I knew what he could do, see." If the material did not come from their own pens, they would often buy out the original composer to get rights to future royalties. Such was Fats' stature that he and Bartholomew were in an unassailable bargaining position, and as a result their files in the BMI archives have reached awesome proportions today.

"I'm Walkin' " was the next big hit, getting to No. 5 in the spring of 1957. It was a great rock 'n' roll record with glorious sax breaks from Herb Hardesty over an insistent parade beat rhythm which was a throwback to the days of the New Orleans marching bands. The simple lyrics were built around the classic rock 'n' roll rhyme of "I'm walkin', I'm talkin'." "It was a very big tune," said Dave Bartholomew, "I knew it was going to be a hit."

What Dave Bartholomew did not know, though, was that the song was going to be covered by a smooth 17-year-old kid, Ricky Nelson. With "A Teenager's Romance" his record was a double-sided smash hit for Verve. Sales did not hinder Domino's version too much, which was already on the way down by the time Nelson's record hit the charts, but it did interest Lew Chudd who promptly signed him to Imperial. Chudd's business sense was right as ever, and along with Domino, Ricky Nelson became the label's star over the next five years.

"Valley Of Tears," Fats' next release, was another massive seller and then followed a string of medium-sized hits. The next big one did not come until the summer of 1958 with "Whole Lotta Loving," another record with the old two-beat parade rhythms. The song reached No. 6 and Fats Domino was re-established in the Top Ten. Incredibly, Gil Webre, a reporter for the "*Times Picayune*," the New Orleans newspaper, attended the session and his report was published in the "*New Orleans Dixie Roto*," a supplement of the "*Times Picayune*." As a living document of Domino and Bartholomew at work in their prime it is invaluable:

"I like to make records," a simple statement with all the more meaning from Antoine Domino, one of the biggest names in disc sales to develop in New Orleans since the emergence of trumpet player-singer, Louis Armstrong.

Antoine—you know him better as "Fats"—has sold almost

thirty million records during the past six years. Walk up to most any jukebox in the nation and you'll see one of Fats' records.

No doubt you've heard many of them: "Blueberry Hill" (it sold three and a half million), "I'm Walking" (almost two million), "In Love Again" (almost two million), "Blue Monday" (one million), "Valley Of Tears" (one million) or "I Want You To Know, Dear" (800,000). Fats, 29, happily married with seven youngsters, is among the élite of his profession. Yet, even after Dame Fortune has arrived, he still enjoys his work—playing and singing rhythm and blues numbers.

Recently he had a tapeing session at Cosimo's Studio on Gov. Nicholls, where he records the majority of his numbers. He went through four songs for Imperial Records. There were old favourites—"I'll Always Be In Love With You," "Margie" and "I Miss You So"—which are expected to be released in an upcoming album. The fourth was one his own creations, "Whole Lot Of Loving," recently released as one of his two sides on a single record.

Fats was neither the first nor the last to arrive for the recording session. It was set for 10 a.m. First to show up was Frank Fields, the base [sic] player. Then came others: Dave Bartholomew, Fats' recording representative and the man who makes all the arrangements for all Fats' records, guitarists Walter Nelson and Ernest McLean, drummer Charles Williams, then tenor saxophonist Warren Bell. At 10.15 Fats arrived. Missing was the second tenor man. A few minutes later Bartholomew decided to call Clarence Ford, an original member of Fats' group, to fill in. The others started rehearsing the first number, "I'll Always Be In Love With You."

"Before the session here," Bartholomew explained, "Fats, Fields, McLean and myself went through the numbers to be recorded. When we get here these pre-recording sessions, or warmups, are so the other members of the group can familiarise themselves with the music."

The warmups went on for about fifteen minutes until Ford came in. Then it was time for the first tape to be made. The tape recording later would be transferred to a master record.

Bartholomew went into the control room.

Quiet prevailed.

From the control room came a voice: " 'I'll Always Be In Love With You,' take one." It was the voice of Cosimo Matassa, operator of the studio, who was at the control board.

The drums rolled, the music started. Fats sang into a microphone suspended in front of him. In the studio, the backing music all but drowned out his voice.

"Cut," came the voice of Bartholomew through the intercom. "Fats, you don't sound like yourself."

"Slow it down," said Bartholomew. "And Fats, hold on to that beginning. Charlie, let's really hear you on drums."

"Take two," droned the voice of Matassa.

The music began. Fats started singing into the mike.

"Cut."

"I can see my mistake," said Fats. "It was on the piano."

"We missed some of the band," said Bartholomew.

Time for a playback; Fats and the other musicians listened critically to the tape, hearing their mistakes.

"Fats, put the same thing in it this time," Bartholomew said.

"Take three."

"Cut! The bass wandered that time," said Bartholomew.

"Take four."

"Cut. Charlie," Bartholomew said, "only use your right hand on the drums. . . .

Oh! you're left handed. . . . Then only use your left."

"Take five."

The group started again, and this time completed the selection.

"I made one little mistake," said Fats. "I turned my head on a word."

"Don't do it again," replied Bartholomew. "Charlie, make it with one hand."

On the ninth take they completed it again and sat back for another playback.

"I made a mistake on my piano," said Fats after hearing it. "Let's keep it but take it over."

"Take ten."

"Hold it! Fats, don't hit 'sweetheart' so hard."

"Take eleven."

Again they complete the song. Then a playback.

"That's a cleaner take," both Fats and Bartholomew agreed. "We'll keep it instead of nine."

After a ten-minute break, the group started on the second standard, "Margie."

After twelve takes, "Margie" was on tape satisfactorily. "I Miss You So" was next and it took twelve takes, too. The group ended the session by quickly recording Fats' own tune, "Whole Lot Of Loving," in six takes.

The session ended at 2 p.m. Fats and his group seemed as fresh as ever.

How did he feel?

"Great. When things go right I can make records all day. After all, I like to make them," says the man to whom they have brought fame and fortune. (November 2, 1958).

There is no reason to believe that this was an untypical Fats recording session. The overall impression is that Fats really enjoyed himself whilst making records, and the happy atmosphere of so many of his records seems to emphasise this point. Also, it confirms that Dave Bartholomew was a firm master, he knew what he wanted, and he made sure he got it.

Fats followed "Whole Lotta Loving" with two minor hits, but came big again with "I Want To Walk You Home" and "Be My Guest" in late 1959. His consistency was quite remarkable, and between 1959 and 1961, both sides of every record that Imperial released made the Top 100 charts. Although it must have been comforting for every side to make the charts, one drawback was the consequent dilution in exposure which explains the lack of a really big hit. However, his records could be safely ordered before they were put on the market, you knew what to expect, albeit with slight variations, and best of all, they would be good.

If consistency was the hallmark of Fats' music at this time, subtle changes were being made in his music. A female chorus was introduced for the first time in 1958 on "Coquette" and unlike so many mindless female groups was tastefully directed. A fuller band sound was evident on "Be My Guest" and a little later, "Tell Me That You Love Me" and "Before I Grow Too Old." And then, showing Bartholomew's great awareness of the times, the use of a violin section, the ultimate commercial weapon. The Drifters' "There Goes My Baby" has a lot to answer for. Violins may have worked well on that particular record but such was its success that seemingly every other session was utilising a bank of local philharmonic men sawing away on their fiddles. The cultured sophistication of the violin

Specialty Branch Office, North Claiborne. PHOTOGRAPH BY JAMES LA ROCCA

Bourbon Street. PHOTOGRAPH BY HANS ANDREASSON

La Salle Street. PHOTOGRAPH BY MIKE ROWE

Little Richard, 1957. PHOTOGRAPH
COURTESY MIKE LEADBITTER

Fats Domino, 1957.
PHOTOGRAPH COURTESY
ELAINE MARS

Clarence 'Frogman' Henry, 1957. PHOTOGRAPH COURTESY BLUES UNLIMITED

The Brass Rail Club, Canal Street. PHOTOGRAPH BY JOHN BROVEN

Bobby Charles, 1956. PHOTOGRAPH COURTESY BILL GREENSMITH

'*Ain't Got No Home*'.

PHOTOGRAPH BY BILL GREENSMITH

'*Blueberry Hill*'.

PHOTOGRAPH BY BILL GREENSMITH

was and is in direct contrast to the spontaneous excitement of blues and R & B.

For all that, "Walking To New Orleans" in getting to No. 6 was one of Fats Domino's biggest hits, and the strings blended in well with the rock-steady triplet piano of Fats. "The strings in the sixties," said Dave Bartholomew, "we got going with the track, put the voice on, then I'd feel what I'd want for the strings. I used to have a guy from the New Orleans Symphony, his name was Whitey. He'd put the strings in but I'd give him my ideas. I'd write him out a lead what I wanted, 'cos I knew he had big ideas and I wanted to keep it as commercial as possible."

"Don't Come Knockin'," "Three Nights A Week," "Put Your Arms Around Me Honey," "Fell In Love On Monday" were all moderate chart successes with strings, and the songs themselves were mostly very ordinary. "Natural Born Lover," a double-sided hit with the more familiar "My Girl Josephine," was another matter. The blend of soaring violins, Herb Hardesty's plaintive sax, and Domino's bluesy piano and emotional vocal was immaculate. The swirling strings in particular conjured up images of the long hot summers of Tennessee William's indolent South and the "Summertime" of George Gershwin where "the living is easy, fish are jumping and the cotton is high." "Rising Sun," issued only on album, captured a similar mood of enchantment.

Talk about Fats Domino's later Imperial releases, and it is almost certain that agreement will be made that there was a marked decline in quality. His records from this period simply do not bear this out. "What A Price" with the same haunting feel of Lloyd Price's "Just Because," the stomping boogie piano on "Ain't That Just Like A Woman," the exciting parade beat of "Shu Rah," the simplicity of "It Keeps Rainin' " and the shuffle beat of "Let The Four Winds Blow" can stand comparison with his best material. By 1962 some older tracks were being released and his Imperial recording sessions were becoming less frequent. Something was in the air. A couple of really good sessions from which came "My Real Name," "Nothing New" and "Dance With Mr Domino" proved to be his last for Imperial, and almost the last for the label itself.

D

On April 6, 1963, *"Billboard"* published a story headed "ABC–Para signs Fats Domino," and announced that "Fats Domino will soon ink a contract with the ABC–Paramount label. Domino, who has been one of the biggest selling artists on Imperial for the past decade, is expected to sign a five-figure pact with ABC–Paramount this week. Bids for Domino by some labels have run as high as $50,000 per year guarantee over a five-year period."

Between them, Fats Domino, Dave Bartholomew and Lew Chudd had created a glorious chapter in the history of American music folklore. You only have to think of all the Fats Domino imitators to justify that statement.

FATS DOMINO ON FILM

The rock 'n' roll film was a phenomenom in the middle and late fifties which was nothing more than an attempt by Hollywood to cash in on the new money-making music craze. The films always seemed to be produced on a shoestring budget, in a maximum amount of haste and the flimsiest of story lines. Speed was essential, everyone was scared that rock 'n' roll was going to collapse overnight, you see. These celluloid epics were no more than a glorified excuse for a procession of artists "lip synching" to their latest records, who were usually filmed in a club scene with annoying camera switches to the hero and heroine sipping their milk shakes whenever there was any sign of a solo from the band.

Fats Domino appeared in "Do Re Mi," "Shake Rattle And Rock," "The Girl Can't Help It," "Disc Jockey Jamboree" and "The Big Beat" before making an appearance in "Let The Good Times Roll" in 1973. "The Girl Can't Help It" with sex idol Jayne Mansfield was by far the most lavish production, and Fats was seen miming to "Blue Monday"—no scene switching for the baritone solo here, it was cut out altogether. But at least the film was in colour and with artists like Eddie Cochran, Gene Vincent and Little Richard it got world-wide exposure. Warner Brothers' "Disc Jockey Jamboree" never had the same impact although its publicity boasted "17 great recording stars, 21 hit tunes." With Jerry Lee Lewis, Charlie Gracie, Lewis Lymon, Slim Whitman, Carl Perkins, Buddy Knox,

Jimmy Bowen, Count Basie and a few more, Fats and "Wait And See" hardly got a look in.

But Fats' business was making music, whether in a recording studio or to a live audience. However, the films did serve a useful publicity service, especially overseas.

Specialty Records, 1956–58

After his successes in New Orleans, Art Rupe felt justified in opening a local branch office on North Claiborne in 1956. He hired a young jazz musician, Harold Battiste, to take over the office, his function being to sign and record local talent. Despite all that had gone before, the office did not succeed too well.

Let Battiste himself take up the story: "When Art Rupe suggested that I should go back to New Orleans to start an office for Specialty there, he hired Sonny Bono, of Sonny & Cher fame, to take my place in Los Angeles. I was a little upset just after when I found out that Sonny was being paid more than me—I was getting $100 a week whilst Sonny was taking home $125 plus gas expenses. What really upset me though was that the records I was cutting in New Orleans began to be subject to what Sonny thought. It was during this period that we lost Chris Kenner, Irma Thomas and a whole lot of people who made it soon after. I did audition tapes, sent them to Sonny and heard no more. But I learned an awful lot from Art Rupe before he went out of business."

JERRY BYRNE

"The most successful thing we actually cut in New Orleans," continued Harold Battiste, "was by a white guy named Jerry Byrne, called 'Lights Out.' It was a Mac Rebennack song by the way. That was at the time that Elvis Presley first came on the scene and I figured that if they wanted white artists who sound black, then I would show them! Because there are more cats around New Orleans who had lived in with black people than these other towns. We had Art Neville on piano on that one by the way."

"Lights Out" is rightly recognised as a rock 'n' roll classic and contains all the power, energy and excitement that is the very essence of rock 'n' roll. Art Neville's pounding piano work was no small contributory factor. But it was strickly a one-off record whose spirit was not captured in the two follow-up records. Jerry Byrne remained popular for a little while, playing hops and dances around the New Orleans area, displaying a strong Ray Charles influence in his style.

ART NEVILLE

Art Neville, having left the Hawketts, had his first solo records on Specialty, and "Cha Dooky-Doo" was a strong local seller. "That was funny because I got some credit for that record I didn't deserve," said Harold Battiste, "because I didn't know what I was doing. The guitar on the session was very loud, over-amplified. I have read several times since then that I was the founder of the distorted guitar sound, the fact was that the guy had a bad amplifier." "Ooh-Whee Baby" also sold well.

Other local artists recorded by Specialty in this period were guitarists Edgar Blanchard and Roy Montrell, the first solo record by Ernie K-Doe (as Ernest Kador), and a lovely Sugar Boy-styled tune by Lil Millet and his Creoles called "Hopeless Love." Best of all, perhaps, was Big Boy Myles's "Who's Been Foolin' You" with some amazing Professor Long-hair·type licks on piano from his brother, Warren Myles.

By now, Art Rupe was losing interest in the record business. Little Richard's sales fell dramatically after his self-imposed, but temporary, retirement to the Church and Larry Williams was unable to sustain a regular series of hits after "Short Fat Fannie" and "Bony Moronie" (Williams, who was born in New Orleans, cut all his records on the West Coast). Bumps Blackwell's departure to Keen Records with Sam Cooke in late 1957 had something to do with it, especially as Sonny Bono produced "clinker after clunker" in Los Angeles after he left, and Harold Battiste was not exactly setting the world on fire in New Orleans. And Art Rupe's renowned refusal to give payola to promote his records must have had a culminative effect.

By 1960 he had effectively closed down the Specialty operation and invested his money in oil, real estate and other business interests, although he had one final fling with Little Richard in 1964. After this he kept the Specialty office in Los Angeles open just to sell existing records to anyone who wanted them, but in 1969 revived the label by re-issuing much of the old material in album form under the wise direction of researcher Barret Hansen.

Looking back over Specialty's involvement in New Orleans, Mac Rebennack's comments about Art Rupe being a "lucky cat" and "in the right place at the right time" carry a certain amount of truth. But such remarks discount Art Rupe's ability to seek out talent, recognise it, record it, market it, and most important sell it. That's what the record industry is all about.

Chess Records, 1956–58

In 1956 Chess began to take a further interest in New Orleans and they took things a little more seriously this time by signing the veteran Paul Gayten as record man for them in New Orleans. It was a kind of rejuvenation for Gayten, who had been such an integral part of the record scene in the late forties.

PAUL GAYTEN (2)

After his association with De Luxe and Regal, Paul Gayten was signed by Okeh and most of his records were cut in New York. He still had his old vocalists, Larry Darnell and Annie Laurie, with him at the time. Between them their output was quite prolific if unexciting; his own "Cow Cow Blues" recorded in a New Orleans radio station in 1953 was probably his best record from this period.

His new contract with Chess brought him back as a person of influence in New Orleans. At this time, his group was resident at the Brass Rail Club on Canal Street. "The Brass Rail was the club where artists would get together before they hit the road," said Mac Rebennack. "And it was through Paul doing arrangements and helping them form themselves as an act. He was one of the true guys who helped most of these artists get it together. He was ideally located at the Brass Rail, and on weekends he would bring in local talent to work with the band, like Earl King. He helped plenty of artists along."

Gayten had several records released on Checker and Argo from 1954 onwards. Some were piano instrumentals like "Yo Yo Walk" and "Nervous Boogie," others were full-blooded New Orleans vocal rock 'n' roll like "The Music Goes Round And Round."

But it was in the role of producer and promotion man that Chess saw his chief role. He was fairly successful but was handicapped by the firm control that Dave Bartholomew now exerted over the New Orleans record scene. Al Reed highlights this conflict when talking about making his own first record:

"I thought it was a good idea to make a record because we could use more work. So Paul Gayten was living right over there on Paris Avenue, just four blocks from my home, so I went to Paul's house one day and asked him about recording. So he asked me to meet him at the recording studio. So I met him at the recording studio and while I was auditioning my songs for him, Dave Bartholomew showed up.

"Dave Bartholomew seemed to have a greater interest in my music than Paul did. Paul said, 'Well, I like you and I'd like to record you but I have to get the O.K. from Leonard Chess up in Chicago, and as soon as I get the O.K. for the session I'll record you.' Dave Bartholomew heard about this and saw me. He said, 'I heard you in the studio and it sounds pretty good. But if you're waiting on him to record you might be waiting around for ever. But if you want to record down here I'm the man, he's got to wait on that white man giving him the O.K. to do anything. But if you record for me, I'll record you tomorrow, because down here I'm the man.' I said, 'Well, prove to me you're the man. Yeah, I'll record tomorrow, I'm as ready as you.' He said, 'O.K. you meet me in the studio tomorrow.'

"We went into the studio, he had the band in there, I auditioned the same songs again. They were writing the arrangements the same time as I was auditioning and I was recorded in the next four hours. I had a complete session and Imperial had a record out on me in less than four months, my first record was called 'She's Rollin''."

CLARENCE "FROGMAN" HENRY (1)

Paul Gayten had more luck with Clarence Henry. Their first record together, "Ain't Got No Home," shot up the charts early in 1957 and got to No. 30 spot on *"Billboard."*

Clarence Henry relates his own story: "I got my start in high school playing in a rock 'n' roll band with Bobby Mitchell and after I left Bobby's band I started with a trio and from there I went with another band to start at the old Joy Lounge and we used to relieve Paul Gayten on Mondays.

"Leonard Chess of Chess/Checker/Argo came down and he heard a song that I had already recorded as a demo called 'I Ain't Got No Home,' about the frog and the girl that didn't have a home. He liked it but I didn't know if it was gonna make it or not. That was my first recording and a disc jockey in New Orleans, his name was Poppa Stoppa, well he took the song— he really was pushing 'Troubles Troubles'—and flipped it over to the Frog song. And everybody liked it, and they didn't know the name of the song, or who wrote it or who was singing it. So he'd say, 'Here's the Frog Song by the Frog Man,' that's how I got my name from the disc jockey, Poppa Stoppa.

"We came to write that song, it was one night at the weekend in Gretna, that used to be a big night, so this was a Sunday morning and we was supposed to get off about 2 o'clock and this was 6 o'clock in the morning. Well, I wasn't the band leader and I really wanted to go home 'cos we had been playing for about eight hours, so I just hit an old riff on the piano and the words just came out of my mouth, because the people didn't have no home, they didn't want to go home. And the longer they stayed there, the longer we had to play, you know. The Frog noises? Well, I used to do that at school time and I used to make the funny sounds of a frog. And I just started to singing it in the club, and I never knew that would come to something."

In an age of gimmicks, "Ain't Got No Home" was quite extraordinary, and it scored. The follow-ups never made it, good though they were. "It Won't Be Long" had a good shuffle beat, and "Lonely Tramp" was a fine slow blues that had a ring of Guitar Slim about it. It seemed as if Frogman Henry was stuck with the novelty tag, his music was not being taken seriously. He toured for six months on the strength of his hit, and then, "things were a bit slack, you know." But he came back again, though not until 1961.

BOBBY CHARLES

Although New Orleans is renowned for its refreshing attitude to racial matters, the colour problem was very real in the 1950's. Segregation was still widespread. Nevertheless the racial climate was freer than any other place in the South, and white singers with talent were beginning to be accepted by the black music community. The results of this musical integration were often good.

Bobby Charles was the first white kid to break into the black music scene, and he did it with the help of Paul Gayten and Chess. Charles had a flat, toneless sort of voice, with a typically unhurried white Southern feel. Life was injected into his records by the enthusiasm of Gayten's backing group which included Lee Allen, Red Tyler and Charles Williams, and the resultant sound was pure New Orleans R & B.

Born as Robert Charles Guidry in Abbeville, Louisiana, in 1938, Bobby Charles's first record, "Later Alligator," was a local hit but was covered by Bill Haley as "See You Later Alligator." The song itself was freely borrowed from Guitar Slim's "Later For You Baby," and with a few jive phrases thrown in it was a natural for the rock 'n' roll market. Publicity photographs of the time even showed Charles sporting a Haley-type "kiss curl," well greased over his forehead.

Later records by Bobby Charles showed him to have the talent to overcome such gimmickry. They followed the standard format of releases in these exciting years, one side a fast jumper, the other a slow blues ballad. It was on the ballad sides that he excelled. "On Bended Knee," "Why Did You Leave," and "Why Can't You" showed him at his best and in their way can be said to be the forerunners of the Louisiana swamp-pop idiom which reached its peak at the turn of the decade with records from Rod Bernard, Joe Barry, Jivin' Gene and other Louisiana artists.

Bobby Charles never tasted real success as a record star, and the move to Imperial did not help. There were a few gems like "I Just Want You," "Bye Bye Baby" and "Those Eyes" which went back to the roots of New Orleans R & B, others were just awful pop records, female choruses and all. But his writing had real quality, and perhaps his best song was "Before I Grow Too Old" on which Fats Domino put in a masterly performance; the most lucrative must have been "But I Do," which he wrote for Clarence Henry, "Walking To New Orleans" for Fats Domino and of course "See You Later Alligator."

Since then he's cut some ordinary C & W records for Jewel in the mid-1960's and cut an album for Bearsville in 1972 which included a good version of "Before I Grow Too Old,"

> *"I'm gonna go out dancin' every night,*
> *And I'm gonna see all the city lights,*
> *And I'm gonna do everything that I've been told,*
> *But I've got to hurry up before I grow too old."*

Paul Gayten also recorded Shreveport bluesman T. V. Slim with a remake of his local hit, "Flat Foot Sam," the great New Orleans drummer Charles Williams on two lively singles, an excellent Eddie Bo record, "Oh Oh," and Arthur & James (Booker) for the Chess group. Apart from the Clarence Henry sessions in 1960 and 1961, this period with Chess marked Paul Gayten's final involvement with New Orleans. In the 1960's he set up his own record company, Pzazz, in Los Angeles. "Put some Pzazz in your Jazz!" was the company's slogan, but whatever he put in there wasn't up to much, and the records were very unremarkable. It seemed that Paul Gayten had left his New Orleans background behind him, but his vast contribution to the New Orleans record scene in the early days cannot be forgotten.

Apollo Records

Yet another independent record company which held sessions in New Orleans in 1956 was the old-established Apollo label from New York which was owned by Ike and Bess Berman, and had a particularly strong gospel catalogue headlined by the old New Orleans gospeller Mahalia Jackson. It was only a fleeting visit, but long enough to record the young Eddie Bo with a song called "I'm Wise", a preceding version of the Little Richard hit, "Slippin' And Slidin'." As were his other Apollo cuts, it was a good record. So too was "Just For A Day" by Chuck Edwards, a pleasant Guitar Slim-styled number. However, more than such niceties were needed to satisfy labels hungry for success, and Apollo did not come back to New Orleans to ask for more.

Modern/RPM Records

The long-established West Coast-based companies of the Bihari Brothers also recorded in New Orleans in 1956. They had a good Fats Domino-inspired session with pianist Jimmy Beasley. Vocalist Richard Berry and local guitarist Eddie Lang were also cut, but by this time the Modern complex was going downhill and they never returned to New Orleans.

Herald/Ember Records

By 1957, Herald and Ember, which were run by Al Silver and Sidney Braverman, were making some sort of reputation as leading R & B labels in New York. They came down to New Orleans, principally to record Tommy Ridgley.

TOMMY RIDGLEY (2)

Tommy Ridgley had mellowed a lot since his early Roy Brown-type blues shouting days with Imperial and Atlantic. He was now singing more refined material. "He was not really a very good piano player," said Mac Rebennack, "but he was a very good blues ballad singer." Let Tommy tell about the Herald period: "Up until 1957, I went with Herald Records, that was Al Silver in New York. And I had 'When I Meet My Girl.' Well this was a big record for me, and then the next one went out, 'Baby Doo Liddle,' next one 'I've Heard That Story Before.' Well, those were the three biggest ones I had on Herald. Hungry was on drums, this particular beat was his style. Nobody could duplicate what he was doing, you know this was a thing I guess all his own. I know Lee Allen was on tenor, Red Tyler on baritone, Melvin Lastie on trumpet, Chuck Badie was on bass. In fact all the other things I did on Herald because Lee Allen had a big record on Ember too, an instrumental. But then it was a downclimb . . . . Herald used to fly down, well, Lee Allen and myself were the two biggest things they had. So whenever I got ready to record he would always fly down.

"Course when I had 'When I Meet My Girl' he came back to record me, he said 'If you make another record like that

I'm gonna buy you a Cadillac.' I said, 'I don't want no Cadillac, give me the money.' I never worried about a Cadillac, it's never been my thing, I like money. . . . I made a little money in the music business, and if I had it to do over again, I would do it again. Because it's my life now, I've never been big car crazy, I never liked all this fancy jewellery. I like women. . . . Like I said, the money I made, this was with 'When I Meet My Girl,' 'cos we got real popular in this town and I played all the colleges, all the fraternities at Tulane, L.S.U. and all over Louisiana and Mississippi. I wasn't particular about New York, no way, the record company, I was supposed to be at the Apollo Theatre on the Thursday but I didn't show up. They called and wanted to know, well what's happened, well I said the money they was offering didn't match up to the money down here. So they tried to set it up but I stayed at home.

"I wasn't particular about going to New York but now, thinking about it, if I could do that all over again, I think I would go."

Whilst in New Orleans, Herald also recorded Joe Jones, Ernie K-Doe and Big Boy Myles. From these sessions Joe Jones and Ernie K-Doe had singles released but they did nothing.

LEE ALLEN (1)

Al Silver's trip was not entirely unproductive for, Tommy Ridgley apart, he also signed star session tenor player, Lee Allen. Allen's first record, "Walkin' With Mr Lee," rose to No. 54 in the *"Billboard"* charts in early 1958.

Lee Allen tells the story behind this record: "We were on a big show with Fats Domino and at the close of the show Fats was playing 'When The Saints Go Marching In' and on this big show they had Paul 'Hucklebuck' Williams Big Band and they were playing with us on that particular last tune. Meanwhile I'd come up with this little riff of mine and these guys from New York City said why didn't I record that. I would play anything the man asked me, that's how it came up. This guy from New York called up and said, 'You got a hit.' It was the time of Dick Clark's 'Bandstand' and the tune had hit Dick Clark's 'Bandstand' and was No. 1 for about six weeks.

"And then I got a little nervous, that was it. Then the record company had me come up there and I'd never made any travelling as an individual artist, I had just worked for so many bands out of New Orleans. Everybody was looking at me!"

Gerri Hall, the vivacious singer with Huey Smith's Clowns, went on tour with Lee Allen: "After the Clowns, I went on the road with 'Walkin' With Mr Lee,' Lee Allen. I was with Lee Allen for two different shows that he made, that's all. One show he made was four or five dates, the other two dates. The band was Placide Adams, drums, Jack Willis, trumpet, Frog Joseph, trombone, Curtis Mitchell, bass, Lee Allen, saxophone, with me lead vocalist. We made Florida, Arkansas, Alabama, Georgia, North Carolina, places like Pensacola, Tampa, Mobile, Charlotte during those two tours.

"Then when he started off next time we were supposed to start off at Washington D.C. and go further up, and he owed me $100 and he paid me $80. So I quit right there in Washington."

"Tic Toc" was a minor hit later in 1958 but nothing else clicked. One of the best records was "Creole Alley," which was a real lowdown and dirty instrumental, but on the whole Lee Allen's solo records seemed to lack the fire which characterised his session work.

By 1957, the independent companies were slowing up in their use of the recording facilities in New Orleans. They didn't stop suddenly, and Vee-Jay, of Chicago, for example, made a lightning visit in 1958 to cut Lee Diamond, Larry Birdsong and Dee Clark, and Carlton, of New York, recorded Big Al Downing.

Imperial Records, 1956–59

Imperial was still very much involved, but even their activities were on a reduced scale after 1957. During 1956, they had sessions with Fats Domino, Smiley Lewis, Dave Bartholomew, the Spiders, Bobby Mitchell, Ruth (Durand) and Al (Reed),

Roy Brown and Sugar Boy, and in 1957 Chris Kenner, Faye Adams and Sugar 'n' Sweet were added to the 1956 roster. But in 1958, the line-up was reduced to Fats Domino, Smiley Lewis, Roy Brown and Bobby Charles, and in 1959 just Fats Domino and Bobby Charles.

The End of the Independents

Why did the independents leave? "The trend of the studio changed," said Earl King. "Firstly, the people wanted the facilities to record in, and Cosimo didn't have the up-to-date facilities and they just wouldn't come down. Next element was, we was posed with a problem like the musicians suffering here in New Orleans because they would be waiting on recording sessions, and everything we did here had to be on the union level, and the trend had changed in New York and Chicago and everybody was cutting non-union and the people was giving different rates. So the people would say, rather than put up with the hassle here with New Orleans musicians they'd get the people that could play like us away from New Orleans, so they used them. And they'd do a deal, so they cut at a different rate maybe lower than the union scale.

"So I was talking to Dave Bartholomew one day, he said, 'Earl, you can beat your head against the wall, man, they don't need us to get our drum sound you're talking about. They can do that.' My experience at Motown, like as a musician, we were paid $30 a session, like $7.50 a side and they were quite big then in 1963, as far as I was concerned. But when we looked at it, what they had on the staff there, they were paying bands, bands and bands, big name bands, and cutting out there, and here we are in New Orleans waiting for a major to record. He ain't coming in here. So this creates a lot of frustration with musicians. And another with production itself. It got so that a lot of writers and producers around here wanted to imitate Motown and so denounce your own identity and do it that way. Many of the producers didn't realise that they were doing excerpts of their own thing chucked back to them in reverse because Motown did a lot of things with New Orleans rhythms and things."

It was an ironical situation. The major independent labels had kept the New Orleans scene alive and yet had given little in return.

"Business wasn't flourishing in the 1950's," said Cosimo Matassa. "Well, we were doing fine, I guess, by our own standards, and within my frame of reference I was doing great. At the risk of repeating myself, I don't think anybody in New Orleans except for a couple of artists that managed to get put on contractual deals, nobody in New Orleans made any money, any real money. I think that's what contributed to it not continuing more or even maintaining it. The New Orleans productions, from that rash over the years when record companies were running from all over the world to record something in New Orleans, most of it didn't amount to anything anyhow. Nothing was left after that because we didn't wind up with a home-grown industry. For all practical purposes I had the only studio, and yet I was looking around, you know, to be able to put the money together to buy another $200 microphone or something. It sounds pretentious to ask what New Orleans has influenced. It contributed its part of it, I guess. It's been a building of things, the originally funky R & B things got diluted by the white artists, and the country thing got into that, and now it's hard to tell where our roots are."

But the end of the serious involvement of the outside independent record companies did not signify the end of the New Orleans record scene. There was in fact exciting recording activity in the late 1950's which carried on well into the 1960's, but this time it was the local music men who were taking a bite at the New Orleans cherry. And as before, everything revolved around the recording studios of Cosimo Matassa.

The Studio Band

It was the sound of the Studio Band which had caught the attention of the record companies, the hit sound of the Studio Band. Only a small group of musicians was used, and it became such a closed shop that at one time it was known as "the clique."

"Little Richard used the original studio band, that consisted of Earl Palmer, Red Tyler and myself, Frank Fields on bass, guitar, and piano was two or three different guys," said Lee Allen. "And then comes Bumps Blackwell with Little Richard. That's when we recorded him and from then on everything else started. Recordings kept being hits and they kept on flying down to us. We had the foot-stomping, hand-clapping thing. Of course, we usually had a lot of fun in the studio as well, I guess, as you can hear on a lot of the stuff we do, this comes straight from the heart. Sometimes we were in the studio all day and half the night on one or two tunes. Course, things now are a little more precise but they weren't strict as they are now. We never heard anything called overtime. After four tunes we had completed one session, and then we'd go on to another session. Those were the good old days, I guess.

"Cosimo would call us, 'Hey, man, like to come and jam in,' and then people started to come to New Orleans asking for us. They'd say who was the guy on so and so . . . and Cosimo would call us and tell us to come down immediately."

Red Tyler was an integral member of the Studio Band. His recollections are strong: "When the independent recording companies came to town, from playing in Dave Bartholomew's band we did a lot of things at Cosimo's recording studios and when these recording companies would come they would say 'I want some musicians,' and we were the nucleus of all the rock that came out of New Orleans, the R & B records which came out of New Orleans.

"I'm gonna name the guys for you, Earl Palmer on drums, Ernest McLean or Justin Adams on guitar, Frank Fields on bass, several piano players, sometimes Salvador Doucette, sometimes Edward Frank, Lee Allen on tenor saxophone and me on baritone. I don't know if it was just luck, I'd like to think that it was just because we were that good, that the first few records we made were hits, so naturally every independent recording company that would come here would use us. So naturally we would record with people like Shirley & Lee, Little Richard, Sam Cooke's first record was made here—not 'You Send Me,' but when he first came out of the gospel field he was known as Dale Cook and one of the first songs he recorded was a song I wrote called 'Forever.'

"I would say these recordings went on for quite a few years. In fact the guys around town said it was a clique, that you couldn't get into it. You know it was nothing that we had to do with it, it was the people that requested the same musicians over and over. It was around the mid-1950's that Earl Palmer left town, and it was then that the other musicians started coming in like Melvin Lastie, Harold Battiste, Allen Toussaint. I was still rather active in the business and later on I was A & R man for Ace Records.

"The nucleus of the Studio Band was out of Dave Bartholomew's band. Not necessarily Dave himself because he had reached a level that other people wouldn't call Dave up and say 'Hey man, do you want to make up a session?', they called other people. So if we needed a trumpet player, nobody would say, 'Hey, Dave, you wanna make a session?' because he would probably say, 'No, man, I don't have time.' But the nucleus of the whole thing, well, Lee Allen played with Paul Gayten and we were old friends, you know, and we jammed around. See that's something else they don't do in the city much, but I remember during the 1950's that the thing to do once you got off your regular gig was to head up to the Dew Drop and have jam sessions till the sun comes up, you know what I mean, just for kicks. But like I said, the bass player was from Dave Bartholomew's band, so was the drummer, myself, the guitarist, Ernest McLean in the beginning, that was really the nucleus of the Studio Band. Now Lee Allen playing with Paul Gayten, naturally he was in it. It wasn't done, hey we're gonna pick this guy, and this guy. I think Cosimo said, 'Well, hey man, we need a baritone sax and a tenor sax, and I know these guys can play, they can play pretty good.' And he called us up. I think it was Cosimo who was more or less responsible for getting us together because he called us on the first date, and luckily by the majority of us playing together it wasn't hard, it wasn't a foreign kind of thing, it wasn't like I'm having to find out what this guy was going to do. I knew how capable he was and where his limits were.

"Rehearsals? Now this is another thing, we were had during this time. I think we were young, we were eager to play. But believe it or not we went into the recording studio and these independent studios got away with not paying for arrangements, they got by without having contracted us. In other words, they'd come into the studio and the guys would say, 'What are you going to do?' and the artist would sing the song, the pianist would catch it, the bass would get the thing, Lee Allen and myself would get together and come up with the riff. We would create the song in the studio. You know, it was trial and error, sometimes we would start playing the riff and we would say that doesn't lay right, so let's come up with something else. And we would make the thing up right then, nothing written, so actually we got by without an arrangement fee and this is why so many independents came to this city. We didn't realise it at the time, plus the fact we were turning out hits too. But also if they had done it in California or New York they would have had to pay an arranger. Now in a sense this may have been why some of the things were so groovy, they were done how we felt, not how it was written and a piece of music written can find you to a degree, and if you do it out of your head either it lays right or it doesn't. If it grooves, it's gonna happen. So what actually happened was that we went into the studio not knowing about the recording business and no one telling us. We went into the studio where it would be a three-hour session or four sides, whichever came first, this is what a session consists of, we might be in the studio say seven hours and we didn't mind because we enjoyed it. But nobody told us we should have got paid overtime. They really got it.

"I recall that we were making $40.25 cents a session or something. But like I said, we didn't get the money we should have, three hours or four sides, but we never got all the overtime money. Every now and then I might be leader which was double. In other words, since there was no band leader as such they would swap leaders around, and we were in the studio a good part of the week, so we were getting a pretty fair living.

"To me, Cosimo's studio was the only one I've ever known, I've never seen another studio. I know it was very raw, it didn't have the plush things I've seen later, like right now his studio on Camp is very primitive, like nothing finished; in fact, if you go up there in the summer-time you are in trouble because it doesn't have an air-conditioner. It's a huge place, it's an old building and kinda primitive. But during that time I didn't know the studios were meant to be other than them. I think Cos learned while we were learning. I think through reading and travelling to other studios, the first thing I noticed was the difference. He said the room was so small so we have got to have separation, so he would build baffles by the drums to keep that sound over here. So I would say, 'Hey, man, this is big time.' So I guess he learned at the same time we learned.

"Today's recording methods makes me know that you don't have to be that good to go into the studio any more. You can goof all the way and they can patch you in. In our time there was a lot of tension that I recall when I first went into the studio because you had to do it right. You got in there, and if you goofed once you didn't do it again because you didn't want the guys to say, 'Oh, man, we almost had this.' So everybody had to take care of business because you didn't want to be the cause to start all over again."

"The importance of the Studio Band? In some ways 'yes,' in some ways 'no,'" was Cosimo's non committal reply. "I know even vocal guys would say, 'Oh, you gotta be in the clique,' you know the studio clique. What really was happening was that some of the guys were contributors, in the same sense as a lot of of the guys that do all the sessions over in Nashville now, for instance, are contributors. They are not just sidemen. They are part of the production. They say, 'How about this, what about that, try that out.' You tell 'em 'I want to do this' they come across with something that says it, or they play it in a way that contributes to what you are trying to produce.

"And there are a few guys that contributed tremendously,

probably Earl Palmer the drummer, a few of the horn men, some of the guitarists too. Strangely I don't recall anybody on the guitar playing side of it that was memorable over the years but some of them were really good. Ernest McLean was probably the best single one of the bunch and yet almost a total introvert. He sat there and you could hardly get him to talk, but he played. Walter Nelson? He recorded, the records that I know of with Fats, and only because he was with Fats' band. He had some things to say, I don't feel that he contributed much particularly to the overall thing that anybody else could have. There was another drummer, Tenoo they called him, Cornelius Coleman, the drummers that stick in mind are Blackwell, people like that, Hungry. He was a thing apart, Hungry Williams."

LEE ALLEN (2)

"Lee Allen was part leader of the Studio Band with Red Tyler. I think he played on more solos on more records, with the exception perhaps of King Curtis. His sound was part of the New Orleans Sound, him and Red Tyler played in intense harmony and also played that unison sound when backing up the singer. It was so strong, and the sound that Lee had when he played solo was so distinctive. Every artist he played behind he put a particular style on it, if it was a Little Richard solo he'd put a Little Richard signature in, if it was Fats Domino he'd do a Fats thing. But he'd always play something around the melody of the song or around the melody of the changes. Every song was a different trip, and he could be very humorous or very funky or bluesy. He was King of the funky saxophone players in the style that was being played in the 1950's. Lee made so many hit records for so many people and got nothing for it except the session fee. He would be a million-aire now if he'd got a percentage out of all those records he'd been on. Instead he just got a little bit of money which was chop-change compared with the work he put in. Considering records in those days were made on one track, everything had to be right for the take, Lee Allen would put in solos from the first or 110th take, and everyone would be just as good." (*Mac Rebennack*)

ALVIN "RED" TYLER

"Red Tyler was the true leader of the Band but he never got full credit. He would sit down and organise almost every song. He would organise the changes, teach the guitar player to change, have the piano run it down for everybody to learn, and also the piano play the correct changes and substitute chords that would be used. Red was always in charge of this although Red himself will tell you that he was lazy. But this was never in the studio, he would always take an hour out to try to get something correct. He got the famous bari sound." (*Mac Rebennack*)

"We were all great friends. They were all great guys, they worked hard for us. Red is a very sweet guy, very quiet, very mannerly, very much of a gentleman. Red Tyler is that. He can just about do anything you ask him. He's a very, very good person for giving himself to create something for somebody else." (*Gerri Hall*)

ERNEST MCLEAN

"None of the guitarists came even close to Ernest McLean. McLean was by far the best musician in Dave Bartholomew's band. He was very soft. You know when he went out to California in the late 1950's, Earl Palmer told me years later, 'Man, if Mac had more of a personality, if he was more of a go-getter he could be in the studios like I am now.' But Mac won't say anything. When he shook your hand he was like this . . . he was that kind of guy. But he was . . . I'll give you an idea of how good he was. Most guitar players, when they voice a chord on guitar, if you say, 'Give me a C9 chord,' they have one or two ways of playing this. They have one or two inversions they know, but Ernest McLean was so good, and maybe all guitarists should be, but you'd say, 'Mac, I want a C9, I want the third on top,' there was no problem for him. He didn't have to say, 'Well let me see . . .' I'm just trying to say how good he was. For instance, sometimes playing with Dave, we had a lot of balls and we'd get the stock music that you'd go down to the store and buy, you know, some popular tunes. They'd say, 'Mac, they have a french horn part, or they have a third alto part that's missing what we want, could you play it?' He'd transpose it at sight. He was just that good.

"This was one of the few musicians I knew that spent ten or eleven hours a day practising. But he was never a go-getter, he was never a guy to push himself. After he got married, I think Earl Palmer went out to the West Coast and told him how good things were and said this was where to make some money and he probably could have but he never pushed. He played with Earl Bostic just before Earl died, he played with him, a very fine musician. He helped found the Fats Domino Sound." (*Red Tyler*)

EDGAR BLANCHARD—JUSTIN "MOTHER-IN-LAW" ADAMS

"Another guy was Edgar Blanchard. Now I'm gonna give you a line of the guitar players in this city. Now Ernest McLean was far above everybody. Now Edgar Blanchard was considered a little better than Justin, I say better from the standpoint of tackling more intricate things. Because at one time Ernest McLean and Edgar Blanchard had a group called the Gondoliers, two guitars, vibes, bass and drums. Out of sight. Terrific. Really, very, very good. And what I'm saying is that Edgar Blanchard was into a few more things than Justin." (*Red Tyler*)

WALTER "PAPOOSE" NELSON

"Walter Nelson was more or less a self-taught musician. His dad was from the old guys . . . one time in the city they had guys who were almost like troubadors. I remember as a kid you might have four or five guys walking down the street and two or three of them would have guitars and they'd just be playing or singing. Or maybe at the local bar on the corner, these guys would get their guitars out and play and sing. It was this kind of thing he was raised in. Now in all probability if you say, 'Walter, now I want you to play this piece of music,' he couldn't play it. Not taking anything away from him, what he played he could play it and he was very good, but he wasn't what I would say in the same category even of Justin Adams. You put music in front of him and it didn't mean anything to him, really. But now if you played the thing for him and say, 'Listen to the way it goes,' he'd probably play as good a part as anybody else. He was pretty hip to what was going on, but he did it from his head, which was not bad, and as I say he was very good." (*Red Tyler*)

"Papoose had a miserable life, like he belonged to a family of musicians. The musicians of that family were put down and he was always the scapegoat of that family. His brother Prince La La, his cousins David and Melvin Lastie, Jessie Hill, all of these people were related. They've had very, very rough lives. They're all from the housing projects in the 9th Ward which is the ultimate in ghettoes in New Orleans—bad conditions, gang wars, just a totally bad and violent situation. These cats that came out of this and done something, I really have to respect and that they lived to make it. Papoose died of a heroin over-dose in 1962." (*Mac Rebennack*)

SALVADOR DOUCETTE—EDWARD FRANK—ALLEN TOUSSAINT

"Salvador Doucette was a very capable pianist and he played with Dave at the time I was in the band, he eventually left the band and went into service french horning, he made it a career in the services.

"But Edward Frank played a lot of things because after I left Dave's band, Earl Palmer left and it was during this time that we were working with a guy by the name of Earl Williams. I think that was one of the finest bands I've ever played in, and that was why Edward Frank was in on some of the sessions.

"Now after Frank had this stroke, Edward Frank was playing piano on most sessions, there was this little guy hanging around that was always interested in what we were doing, Allen Toussaint. He was a youngster and sometimes I recall I used to fiddle around on piano and he always used to bug me about changes, you know, 'Show me that,' and the next thing I knew he was making recording sessions on the same sessions as me." (*Red Tyler*)

FRANK FIELDS

"Frank Fields was about the most steady bass player I've ever worked with. If you set a tempo, he's got it. He plays correct, nothing fancy, very strong and dominant in his bass playing. But similar to Ernest McLean, very soft, very quiet, never pushing himself. So naturally he wasn't one of the guys, he was a little older than the rest of us too. Whereas maybe Earl Palmer, Edward Frank, Lee Allen and myself used to hang together when we got off gigs, he'd go off another way because he was from another age bracket. He's still playing and to show you the kind of guy he was, even back during that time he used to repair televisions and that's what he does as a sideline, as far back as that time." (*Red Tyler*)

EARL PALMER

"You know, they had a TV Special come on a Friday night from California, Paul Anka, Bobby Darin, well, the drummer, he was Earl Palmer, the drummer from New Orleans. We sorta started this trend with this type of drumming, you know, this beat. Earl Palmer was really one of the foundations of this type of beat." (*Tommy Ridgley*)

"Now the guy I keep mentioning is Earl Palmer, the drummer. Now he was one of the influences in Dave's band because he was such a steady drummer. He was capable of playing all types, no matter if it was jazz, rock 'n' roll and rhythm and blues. Whatever it was he was very capable. Now he is the top studio drummer on the West Coast." (*Red Tyler*)

"When things first started, Earl Palmer had the scene tied up. He was offered a lot of money so he went out to California, and they used to say they had to use two drummers in his place when he wasn't playing. In New Orleans, they tried out Edward Blackwell, who was too hip, too jazzy and June Gardner who was too straight. Every session had a different drummer until Charles Williams." (*Mac Rebennack*)

CHARLES "HUNGRY" WILLIAMS

"Like New Orleans had a point, like Lee Allen, man, like they began to concentrate on making sessions at a commercial level, just for the money and not for the production of its product. And it started getting stagnant and even in the Little Richard era you'd notice that many times, like I'd be looking at Lee Allen and he'd say 'Man, you can't get it no better than that, that's it.' " (*Earl King*)

"The change came when Funky Charles started playing

drums, that was when all the shit changed. Hungry, yeah, and a whole lot of people right now aren't hip to his contribution to rock. He was the funkiest thing out. He was crazy, Hungry he'd be on drums clowning, just clowning, and the shit he'd do. He could clown and play better than the average guy could concentrating." (*Al Reed*)

"I remember when Charles broke his leg and he was playing with his right leg in a caste. He was playing with his left foot which was so fast and his left hand was phenomenal. I've seen him do things with his left hand, I'm still waiting for another drummer to do it. It would go off like a machine-gun, man, *brrrrr* . . . real fast and you look at it and you don't believe it, but you've seen it, and you'd say, 'Wow, man. . . .' But really, Charles' playing emanated out of the calypso type stuff, that Latin type stuff. When I first heard him he sounded really Latin, he used to play with that Cuban guy, Rico, somethin' like that. Every Latin rhythm he could play, Charles could duplicate on the set, they used to have battles at the Club Tijuana. But he was one of those who drifted off and got into this whirl and that was it. He's around New York somewhere. Charles Williams, a hell of a drummer." (*Earl King*)

"Now Hungry Williams came into his own after Earl Palmer left. Now this guy had more natural ability than all of them put together. He was another musician that couldn't read a note, but as far as feeling, he would do things on the drums most drummers would say, 'How does he do that?' And it was only because he didn't know he wasn't supposed to do it. In fact, Earl Palmer and I used to get off our job and go to the place Hungry was working at. He had a thing that sounded like a roll with one hand, he didn't know you weren't supposed to do this. He did a lot of things and go into passages that better drummers would say, 'He's not going to come out of it in time,' but he did. He just had a natural talent. The whole feeling had something to do with the popularity of the records as well." (*Red Tyler*)

The Clubs

"Well, in the old days, the clubs were places for musicians to meet," said Al Reed. "There were two clubs that were most predominantly frequented by the musicians, they were the Dew Drop and the Club Tijuana. All the musicians in town would come to these clubs, to hear other musicians play, but they would enjoy listening to other musicians. And many times they had a chance to participate. And each guy would take a turn to play, and he would play or sing or whatever. It was an atmosphere like that today would be a producers' paradise, if someone would open such a club. Because you did not have to be a well-known musician, you did not have to be a known musician, you could be an unknown. If you could play an instrument or sing you were allowed up to the mike or you could play an instrument. And we would do our gigs and rush back to town, well, we played mostly out of town in those days anyway, mostly maybe 45–50 miles from town. But we always knew that we could go to the Dew Drop because it was open all night and something was happening all night, that we could sit in after hours and play. And we enjoyed playing for free more than we enjoyed playing for money. And it was at these clubs that guys really stretched and showed what they really could do. Because each guy wanted to show the other musicians or singers that they were as good as he was, and they would do their best songs or play their best tunes. It was like a competition, but no prizes involved, only the attitudes. It was mostly attitudes."

THE DEW DROP INN

The most important and influential club was the Dew Drop Inn, which was situated at (and still is) 2836, La Salle. It was managed in its heyday by the late Frank Painia, who looked after the promotions through his own firm.

"The Dew Drop Inn was the real hang-out," said Mac Rebennack, "it was where Charles Brown, Ray Charles and all your top acts would play. It's a hotel, night club and restaurant. Next door was Leroy's Steak House, now no more, where musicians would hang out. You could go in there any time and find Earl King, Huey Smith who would be there writing songs and then rehearsing in the Dew Drop when Leroy's closed. George Davis, Earl King and myself would rehearse for recording sessions at the Dew Drop because it was the only place open at 9 o'clock in the morning. All the other joints would be closed to clean up but the Dew Drop would be open because it was a hotel and restaurant. You used to just work at places like the Brass Rail and the Texas Lounge, but the Dew Drop was different. It was a scene where all the cats could find the other guys, where all the marijuana and things was, it was like a sort of headquarters and musicians' club."

"We all got something out of the Dew Drop," said Earl King, "it was an era. Man, if you wanted a band you'd go round the Dew Drop and there they were. Like Friday, Saturday and Sunday, man, you'd have thought it was the Union Hall. They should have made the Dew Drop the Union Hall upstairs because that's how many they had down there. You could always find bands. I think this was what caused a lot of musicians to communicate because a lot of them would be around here everyday, and every weekend they used to cram round there. They had jam sessions and used to play with one another, everybody knew one another."

THE CLUB TIJUANA

"I think the Club Tijuana which was located off North Claiborne coming along as a later club to the Dew Drop, was the greatest of meeting places," said Al Reed, "because the atmosphere was less formal, it was far more informal. Because the Dew Drop had the nice tables, the nice walls, and the nice bandstand, whereas the bandstand at the Tijuana was a plain old board or a plank for a stage. But it was so doggone big, you know, something about 30 feet long but only about 10 feet wide. And up there the people danced and the bands played, and this was where everybody formed on this stage. And they had the folding chairs and the plain old tables, but they had tablecloths on them, you know, and it was the type of place where the down-outters could go. You might call it a cheap joint. But by having a cheap joint they attracted the type of people who would spend only $3 or $4, whereas the

Dew Drop, you could expect to spend at least $10. Well, if a guy couldn't afford to spend $10, well he wouldn't go to the Dew Drop, he'd go to the Club Tijuana. This caused the place to be crowded most of the time, this crowd was most big, oh, the best crowd you could ever play for, this crowd really loved their music. But it was the poor type of people that really made the Club Tijuana what it was. It was this club which made musicians and turned out such musicians as Huey Smith, this was one of the places where Huey really reached his peak, at the old Club Tijuana. Huey Smith and the Clowns. Ernie K-Doe and his group called the (Blue) Diamonds, a vocal group. And of course a lot of people came into town and played there, who wouldn't and didn't play at the Dew Drop, like Little Richard. I don't recall him playing at the Dew Drop until after he had become popular. But you see, the Club Tijuana was actually the jumping off spot for the unpopular artists, people who had not yet made it. You had to have a name to play at the Dew Drop, but you didn't need a name to play at the Club Tijuana, and this was where the locals and everybody else congregated.

"In later years the Hi-Hat became the same sort of place, that was located down on Orleans Avenue, Orleans and Hillary, and the Old Gypsy Tea Room, but they never reached the same heights as the Dew Drop and Club Tijuana."

The talent nights at the Tijuana were immensely popular, with musicians and record men alike. "The Tijuana had always had talent nights for a long time," said Mac Rebennack. "I never went to the talent nights but I hear they were pretty much fixed. Guys like Lee Diamond who were professional musicians would come in with their bands and would compete with non-professional bands that did not have a chance. Lee had a group with George Davis, Big Boy Myles and Art Neville in his band and he would walk off with the show. The prizes were about $25 but, more important, they would pick up gigs from booking agents. For example, Bill Sinigal knew there would be booking agents, record company people there. The guys were just trying to get the breaks."

Johnny Vincent was one record company man who used to be a regular visitor to the Club. "Johnny would come round to listen to the talent," said Earl King. "There was Billy Tate and Hungry and Eddie Bo who at the time was calling himself Spider Bocage and Albert Scott, the guitarist, they all played there for the house band at the club. So quite naturally you could hear some good music because they really put it in. Every group that came in, they would support the acts and Robert Parker was in the group as the leader. It switched around such a lot—at one time Eddie had a band and Robert had the group, then Billy Tate. Them three, Billy Tate, Hungry and Robert just stayed there like wallpaper, because they were the house band. There wasn't too many other things at the Tijuana that had significance for Johnny but the people he found out there were people like Izzy Coo, Guitar Slim." Other popular clubs were The Dream Room, Natal's, The Safari Room, The Sands, F & M Patio as well as Lincoln Beach.

On the Road

The New Orleans club scene was unable to provide work for all the musicians in the city and much time was spent on the road playing at small clubs and dance halls throughout the South. You only went North if you had a national hit.

The circuit extended along the Gulf Coast towns in Texas, Louisiana, Mississippi, Alabama and Florida and on inland to take in Georgia, the Carolinas, and Arkansas. Touring the South was not all fun for black artists in the 1950's, especially up-country in the "redneck" towns like Slidell, Bogalusa and Lacombe, Louisiana, where the colour bigotry was such that black bands used to have to play behind curtains to a white audience. The small country Mississippi towns were particularly bad and you only played those places when times were really hard. It was nothing for a white kid, loaded with moonshine, to approach the band and demand they played his song, and he had a loaded derringer to make sure they did. Among the more notorious venues were the Louisiana offshore islands, where the musicians had to stay overnight, sleeping on poolroom tables with the "left overs" provided for meals; there was no room for complaint as the only way out was across the water. Gigs in small South Louisiana towns were better, places like

Houma, Golden Meadow, Raceland and Galliano. Bands were instructed to be ready to play at 9 o'clock and usually when the signal was given for them to start playing, there would be nobody around. And yet Mac Rebennack can recall occasions when, half an hour later, the dances would be packed with a thousand teenagers who had come literally from nowhere out of the swamplands.

"Well, we just travelled across the country," said Earl King. "At the time I was booked out of Buffalo Booking Agency in Houston, Texas, that was Don Robey. As a matter of fact he was highly influential in making 'Lonely Lonely Nights' a success because we had problems when the recording first came out, and after he started booking he was really trying to project the recording as far as he could for Johnny Vincent. At Buffalo, Evelyn Johnson was in charge and she would say, 'Tomorrow you gotta go just right up the street, so be on time for the gig.' And like that would be 700 miles! And we used to complain among the band, we used to complain how we'd jump. When we got a job say, 300/400 miles, that was nothing. Man you name it, we played it, we played so many places."

Al Reed can recall a tour he undertook with Roy Brown's band in 1956: "There was a guy down the street named Clarence, they called him Mo'. Mo' came around here early one morning about 5 o'clock and he knocked on my door. He said, 'Hey, man, I'm going on the road with Roy Brown, and the dude needs a piano player, how'd you like to go on the road with Roy?' I said, 'I don't mind.' He said, 'Well we got a gig in High Point, North Carolina, tonight, and we're gonna be leaving out in about an hour, will you be ready?' I said yes, so I got my shit together: 7 o'clock came, he hadn't left yet, so around 8 o'clock we split out of New Orleans for High Point, North Carolina. Of course, we missed the gig, my very first gig with Roy Brown. So we left out of High Point, the next gig was in Macon, Georgia, and we broke down in South Carolina. We broke a rear axle. We slept out on the highway, of course, I hadn't made any money so I didn't have any money other than a few bucks I had on me. On the road when you break down, you sleep on the wagon, course there were seven of us. We slept on the wagon, on top of the wagon or wherever we could. So we made it, eating beans out of the can, 'cos we didn't have a whole lot of money, so we finally got everything together and the gigs started coming through.

"We played the entire Palms chain in Florida, we played just about every nook and cranny in Florida that you could name. But Roy was very popular in the South. His popularity had waned in the Northern cities and in the West but on the South East he was still a big draw. We played some of the finer clubs, we played the Royal Peacock Supper Club in Atlanta, Georgia, we played there quite regularly, we played in the Meadowbrook in Savannah, we played all over Alabama, Mississippi—Vicksburg, Jackson, Mobile (Alabama), Pensacola (Florida). It was a lot of fun.

"At the time in Roy's band we had Batman (Leroy Rankin) on tenor, we had Freddy Domino, Fats' cousin, on trumpet, we only had those two horns, I played piano and we had a little guy named Vic on drums and Junior played guitar, I don't think we had a bass player, I played bass on the piano. Those were the guys in the band, and the damnedest thing was the guys could not read music, that was the reason why we had to rehearse so often. And always whenever we would run into a singer or a dancer who brought their own music, the guys had to stumble through it. And Freddy could read and I could read, so we would read out these parts and play them, and the other guys would pick them up. It was quite a hassle.

"Of course, the guys didn't get along very well with each other in the band, we always had a lot of arguments, quite a few fights. But it was a lot of fun in that you can learn from a man like Roy Brown, and Roy, he started his beginning musicians off at $18 a night, top salary was 27 bucks a night, and of course his band leader made 35 dollars. But the faster you learned to play his music the faster you got raises in pay. So I started out with Roy at 18 dollars, we rehearsed every day, we rehearsed only his music, and after the first week I was raised 3 dollars; now after the second week I was up to $25, after that I was up to top salary, $27. I played his music the way that he wanted to play and this is really all that mattered to him, having it played like he wanted it played and of course I had to learn to play in keys that I was unfamiliar with. Keys such as D flat, A flat, E flat was an easy key, but he sang a lot in D flat and A flat with different things in F sharp, and this was the way he was. Except when he wanted a real swinging thing, he used B flat, man.

"He was a joy to work with, and the man had so much soul, and he had a rhythmic like not many singers have, because there were many breaks in his songs and his music and this was where he reached for his soul. He reached for his soul during those breaks, it seemed like to him a break was opening up a door upon another horizon. And then he would venture there for awhile until he was ready to go out upon another. This was how Roy was, and I could just sit there and play with Roy and just listen to Roy. And I think what many musicians today, they never had a chance to travel on the road with more experienced talent, they miss a lot of their musical education."

Promotions

"The proprietor of the Dew Drop, Frank Painia, had something to do with Earl King, Gatemouth Brown, Chris Kenner, he booked Irma Thomas," said Tommy Ridgley. "In fact he booked anybody local. I tell you what else happened. There was a group there called the Spiders, well we were booked on a show with the colleges in Hattiesburg. Well, anyway, Frank Painia booked us and it was on a Monday night. He say, 'We gonna get you $250,' and during that time they never asked you how much you want, they tell you how much you're gonna get. He say, 'We gonna get you $250.' O.K., $250 on a Monday night, that's pretty good. This was in the 1950's too. So we get over there, he told me the man was going to give me an envelope, and I was to take it to this other fellow. Well, anyway, the man gave me the envelope and naturally I looked in the envelope—it was $750. I gave the envelope to this man, this man took that and gave me another one. So I saw that, I might as well see all the rest of them. I opened that up and they had $250. That man took $250 and Frank Painia took the other $250. Well, that's the way it was done."

"I didn't get involved with promotion," asserted Cosimo Matassa. "In one case I came across a group called the Spiders.

The Studio Band, 1957. Left to Right: Justin Adams, Edward Frank, Leonard Lee, Shirley Goodman, Lee Allen, Red Tyler.
PHOTOGRAPH COURTESY ALVIN 'RED' TYLER

Alvin 'Red' Tyler, 1973.
PHOTOGRAPH BY
JOHN BROVEN

Lee Allen, Leonard Lee, Justin Adams, Shirley Goodman, 1957. PHOTOGRAPH
BY ALVIN 'RED' TYLER

Justin Adams, with Al Smith, 1973. PHOTOGRAPH BY VALERIE WILMER

Edward Frank, Peter 'Chuck' Badie, Blanche Thomas, c. 1956.
PHOTOGRAPH BY ALVIN 'RED' TYLER

Frank Fields, bass, with Papa French Band, 1973.
PHOTOGRAPH BY JOHN BROVEN

Earl Palmer at the Dew Drop Inn,
c. 1954. PHOTOGRAPH COURTESY
TOMMY RIDGLEY

Charles 'Hungry' Williams at Cosimo's Studio, c. 1957. PHOTOGRAPH BY
ALVIN 'RED' TYLER

The Dew Drop Inn. PHOTOGRAPH BY MIKE ROWE

Restaurant and Bar, South Rampart Street. PHOTOGRAPH BY JAMES LA ROCCA

So I signed them up, I was going to be their manager, I was. I bought them each two suits, put a down-payment on a Plymouth Suburban station wagon. The girl that worked for me then, named Phyllis Boone, now in Miami, used to go on the road with them as much as to keep them together, because that was the death of all unsophisticated guys. Just as soon as they made over $50, crack! they had a personal discipline. Save your money, pay your bills, make it to the next gig, that kind of thing, show up on the job.

"Incidentally I think that lack of personal discipline probably hurt more New Orleans men than any other thing I can think of. I know of instances when a guy got his first royalty cheque, well you ought to talk to Joe Banashak, he owned the Minit thing, other than that he was a distributor, A-1 Record Distributors, he had all the independent lines that amounted to anything. Anyway, he can tell you tales of guys coming in and picking up his royalty cheque, and the Cadillac dealer was in the next block up from him and in at least one instance, a guy didn't even as much put the cheque in his pocket. He just ran down the street with it in his hands, 'I gotta put a down-payment on a car.' That's sad. I've seen a lot of these guys who could be a lot better off materially. Aside from having a home, a couple of cars, be able to send his kids to a nice school, do nice things for them and himself and to have security, and maybe be more productive in himself. Also what it meant inspirationally and that sort of thing."

Two local disc jockeys, Larry McKinley and Jim Stewart, were actively involved in promotion, arranging concerts and hops, as well as breaking records by local artists. Jim Stewart, who has been a jock with WNOE since 1957, learnt pretty quickly that when you promoted a dance, it paid to stand on the door and collect the proceeds yourself. Stewart helped to arrange the shows and concerts at the Municipal Auditorium on Orleans and St Ann between 1957 and 1965.

The Auditorium Shows

The shows at the Auditorium were typical of the mass package shows which proliferated during the rock 'n' roll era.

E

Often there would be twenty acts, averaging around $20 a time. "The white acts used to go on first," said Jim Stewart, "and then the blacks, because the blacks were always the strongest." Tommy Ridgley and his band, the Untouchables, provided the backing support throughout.

"It was a big turning point for me," said Tommy Ridgley. "I can remember when Bobby Darin and I were on the show together at the Auditorium in 1957, and back at that time you had the white show and the coloured show. The white show would come on and we would always close the show. Well, Bobby Darin had 'Splish Splash,' so at the end of his performace he had four encores, so when we came on we had five encores. And then for the grand finale, everybody came on stage and that was a beautiful moment for me. There was James Brown in 1961. They saw me and my band, James Brown came out of the dressing-room when I upset his house, like 11,000 people. When I finished, like the people tore the house down. James Brown came out of the dressing-room, like in his underclothes, he grabbed a robe and came out there and wanted to find out who I was. I said just a local. I played with just about everybody who was somebody in the rock 'n' roll era, like Little Willie John, Sam Cooke, James Brown, just about all the ones that were really big."

The Disc Jockeys

"Radio exposure was pretty heavy," said Mac Rebennack. "We had Poppa Stoppa who stuck by all the local artists whether they had hits or misses, Okey Dokey who used to play blues, and Larry McKinley who also stuck by the local artists. From Ernie The Whip, Larry McKinley, Bob Hudson, Okey Dokey, Jack The Cat, Poppa Stoppa, all of these dee-jays favoured the New Orleans artists. They didn't give a damn about payola but they took it if it came. If there was a local artist trying to make it they would try to help him along, and there were very few New Orleans artists who didn't get any airplay. The main stations which pushed R & B were WMOY which has changed its name to WYLD, WBOK, WJMR where

Poppa Stoppa was, and WWEZ where Jack The Cat and Doctor Daddy-O, who had a gospel show, were."

"In New Orleans a couple of guys dominated the industry," said Cosimo Matassa. "There was one show on the air in the early days, called the Poppa Stoppa Show on WJMR, the local AM daytime-only show. That was probably the single greatest influence on the record business in town. Incidentally the first guy that was a jock on that thing, to be accurate all of them, but the prime mover, this guy had the whole concept of the show, all the material, the format everything, was a local college guy who's now on another radio station as a gospel thing, he's also a professor out at a local university, a fine guy and a talented writer. Vernon Winslow is his name and he's on the air as 'Doctor Daddy-O.' He formatted, and wrote, and he was literally the producer of that original Poppa Stoppa show, but because of the race thing, they wouldn't put him on the air. I don't know if they ever said it, but he knew, and I knew, and I guess everybody else did. He did a show as Doctor Daddy-O and the first few years that he did that, he did it from our studio because they wouldn't let him into the hotel where the radio station was. So he went into, he went up the crate elevator, crap like that. The situation in that respect is better now. An Italian boy like myself is prejudiced now and then!

"The jocks played a lot of local material, not just here in New Orleans but everywhere. I think jock's really prided themselves on making a new record, finding something that his head said was going to be a hit record and playing it first, or even jamming it down the throats of an as yet unsuspecting audience. He knew they were going to like it and he had to convince them. I can remember records being played three or four times in a row, a guy coming on the air with some jive talk and skip the record back, the record played seven minutes, that kinda thing. Another use of this kinda thing too, this Vern Winslow, Doctor Daddy-O used it all the time. Blues records in those days had a blue lyric or word or something and he would just come in and talk right over that piece or turned the level of the record down, all sorts of horrifying words in those days that today nobody even notices. Even 'damn' or something like that was too much. Those were the days literally when the F.C.C. had a blue book, literally a list of words, just the words, forget the context. Imagine the trouble they had with a thing like 'I Love You Body And Soul.'"

The Jukeboxes

"The jukebox was a great moving force when I was on Gov. Nicholls and doing all the R & B things," said Cosimo Matassa, "because, well, TV had not become the universal medium that it is now, so the jukebox and the taverns were the prime sources of sales. Direct sales used in the phonographs, I suppose at that time there must have been thousands of jukeboxes in the R & B segment and that was about a 100,000 records that somebody had to buy. It's not quite the same thing now. I don't think they change so many records, the huge library if you will on the machine, most of them have at least 40 records in them, some 50 and a few 100. So they don't need to put so much new stuff on them as they did and they stay on longer, and technology being what it is, they last longer.

"Right after World War II, a hit record would get worn out every week on the jukebox, because shellac supplies were scarce and record formulations were poor, and in those days they were big old dynamic, magnetic playback heads, weighed about four ounces and ploughed up the records, literally, so a hit was worn out every week. It got played 100/110 times and it was worn out. So a hit record kept on selling and selling. What would fit in that era? 'Blueberry Hill' by Fats Domino. I'll bet that there were jukeboxes that wore out six discs of that on the box, because it was a long-lived record, it was popular for a while. A decent location went through six copies of that . . . wow! Think of that in volume for the manufacturer.

"It was an integral part of the industry. Plus the exposure. It would merchandise it for you, people would hear it and would buy it for themselves. That still takes place of course but now it's more orientated to what they hear on the radio and with the so-called tight play lists and selective programming, a lot of records just never get heard and never reach any kind of market size."

The Musicians' Union

There are a lot of stories about the local branch of the Musicians' Union, the American Federation of Musicians, and not all of them are good. There was no union in New Orleans just before the War, and with the increased musical activity bad deals abounded. The Union was therefore set up to protect the musicians' interests, with musicians taking an active part in its day-to-day operations. Admirable so far, but the Union seemed to have a blind spot over recording matters.

"I've nothing against Mr Winstein (President) or Mr Cottrell (Vice-President)," said a local musician, "but if either one had got into the record scene when it was alive in New Orleans, they may have helped keep it alive. They continually chased companies and artists away from New Orleans. From Fats Domino who was forced to record in Los Angeles to other artists being forced to record in New York, Los Angeles, Jackson, Texas whatever. I blame plenty of this on the Musicians' Union."

Cosimo Matassa has never been one to keep his thoughts silent about the Union but they have mellowed over the years. "We had a little trouble," he said, "there was a time when I was blaming them for it, but at this point, it's more under-standing what happened. So looking back on it, it's not as bad a viewpoint as I had at the time. We had things happen, like a company has to have a union licence to hire musicians to do recording sessions. They sign up an advance with the M.U. and agree to certain terms, rates and things like that. They have what is called a licence. I could recall instances like a company would come to New Orleans, set up a recording session, be in the middle of it or about to start when a representative of one of the locals—we had two in those days, a black one and a white one—would show up and say, 'You can't record because we don't have you on our list of companies that are on the Union list of licensees.' They probably publish that once a year or something like that, or a company might be an affiliate, or when they started this proliferation of labels, the guy might say, 'I'm with Wing Records,' but that was really Mercury. So we had a communications problem. But the guy would come in and say, 'Stop the session, you can't go on.' Then there was an hour, half-hour, hour-and-a-half orgy of long-distance telephoning to get the thing straight. I can remember one instance where the Union President, we had an insurance debit, he went out and collected from people who paid nominal weekly amounts for their life insurance, burial insurance, so he's out on his rounds walking, can't be reached, and the fella he delegated to come in and investigate about the session due to take place, stops the session. They get on the phone, two hours later, 'Yeah, O.K., this company is O.K. to record.' He says, 'Well, I only have authority to stop the session, not to let it start again.' So four hours later, five hours later, maybe the next day, maybe never, and the guy, at the last minute before he had to be somewhere else, was recorded under the worst possible mental conditions. Things like that. What bothered me was that when something like that happened, the next time it would happen again. It never progressed.

"The President of the white local, Mr David Winstein, a knowledgeable nice guy, seemed to have a brontosaurus attitude, you know, big and powerful but not very communicative. They didn't help at all. They always seemed to be around when there was something to stop or impede or make difficult.

"The other guys were running in with their little, millions of them I think, the little Magnachord portable tape machines PT6, two-head portable machines, good machines mainly intended for radio stations, things like news and spots, delayed news and junk. But record producers, especially little independents and that type of thing, were running all over the country and I guess the world with those little Magnachords doing on the spot sessions. And I'd be sitting in the studio with a union problem and there'd be three sessions going somewhere in some dance hall or something, and nothing ever happened on that. There was a lot of that.

"There were non-union sessions at our studios. We never took the position that if it wasn't union we wouldn't do it. There never were, officially at any rate, mixed sessions where union and non-union worked together except on a couple of rare occasions where either the producer sneaked it and we went along with it on the basis, well if they come in, it's your baby not ours. The guys are working for you, we just hired the hall. Or they got special arrangements to do it like with John Handy where when his money came in they would take their dues out of it. A lot of that took place.

"We had a rash of activity where AGVA, the Vocalists' Union, got into the picture when the first road shows, R & B shows with four or five stars, hit record type people, who'd come in and play the Auditorium, and they wanted to hire people to do extra parts and that, they all had to join AGVA, but if they came up with their 50 bucks for the one-shot AGVA never worried them again. That kind of union activity impeded, made for a bad situation, but that didn't apply only to New Orleans. I think that's kind of union thinking."

PART III

The Local Record Scene, 1955-63

Ace Records

Ace Records was the first local record company to operate out of New Orleans. Even then it was based at Jackson, Mississippi, but the 196-mile journey was short enough in American terms to make it a local label. Its business, however, was centred in New Orleans.

The other local record companies didn't come into the picture until the tail-end of the lucrative rock 'n' roll period, and missed a lot of the jam which the independents had enjoyed. Nevertheless, it was an eventful period which at its peak encompassed the watering down of rock 'n' roll and a revival in black R & B with a mass of dance crazes headed by the Twist. More important, New Orleans created a further development of its own sound which was climaxed by an unprecedented number of hit records in the early 1960's. It was a golden era which lasted until the Beatles turned the American music industry upside down in 1963.

The importance of Ace Records to New Orleans is amplified by Earl King, who was an early artist with them. "We only had one studio over all these years, and I don't know why," he said, "but it just made New Orleans stagnant in productions, and people say 'Why isn't New Orleans popular like it was?' At that point in the game, like, New Orleans was dealing with a lot of major companies and major companies would come in every week to do a lot of recording. So this kept New Orleans alive because this was the major companies coming, and when they stopped coming, well, it was a case of many things. A lot of people think maybe it's the musicians or the music . . ., it's just the fact that it's not like it used to be, because even Imperial, you couldn't call it a local company because it was a national company, they just had a branch office. They had a chance to project the local talent by having an office here but they were a major and we had Specialty. The only local label we had of any significance was Ace. Not even Joe Banashak who reached out in the direction of Lew Chudd out of Hollywood. It was really Johnny that had a company."

An announcement was made in the August 13, 1955, issue of "*Cash Box*" stating, "John Vincent, formerly of Specialty, formed Ace Records with home offices in Jackson, Miss. First release is 'Those Lonely Lonely Nights' by Earl King. New label has also signed Big Boy Crudup, Lightnin' Slim, Kenzie Moore, Joe Dyson, Lou Millet and Jimmy & Jack." One or two details weren't entirely correct but it did not matter because Johnny Vincent had got the publicity he wanted for his brand new baby. And from such humble beginnings, Ace Records was to grow into a major independent label whose foundations were firmly entrenched in the New Orleans R & B scene.

Johnny Vincent was of American-Italian stock, his full name being Vincent Imbragulio which he stopped using at Art Rupe's insistence because it was such a mouthful to say. He had started out in the record business in the War years when he bought six jukeboxes in Laurel, a small town in Mississippi, and it was not too long before he realised there was a ready market to be tapped in "race" records. "In Mississippi back in those days, a lot of people wouldn't even let you put a R & B record on their jukebox," he said, "but when the kids could hear the records they did want them, and they especially went for Roy Milton's 'RM Blues' and Goree Carter's 'Rock Awhile.' And the spirituals were big back then too, there was Sister Rosetta Tharpe and then Marie Knight came up with beat gospel records. We could sell 50 or 100,000 of some of those old gospel records back in those days."

After setting up a small shop in Laurel, Vincent moved to Jackson and went out on the road for a local distributor called William B. Allen Supplies. "That was also about the time that Chess started," he said, "he had a label called Aristocrat. I noticed that he was selling them to distributors for about 35 cents (they retailed even then between 79 and 98 cents) and I realised there was something more to this than I first imagined." Vincent did some recording with a little tape recorder, "in those days you'd see guys playing blues on every street corner," and started his own label, Champion, which was mainly hillbilly.

He did release a blues record by Arthur "Big Boy" Crudup on Champion which was later reissued on Ace. As Crudup was under contract to RCA Victor at the time, the record came out under the name of "Arthur 'Blues' Crump & His Guitar." Johnny Vincent also claims to have recorded Little Junior Parker and James Cotton in this period. In 1949 he started the "John Vincent Distributing Company" at 241, North Farish, Jackson, which ran successfully for four years.

By 1952 Art Rupe of Specialty Records was seeking to set up a chain of distributors for his label throughout the South and had caught word of the reputation that Vincent was building up as a hustling salesman. He called in whilst on his Southern trip. "He told me he had driven in from New Orleans," said Johnny Vincent, "and how he'd heard a lot about me and wanted me to come to work for him. So I went down to New Orleans for the weekend and took the job, not for the money but the experience. I knew then that the record industry was in a changing state because the big companies that I knew, such as Modern, were beginning to fade and I couldn't understand why. Savoy and Miracle were two others who'd had hit records but were just disappearing. Most of the guys were sharp and only interested in making a bit of money fast and then drop out."

Johnny Vincent's commitment to Specialty was total, or at least for the time being, when Art Rupe bought out his Champion label. An announcement of the purchase appeared in "*Cash Box*" on April 4, 1953. His duties for Specialty included promoting, scouting and recording talent throughout the South. His biggest success, though, was in New Orleans with Guitar Slim and "The Things That I Used To Do." Art Rupe was naturally upset when Vincent left to form his own label in 1955 after he had ploughed a lot of money into setting him up, and relations were not improved when Vincent took some of Specialty's most promising talent with him, including Earl King and Huey Smith.

Ace Records was a great name. Short, sharp, slick. Apart from the obvious marketing merits of the name, Vincent was quick to spot that by its alphabetical pre-eminence any bills due to Ace would be at the top of their debtor's pile for payment. In a nutshell, this is the mind of an alert businessman at work, and a successful one, too.

The first releases on Ace were by New Orleans artists Al

Collins, Little Bo (Eddie Bo), plus Bobby Fields. The plodding arrangements gave the records a very dated feel and the weak recording quality did not help, either; the same criticism could be levelled at some of his Specialty sessions which suggests that Johnny Vincent was not a natural producer. He was still learning. The Al Collins release has some academic interest, overlooking its value to collectors as the first release on Ace, because the song "I Got The Blues For You" was later recorded with changed lyrics by Eddie Bo on Apollo as "I'm Wise," and then more famously by Little Richard, again with revised lyrics, as the rock 'n' roll classic, "Slippin' And Slidin'." Collins' version sold fairly well, but its chances were limited after the disc jockeys wouldn't play the record because of its obscene lyrics, *"Baby with the big box, tell me where your next stop is, I got the blues for you."*

At first, Vincent concentrated more on blues artists, having been impressed with the success of Chess and Modern in this field. "I had formed Ace as a small independent label just to record blues artists and any local people I liked, Big Boy Crudup for example." So he leased material by Sonny Boy Williamson and Elmore James from his friend Lilian Mc-Murry, who owned Trumpet Records out of Jackson. Lightnin' Slim was brought in by country singer, Lou Millet, whilst still under contract to Jay Miller ("Jay was mad," said Vincent) and he also cut star Texas bluesman, Lightnin' Hopkins. Unluckily for Vincent, the blues market was rapidly tailing off at this time and the demand for this type of music was fading fast in spite of his all-star roster. The blues records did not sell, and he did not have much better luck with his white country artists, Al Terry and his Louisiana Hayriders, Jimmy & Jack, Lou Millet and J. W. Meredith.

EARL KING (I)

It was different with his New Orleans artists, though. "In those days, New Orleans had a particular sound," said Vincent. "It was a case of getting the breaks because they all had talent." The first big hit on Ace came with Earl King's blues ballad, "Those Lonely Lonely Nights," which sold 250,000 copies. "Lonely Lonely Nights," said Earl King, "that was cut at the

McMurry Studio in Jackson, Miss. It was just a little home studio and we cut from about 9 o'clock in the morning till 6 o'clock in the evening, just cutting different songs."

Earl King is a major New Orleans artist and he tells how he started out in the early 1950's: "Basically I did gospel and through a man called Victor Augustine who was a talent scout and he used to have a lot of entertainers come by his place just to jam and sit around and hopefully some recording companies would come to town and hear the talent. And around that point I met Huey Smith and we started playing little weekend engagements at a place called the Moonlight Inn in Algiers and from that we started playing together quite regular. I was just singing then and the guy at the club some-time said, 'Man, the people over here are interested in guitar music,' and he says, 'We can't afford to pay the band any money, we have a certain budget, man. We either gonna let you go or get someone who can play the guitar.' So I started fiddlin' around with the guitar, trying to learn how to play it. Then I got interested in it and really getting down with it.

"A year later I started making records and that was when we came into 'A Mother's Love.' I had one prior to that on Savoy. The Savoy came about when I met the talent scout, A & R man Lee Maghid, and he happened to be down there audition-ing songs and stuff, and I just had a whole lot of songs I was trying to get someone to sing. This guy said, 'Well, you sing them, you put them down,' so we recorded them that day. Two of the selections came out and nothing happened with them.

"So about three months later I went with Specialty because I had met Johnny Vincent as he was A & R man with Specialty at the time. He used to come around Victor Augustine's place to pick up talent and I met him at the time I was playing with Huey. Huey used to be house pianist, he played for all the talent, that kind of stuff. Well, anyway, the Johnny Vincent episode began our relationship with Specialty and we did 'A Mother's Love' and maybe six more sides. The Kings was on Specialty too, we did a thing called 'What Can I Do,' 'Till I Say Well Done,' but they were putting out records on me at the time as Earl King and the group, the guys in the band called themselves the Kings and so they were doubling up.

"Going into the Ace situation, I left Specialty when Johnny formed his label. Well, he had talked to me during the time he was with Specialty and he said, 'Well, look, Earl, I'm going into business, I think I'm gonna make a go of it.' So he said, 'If I set up a thing, your contract is just about up with Specialty, come with me.' And so that is what happened and the first thing I did with him was 'Lonely Lonely Nights' and we had success on the first record. And here I had Huey and the group with me at the time, he was on piano on most of my recordings on Ace. He was from Specialty and I always had the piano solos and the little guitar things and it was always Huey, so we started that. So that began the episode on Ace."

"Those Lonely Lonely Nights" is what Mac Rebennack has called "a classic South Louisiana two-chord (E-flat B-flat) slow ballad." It was a progression from the same melodies that Guitar Slim was using and it went on to influence the Louisiana swamp-pop style. The follow-up records were really too similar to succeed and it was not until 1958 that Earl King managed to get away from the sound of his hit record.

But "Well-O, Well-O, Well-O Baby" was worth waiting for. It was in the famous Ace rocking R & B groove which was being made famous by Huey Smith, and it was New Orleans at its very best. The record was compulsively irresistible yet made little noise, nor did the next release which was just as good, "Everybody's Carried Away" (by Rock 'n' Roll) and "A Weary Silent Night." Better results came from "Everybody Has To Cry Sometime" which was released on Vin, a subsidiary of Ace, under the pseudonym of Handsome Earl. "Johnny Vincent was a sorta superstitious person at the point," said Earl. "He believed he could do all sorts of things to change his luck so he formed Vin Records. 'Everybody Has To Cry' almost took off, it did 70–80,000 records, a little regional thing. He called me Handsome Earl on the recording and nobody knew it was me, but the dee-jays and the locals knew it was me so they told the people, but I really blew a good record because the record really took off here. That was some of Johnny's tricks, he was always doing things like that, man. If it was possible, if Johnny could have got away with it, he would release five records of you at once, he would try that, you know."

Earl King was popular. "Like, we played the circuits," he said, "and mass crowds were coming out. You could take an artist and a band and draw capacity crowds. Like, Fats didn't become popular until 1954 but he was drawing crowds, tremendous crowds from 1949 on up, the people knew that they were coming. And the same with me. When we played engagements a guy who knew the business would say, 'Man, there must be a big, big record man pulling all those people,' but the situation was much different from what it is now. You didn't have TV shows, way back then you didn't have anything to cater for the rock music and stuff. So they saw this and said, 'Man. . . .' "

It was during this time that Earl quit the big time. "We went to Mexico with the Buffalo Booking Agency," he said, "they worked us, and one day I just quit and didn't go back on the road again. It may seem funny but I was in the middle of Texas, in the middle of a wind and sand storm, and I never witnessed a sand storm. The sky got black, the sand started running. I can't stand the dust, man, and I took out, left my car with the band, caught the bus. And that was it, I've never been back working on the road like that for any agency. So I started working in and out of New Orleans, playing."

THE ROCKING BLUES

Johnny Vincent had got off to a good start with Earl King, but this did not mean a complete rejection of the country-based blues artists. The change was gradual and before the label took on a much more commercial outlook, Vincent continued to record excellent blues. But the old backporch country sound had gone, the records were more modern and they rocked. Frankie Lee Sims, an older Texas bluesman, who had been recorded by Vincent when he was working for Specialty, had one of the best records with "Walking With Frankie," a tune which is still heard in the South today. Vincent certainly had a penchant for rhythmic records, and another strong rocking blues disc was cut by Sims's drummer, Jimmy "Mercy Baby" Mullins with "Marked Deck" and "Rock And Roll Baby," using the same combo that backed Frankie Lee Sims. "Sleeping In The Ground" by harmonica player, Sammy Myers from Jackson, Miss., is recognised as one of the best blues cut in the Jimmy Reed "walking" blues idiom; Myers was backed by the splendidly named King Mose Royal Rockers.

These rocking blues records bridged the gap between the old and modern R & B sounds and were so good that it was a pity that the period of incubation could not have been longer.

During this time in 1956 and early 1957, Johnny Vincent recorded several New Orleans-styled artists. Drummer Joe Dyson did a remake of the old Tommy Ridgley song, "Looped," and guitarist Albert Scott had "I'm So Glad You're Mine." Scott had a follow-up on Vin called "Can't Let You Go, I Love You So" in 1958 which had the pulsating New Orleans beat and sold well locally. The Supremes' "Don't Leave Me Here To Cry" is now a collectors' item whilst the Blue Dots displayed an enthusiastic form of gospel rock on "Saturday Night Fish Fry." The real success of Ace, however, was started by Huey Smith.

HUEY "PIANO" SMITH AND THE CLOWNS

Ace had their first national hit record when Huey Smith and the Clowns cut "Rockin' Pneumonia And The Boogie Woogie Flu." It established the company and ensured their future involvement in New Orleans.

"Rockin' Pneumonia" was not a particularly good record in itself, and recorded in Jackson, it adds some weight to the frequent argument that New Orleans music does not travel well. Certainly much of the flair of Smith's later recordings was missing, although it did set a pattern with his vocal group, the Clowns, chanting and shouting the novelty lyrics over the rhythmic shuffle beat and Smith's insistent piano work. "Rockin' Pneumonia" was inspired by the success of Chuck Berry's "Roll Over Beethoven" and came at a time when jive lyrics were in favour. It made No. 52 on *"Billboard's"* Top 100.

Huey Smith was no overnight success. He had been playing the clubs since 1949 when he started out with Guitar Slim, and later he joined forces with Earl King. During the early 1950's he became more and more involved in session work, most notably with Lloyd Price, Smiley Lewis and Little Richard. Once Huey had said, "What was typical about my style is the heavy left-hand rhythm," and he's right. But everyone in New Orleans agrees that heavy traces of Professor Longhair's work can be seen in his more refined, sophisticated style. At one time Dave Bartholomew told him he was technically too perfect and he should hit a few wrong notes sometime, "like Little Richard." His career as a solo artist was hampered because he did not like singing, and this encouraged the formation of the Clowns vocal group. The first Clowns were comprised of Junior Gordon (real name Izzy Cougarten), Dave Dixon and Roland Cook, and they appeared on the first Huey Smith sessions for Ace, as well as having several releases in their own names. If it may have been like fitting a quart into a pint pot, Johnny Vincent was just using an old trick to increase the "depth and variety" of his catalogue. For a while the personnel of the Clowns was very fluid. Bobby Marchan, who had a minor hit with "Little Chickee Wah Wah," was brought in as lead vocalist and he added the distinctiveness that was needed to give the Clowns an original sound. With Marchan on "Rockin' Pneumonia" were "Scarface" John Williams and James Black but this group broke up, which led to the formation of the most famous collection of Clowns featuring Bobby Marchan, Gerri Hall, Eugene Francis and Billy Roosevelt. But it seemed no matter who was in the group, they almost always managed to capture the enthusiasm of the good time music that Huey Smith was putting down.

After the success of "Rockin' Pneumonia," Huey kept on the novelty gimmick kick. "No harmony singing for us," he said, "there were so many harmony group records around, but we sold records." The crazy vocals had something of the feel of the Coasters' humorous approach. "Huey was the driving force of his sessions," said Cosimo Matassa, "he had the good fortune to get together a couple of real funky background singers and they drove the sessions as much as the instrumentalists might." It was a combined effort, though, and the socking beat set up by Charles Williams with Lee Allen and Red Tyler blasting away on their horns was all part of it.

"All the Huey Smith sessions were very, very happy," said Red Tyler. "I think all of us were making enough money and I imagine we thought that this would never end. It was a happy time, very much so." Johnny Vincent played his part. He said his main aim at sessions was to get the "*chugga chugga*" drum sound, the old parade beat. "Johnny had a real gift of the gab and had a silver tongue," said Mac Rebennack. "He inspired musicians a lot with his cornball stuff. He didn't know anything about music but he'd say, 'Hungry, put some shit into it.' He pronounced everything so funny that he overused his country Jackson accent and had everybody falling about laughing."

The follow-up to "Rockin' Pneumonia" did nothing, but then "Don't You Just Know It" and "High Blood Pressure" became a monster double-sided smash hit which got to No. 9 on "*Billboard*" in the spring of 1958. "It just grew into something phenomenal," said Johnny Vincent. The alchemy of Bobby Marchan's high-flying vocals and the booming bass lines of Billy Roosevelt was explosive. "*Ah ha ha ha, hey you, gooba, gooba, gooba*" was the call-and-response theme set up by Marchan and the rest of the Clowns with the rich horn riff of Lee Allen and Red Tyler, and the driving beat of Charles Williams all cascading in together. "*Hey pretty baby, can we go strolling*," bellowed Roosevelt, "*Don't you just know it*," came the unison reply from the Clowns. And then Gerri Hall, "*You got me rocking when I ought to be rolling*." It was pure nonsense but great fun.

"It was a very strange way that 'Don't You Just Know It' was created," said Gerri Hall. "There was a gentlemen that was called Rudy Ray Moore, well at that time he was an associate of Bobby Marchan, our leader, and he was travelling with us, he was driving for us, and would say, 'Don't you know it, honey, don't you just know it.' And we were travelling, riding between Baltimore and Washington D.C. and we made 'Don't You Just Know It' up, and that was how it came about. That same night we came up with a lot of the words for 'High Blood Pressure' and who was going to sing what part, and who was going to say what part."

"*I get a high blood pressure when you call my name*" was the first line of "High Blood Pressure" with Bobby Marchan taking the lead. This time the highlight was the rolling piano of Huey Smith in the middle-break and the fade-out. He had used similar phrases on "I Hear You Knocking" by Smiley Lewis and "Those Lonely Lonely Nights" by Earl King. "People started to complain when I had done it three times," said Huey, "but it was such a damn good piano solo."

In a way it was a pity that two of Huey Smith's greatest records were paired together, especially as he was unable to find a real follow-up to this million selling double hit apart from "Don't You Know Yockomo," which climbed to No. 56 in the early months of 1959.

HUEY SMITH ON STAGE

The combustive, energetic sound that Huey Smith got in the recording studios must have been difficult to reproduce on stage. But he did just that and more. It was not unusual for Huey to stand up and play, just hitting the piano from time to time, while the Clowns were jumping around and singing leads at different parts. "That was one of the strangest groups that I've ever seen," said Gerri Hall, "they did things different from what other people did. We were just like a bunch of nomads, all of us had our own say and all of us could say what we felt. If we had something to say, we'd say it, and that was how we got along. We all loved it, we had a lot of fun. Like when Huey and Bobby Marchan, who was leader of our group at the time, had a thing going where Bobby didn't tell the people that he wasn't Huey Smith and Huey was playing on the piano and not singing."

"Huey Smith and the Clowns did a better job live than they did on record, they did a much better job in person than on record," said Al Reed, "I think their records were sterile when compared with their live performances, and their

performances in New Orleans far surpassed the performances
they did, like at the Apollo, New York. Because they weren't
really at ease, not at a place like the Apollo, they performed
and they performed but it wasn't like performing at home
because they were here among familiar people, familiar faces,
familiar surroundings. And Huey Smith and the Clowns were
a bunch of clowns, they were. Like Scarface John, he was
one of the greatest Clowns ever, and he was the lead singer,
he was killed last year, some guy shot him. He was a buddy of
mine, a real nice guy. But they would clown anywhere they'd
go, man, these guys would walk down the street clownin',
goose each other in the behind or something, or one would
walk down the street with his handkerchief around his head,
his hand around his hip playing gay or something, you know,
and then all the people would stop and they would draw a
crowd. These boys would go on Canal Street and do that.
They were clowns, you know. And this was not just I think
during professional performances, they did this everyday, man,
they were natural clowns, they were very good.

"After a while they changed personnel, and as they changed
personnel, they lost a lot of what they had of the original
Clowns, that's what success does. It brings about personal
conflict within the group and naturally it happened to the
Clowns. They were not really the same."

GERRI HALL

"Our life together was beautiful," said Gerri Hall, "with the
Clowns I went everywhere but to Canada, I left when they
sorta went to Canada. I stayed with Huey some two or three years,
we did just about every part of the United States. Were Huey
Smith and the Clowns that big? Oh, man, I have signed so
many autographs, whoo, I say is this me, has this really
happened, is it really me? I enjoyed my work, you know, it is
so much like living with it, being so much part of it. You know
it's not like a job. You'll work hard, and can be on the highway,
live out of suitcases and eat different types of food and make
800 mile jumps in an automobile in one or two days. For
me this was all beauty. The Clowns was a good name for the
group. But we were well known. I was not the featured dancer,

we all danced. But everybody had a way of pointing at me when I did my thing, you know. It made me kinda ashamed at first but I didn't mind after a little bit. When the stage fright leaves, you sorta get bold and you know you're going to do your thing so you get it ready. And all I did was to sing and dance, that's all. What I like to do, sing and dance."

The contribution of Gerri Hall to the Clowns was huge. She's a super singer and really excelled when harmonising with the rest of the group. Besides appearing on many of the Clowns Ace sessions, she had a single on Ace, "I'm The One," and a joint effort with Huey Smith as "Huey and Jerry" on Vin called "I Think You Jivin' Me." "I used to make Huey sing," she said. "He's not a singer, he's a person if you tout him the right way, he'll sing, you know, but he's not going to do much of it. He'll answer a few words that you might sing, but if you say, 'Huey, let's sing in the group,' he'll say, 'Aahh, I'll play.' But with Huey and Jerry we couldn't find anybody else to sing the boy's part so he sang it." "I Think You Jivin' Me" was good and catchy enough to become a hit, but it wasn't.

"She used to sing with the Raelets as well," said Mac Rebennack, "and she was a good singer and good looking too. She was very together, and you had to keep it together after singing with Bobby Marchan and the Clowns. She was the only chick and she used to joke she was more 'man' than the other guys in the Clowns."

HUEY SMITH—THE LATER YEARS

By 1959, the novelty R & B sounds of Huey Smith were going out of fashion. "Tu-ber-cu-lucas & The Sinus Blues," a variation of "Rockin' Pneumonia" and by its title it had to be, the doo-wop sounds of "Dearest Darling" and the socially aware "Beatnik Blues" were too good to be ignored, but they were. Suddenly Johnny Vincent had lost interest and in 1960 Smith was signed by Imperial.

Like most of the Imperial sessions at this time, Huey Smith's records were very good and the sound was an extension of the Ace sides, which wasn't bad. "Behind The Wheel," with its motor-revving noises, "Sassy Sara," which was Huey's description of Gerri Hall and on which Gerri took lead,

"Snag-A-Tooth Jeannie" and "The Little Moron," with their infectious shuffle rhythms, and "Don't Knock It," with some more doo-wop sounds, were the pick of a good bunch.

Curley Moore took over as lead vocalist and if he lacked the sparkle of Bobby Marchan, he fitted in well with Gerri Hall and the others. "They were on the way down when I joined them and on the way out when I left," he said. He was not too happy with the style of singing he had to adopt with the Clowns. "To shout '*I wanna jump*' or '*popeye*' once in a while just ain't singing," he said. Moore had a good local hit in 1966 with "Soul Train" on Hotline.

Huey Smith's next records reappeared on Ace, and Johnny Vincent got him back through some contractual technicality. It must have been upsetting for Lew Chudd and Imperial when the second record after the return to Ace, "Pop-Eye," was a No. 51 hit. Vincent had merely added the vocals of Johnny Williams, Billy Roosevelt and Gerri Hall to an old backing track with Lee Allen and Red Tyler, but it was enough to make the record the biggest in the "Popeye" dance craze which came out of New Orleans early in 1962.

After this the downhill slide continued, although Vincent did get three albums on the market before the group folded. "Having A Good Time" was released when Huey was hot and "For Dancing" and "Twas The Night Before Christmas" came from the second period. All were superb. The first two albums were mainly collections of past singles; "Twas The Night Before Christmas" was something else. "Jingle Bells," "Silent Night" and "White Christmas," done in best New Orleans R & B style, must be heard to be believed. However, the reaction to Huey's rocking treatment of these sacred tunes was so bad that Johnny Vincent had to withdraw the album from sale just after it was released in 1962.

By now the record industry was feeling the effects of the change brought about first by the Beatles and then the Soul revolution, and to compromise Huey Smith had to adjust his time-tested style. He had a few soul singles out with acts like the Soulshakers and the Pitter Pats on his own Pity-Pat label, and even recorded himself as Shindig Smith and the Soul-shakers. "Blues '67" for White Cliffs was more like the old

Huey Smith, as were the singles on Instant by the Pitter Pats with him on piano and occasional vocal. He became more involved in production work and had a local hit in 1968 with the Hueys and "Coo Coo Over You" on Instant, as well as putting out some really good funky soul records in his own name on that label in 1969.

By any yardstick, his fortunes took a dip in the 1960's. It was all too much for him and he has now taken up the Jehovah's Witnesses as a form of salvation. If he plays no more, his past exploits have been enough to put him on a pedestal alongside Fats Domino and Professor Longhair in a New Orleans "Hall of Fame." His contribution has been vast.

"Huey Smith is a very rare individual, very rare, because he has his own way with just about anything he does," said Gerri Hall. "He's a person who's not very easily influenced by other people, he has his own ideas. And he's deep, he has depth in his thoughts, he gets inside of himself, he has his own ideas of what he wants to do and he knows how to go about making them come true, to being, which is what a lot of people don't have. Huey has that. He's a very very sweet person, he's very humble, all he asks of you is that you do your work, get to work on time, and don't give him a lot of trouble. He's very good to work for. We used to ride down the highway, we always had fun together, we always rode in the station wagon, we used to do things like sing amongst ourselves, other people's tunes that we liked, we'd be ridin' 'n' singin'."

JIMMY CLANTON

With Huey Smith's records keeping the cash registers busy, Johnny Vincent was a happy man. But his mind soon took on a far more commercial outlook when the white artists on his label roster started to sell. The overall quality started to fall as well. If Earl King and Huey Smith had taken Ace Records into R & B and New Orleans then Jimmy Clanton and Frankie Ford were taking them out.

On the face of it, Jimmy Clanton was too good to be true. A good looking white kid of 17 who with a bit of grooming could be turned into an all-American "pop" idol in the company of Frankie Avalon, Bobby Rydell, Fabian and Ricky Nelson. Johnny Vincent wasn't too keen at first.

"All he could hear was Huey," said Earl King, "he missed Allen Toussaint, Little Richard, the Spiders, many incidents like that. Jimmy Clanton and Frankie Ford started a new thing for Johnny but that's another one that Johnny didn't want to record, Jimmy Clanton. I influenced him to cut Clanton, and in spite of Clanton's manager which was Cosimo Matassa, Johnny still didn't want to record him. He had this song, 'Just A Dream,' I was playing guitar, Huey on piano, Lee Allen, Red Tyler, same crew. I said to Johnny, just making a joke with him, 'It's a hit record.' He said, 'No, man, I don't like it, I don't like it.' It took off like wildfire."

Clanton's next record, "A Letter To An Angel," showed influences of the late Duke star, Johnny Ace, but from this point the R & B content was quietly extinguished. He had a string of hits, a couple of films, and between 1959 and 1961 he was a real, living teen-idol.

"Jimmy Clanton was another artist I got involved in," said Cosimo Matassa, "probably the most extensive thing. With him I actually hired some people to work in the studio and I actually went on the road with him and for him, and spent an awful amount of time trying to do something. I was moderately successful, unfortunately about the time that first contract I had with him was expiring, he was looking in other directions for direction, and he didn't renew my agreement. Probably to the detriment of both of us!"

FRANKIE FORD (1)

There was far more energy about Frankie Ford's work and he had a genuine feel for blues and R & B. He started playing in high school bands in Gretna and Algiers, just across the river from New Orleans. His first record, "Cheatin' Woman," was a local hit, but "Sea Cruise," his next, shot up to No. 14 on *"Billboard"* in spring, 1959.

"Sea Cruise" was a great song. The title alone was different enough to attract attention, and the ships' bells and foghorns were a great opener. You had to sit up and take notice. "I was opposed to the horns at the time," said Mac Rebennack, who was just starting to do studio work with Johnny Vincent, "but Joe Caronna can take credit for the great idea to overdub bells and foghorns. It sold, so I guess I was wrong, but the foghorns were out of tune with an unusually good horn section." Ford really captured the sensuous feel of the song as he sang,

> *"Old man rhythm gets in my shoes,*
> *It's no use sitting and singing the blues,*
> *So be my guest you've got nothing to lose,*
> *Let me take you on a Sea Cruise,*
> *Ooh ee, ooh ee, baby. . . ."*

What wasn't known at the time was that Huey Smith had recorded his own song with Gerri Hall and himself taking the vocals. "It was one of the heavier sounds Huey came up with," said Rebennack, but Vincent had simply taken off the vocal track, left the tremendous rhythmic backing track and had overdubbed Frankie's vocal. The same thing was done with the flip "Roberta" which had Huey's piano boogieing away over another electric riff from the hornmen, and also the follow-up, the amusing "Alimony." Frankie Ford had three more singles on Ace, had a couple of very minor hits on Imperial, never made it again, and now sings standard songs in night clubs in and around New Orleans.

MORE R & B ON ACE

There were still good things being done on Ace. Records like "Open The Door" by Little Booker, "You Little Baby Face Thing" by Joe Tex, "I Love To Rock 'n' Roll" by Eddie Bo, "Educated Fool" by Charles Brown and Amos Milburn, "Gee Baby" by Joe and Ann, "Mercy Mercy" by Gene and Al, and "New Orleans" by Big Boy Myles. Most of the latter sessions were supervised by Red Tyler who had a couple of records out himself, "Junk Village" and "Walk On." It still sounded as if everybody was enjoying themselves.

"It was very relaxed around Cosimo's," said Red Tyler. "You had guys drifting in and out, you know, people that liked the music. You might have seven musicians and twenty-five people sitting in the studios. This was how it was. James Booker and Allen Toussaint used to hang around. Strange as

it may seem they really weren't interested in you showing them
about rock or rhythm and blues, they wanted to learn the
more modern things, because we were the guys around town
that, even though we were in the studio playing rock, we
played all the jazz gigs. So more or less, when guys came into
us they would ask us about a jazz tune rather than a rock
tune, because they were pretty hip to the rock thing. They
wanted us to show them the little be-bop tunes, the Diz and
Miles and all these people. After hearing them play, you'd
say, 'Hey, man, you're capable of making a session.'

"The Ace period, that was when Cosimo contacted me to
do A & R work for Johnny Vincent and this was when we
did the Huey Smith, Jimmy Clanton, Frankie Ford, people
like this, and I did most of the work on this as arranger. I
enjoyed that period, it was beautiful. I didn't make much
money, got a lot of promises! The Ace session personnel was
when it started to change somewhat. Earl Palmer had left,
Lee Allen was still in town, I think I was using Melvin Lastie
on trumpet, er, cornet really, Lee Allen on tenor, myself tenor
and baritone, Allen Toussaint on piano, Frank Fields was still
playing bass at the time, Justin Adams on guitar and Hungry
Williams on drums."

ACE AND POP MUSIC

But times were a-changing. "Johnny saw a goldmine in the
sky with pop records," said Mac Rebennack, "and he jumped
in and got Bob Mersey to do big New York pop arrangements.
It was a total fiasco. The cats could read simple New Orleans
arrangements but not real precise, correct New York type
arrangements." Artists like Roland Stone and Johnny Fairchild
had some bite, Ike Clanton, Jimmy's brother, had a lot of
boyish charm but David Wayne Dyess and Fifi Barton had
nothing records, just like the later efforts by Jimmy Clanton
and Frankie Ford. The catalogue, by 1960, was now generally
banal, insipid pap which was meant to be popular music
but wasn't.

Rhythm and blues made a comeback in 1961 and 1962 with records by Huey Smith, Big Boy Myles, Sugar Boy Crawford, Gerri Hall, Benny Spellman and Curley Moore. On the whole they were nice but never sold well apart from "Pop-Eye." Some of the sessions were produced by Mac Rebennack but he rarely got a really good record.

THE ACE ADMINISTRATION

But as the label grew, the administration side began to fall into disarray. With the rapid increase in business, fellow American-Italians, Joe Ruffino, Joe Caronna and Cosimo Matassa were brought into the management line-up. "Joe Ruffino and Joe Caronna worked for Johnny Vincent as sales road guys and all before they became record cats on their own," said Mac Rebennack. "They were Johnny's stone hustling partners and eventually they got too much going for themselves and were scattering Johnny too far. Like Joe Caronna was managing Frankie Ford, Cosimo Matassa and Joe Caronna were managing Jimmy Clanton and Joe Ruffino was managing Lenny Capello. There were starting to be splits in the works and before the whole thing went down Johnny cut 'em a-loose. He kept Frankie and Jimmy as artists, let Lenny Capello go to Joe Ruffino and let Joe Caronna get more into management and distributing."

THE VEE-JAY DEAL

The heady days of unlimited success were over and in 1962 Johnny Vincent signed a distribution deal with Vee-Jay Records of Chicago. "Breaking Ground, Ace-Vee-Jay Deal Called Biggest Ever Of Its Kind," ran the headlines of the story in "*Billboard*". It went on:

> "The exclusive distribution deal, recently concluded between Ace Records and Vee-Jay Records in Chicago, is believed to be one of the biggest of its kind ever negotiated in the independent disk business.
> "The move will see Vee-Jay taking over all Ace promotion, sales and distribution and will soon result in a permanent move from here to New Orleans by Johnny Vincent, owner of the Ace label and the New Orleans distributorship, Record Sales.

"The deal calls for Vincent to devote himself exclusively to producing records and developing new artists. The Ace label will be maintained as it is, with three currently important artists, Jimmy Clanton, Frankie Ford and Huey Smith expected to be joined by others soon. Vincent will turn out product for release under the Vee-Jay banner as well.

"Vincent will get a guarantee of $500,000 for the life of the contract, which is expected to run for at least five years. Paul Marshall, Vee-Jay attorney, who represented Vee-Jay exec. Ewart G. Abner, Jr. in the negotiations said: 'I've been involved in a number of contract negotiations for independent producing deals, and believe me, this is twice as big as any I've ever seen.'

Johnny Vincent's reply is important because it pinpoints the problems facing independent companies in the early 1960's. The report continued:

"Vincent was frankly elated and said: "It's the only real answer for an indie company today. We simply did not have the power to keep pushing out the volume of releases that give you a chance of having a continuing string of hits. And if you don't have a string of them, the little guy, like me, gets hung up for money. The distributors will eat you alive. That's been our problem.

"We wanted to go in with someone in the same level of size that we were. We know we can turn out the product. But it takes push to get hits building up. If we didn't have the hits, we didn't have a big enough catalogue to have a decent exchange deal. The result was that we just had to eat our returns. With Vee-Jay we're with some people who have the staff and the organisation to promote and sell records. That's what we must have.

"I'm letting my whole promotion staff go and I'm closing up my shop in Jackson. I'm opening my own studio in New Orleans, and I'll be busy there producing for Ace and Vee-Jay (the deal calls for a dozen albums during the first year) and running my distributorship.

"This is the kind of arrangement that more and more of the smaller indie companies are going to have to consider. Otherwise, they don't have a chance, because indie distributors for the most part, just don't care about us. I'm happy, man, I can see great things coming out of all this."

The great things were not to be. Before long, Vee-Jay was to come across the same problems as Ace, only on a far larger scale. The company eventually collapsed in 1965, and left a trail of debris in its wake. Johnny Vincent's "biggest ever deal of its kind" fizzled out some time before Vee-Jay went broke. "Our first record with Vee-Jay was a monster record by Jimmy Clanton called 'Venus In Blue Jeans'," Vincent said, "and it sold a million and a half. But shortly afterwards Vee-Jay changed hands and went downhill. I couldn't get my records released, I couldn't get my masters back and I couldn't get my money. I couldn't afford to keep going with them and so I dropped out on the deal. 1963 and 1964 were bad years for all of the smaller independents, they all went through a hard time, even the bigger labels. And today there are hardly any independents."

With the end of the Vee-Jay deal, Vincent continued to release a few more records on Ace before giving up the record business in favour of other commercial activities. He has always been willing to talk about Ace Records which has meant the label has been better documented than most. Perhaps inspired by frequent visits from collectors, he reactivated the Ace label in 1971 with Little Shelton, who did a good version of "Sea Cruise" using the original backing track with updated electronic embellishments, and bluesman Guitar Reed. It was not quite the same as before, though.

Rex Records

Rex Records was Cosimo Matassa's own label which he started in 1958 under the close supervision of Ace, who were the distributors.

"That was my label," said Cosimo, "it probably doesn't mean much to people out of New Orleans. At the time, and even until now, Rex is the premier carnival organisation Mardi Gras group. It may not be for long, there is another group that is fast giving it a go for its money, but anyway Rex was the prestige carnival organisation, the real blue bloods belonged to it. It was kind of mock royalty but it was synonomous with Mardi Gras and New Orleans. So I had a little label with a crown, 'Rex' on the band of the crown, and it was purple, gold and green, the colours of Mardi Gras. And I did New Orleans things and a couple of country things. Mac Rebennack played on a lot of sessions, didn't help do 'em, you know. It was more than playing, he contributed, he came up with things that made it go."

MAC REBENNACK AND DR JOHN

Chuck Carbo, the former lead with the Spiders, rocker Mickey Gilley, bluesman Jerry McCain and Earl King all recorded for Rex. So did Mac Rebennack, who had a good instrumental, "Storm Warning," which was supercharged with the excitement and fears of an oncoming storm. "I was an artist for Ace and recorded an album for Rex, then cut another album for Ace," said Rebennack. "There were no contract hassles, and there was some kind of partnership deal between them."

Mac Rebennack has since made his name as Dr John and has given the New Orleans musicians a lot of publicity. He has probably overstated his own contribution to the New Orleans record scene in the late 1950's and early 1960's but he is remembered and well liked by the local musicians.

"John, Dr John is very, very close," said Earl King. "We've been in the producing thing and writing thing, and you know, we've really paid some of the similar dues, man, we've shared some of the same headaches and problems, trying to come up with something. John would say, like, 'I'm trying to get

Baronne Street. PHOTOGRAPH BY JAMES LA ROCCA

'Home from Church'. PHOTOGRAPH BY MIKE ROWE

Gerri Hall, 1973.
PHOTOGRAPH COURTESY
GERRI HALL

Huey Smith, 1970. PHOTOGRAPH BY
JOHN BROVEN

Bobby Marchan, 1957. PHOTOGRAPH COURTESY
ELAINE MARS

BOBBY MARCHAN

'*Pop-Eye*'. PHOTOGRAPH BY BILL GREENSMITH

*Ace advertisement, '*Billboard*', 1962.* PHOTOGRAPH BY BILL GREENSMITH

Jimmy Clanton and Cosimo Matassa, 1958.

PHOTOGRAPH BY
ALVIN 'RED' TYLER

Frankie Ford, 1959.

PHOTOGRAPH
COURTESY MIKE
LEADBITTER

Dr John, c. 1967. PHOTOGRAPH COURTESY
FRANK ODDO

Mac Rebennack, guitar, and Band, with Jerry Byrne, vocal, c. 1958. PHOTOGRAPH
COURTESY FRANK ODDO

Edgar Blanchard and the Gondoliers, 1959. Left to Right: Alonzo Stewart, Lawrence Cotton, Edgar Blanchard, August 'Dimes' Dupont. PHOTOGRAPH COURTESY TOMMY RIDGLEY

Allen Toussaint and Tommy Ridgley (standing) at the Dew Drop Inn, c. 1959.

PHOTOGRAPH COURTESY

ALVIN 'RED' TYLER

Battiste Joins Ric A&R Staff

HAROLD BATTISTE, JR.

NEW YORK.—Harold Battiste, Jr. has joined Ric Records of New Orleans as an A&R man. Battiste did the Joe Jones," session of "You Talk Too Much," the smash which was originally released on Ric and later taken over by Roulette. While with Specialty Records, he A&R'd successes by Little Richard and Larry Williams. Presently, he is responsible for two Ric singles, "You Can Make It If You Try" and "Closer" by Johnny Adams and "What A Fool I've Been" by Eddie Bo. He is set for eastern-mid-western promo tour on behalf of the singles. He will also be on the lookout for new talent and materials.

The Cash Box—January 28, 1961

Harold Battiste article, 'Cash Box', 1961. PHOTOGRAPH BY BILL GREENSMITH

somebody, man, to do some of my compositions,' and he'd say, 'Let's get together and write something, let's do something, 'cos it's a bug, man, sitting here day after day just getting a few sessions,' and stuff like that. But Max has always been a conscious person, very much aware of situations and conditions in the music situation. Prior to his success as Dr John I think Max was on the West Coast with Harold Battiste and I talked to him one time when he came home, and he still wouldn't give up. At one time he was talking about just quit playing for a period, and I guess you go over your history and think of all the hassles you've been through and it ain't getting no better. But Max was just one of those, George Davis was one of those too, he played a lot of instruments, he just liked to play, you know. He was the only white guy during that period.

"Put it this way in rock piano, and guitar, more piano though, we had three piano players here that was putting a lot of influence on rock and that was Huey Smith, well Professor didn't play, too many people didn't record him, he did his own thing, but Max, and Allen and later we got Jake Myles, Booker and Marcel Richards' period, that was way up in the 1960's. The objective of it is that Max, not being just white, he was one of the few piano players around here that could hear, that could tell where things were going and what was happening. Max, he was a hip dude period, man, you know. He's just fine. To sum up Max, he's very much aware and a beautiful person. I was always laughing at him and say, 'When you gonna wake up, you'll never wake up man,' and he's always in a haze. I had a job playing once and I went and got Max, got him out of bed, and his mother said, 'If you can get him up, you'll ruin him, he's lying in there sleeping.' Real difficult. 'We gotta get him out of bed.' 'What's up?' But he was like that all day. Too much."

"I remember when he used to play local gigs," said disc jockey Jim Stewart. "He and his band were always high, always late."

During the 1960's Mac Rebennack lived most of the time on the West Coast and he kept in close contact with fellow "exiled" New Orleans musicians and artists like Jessie Hill, Alvin Robinson, Shirley Goodman and Ernest McLean. It was

F

with another Orleanian, Harold Battiste, that he created the
Dr John character, specialising in Voodoo Rock. However, his
fifth album, "Gumbo," in 1972, was a faithful recreation of
the real music of his home town and a tribute to artists like
Huey Smith, Archibald, Earl King and Professor Longhair. It
created a lot of interest in New Orleans music amongst the
"*Rolling Stone*" magazine type intelligentsia and in the record
business itself. In 1973 "Right Place Wrong Time" was a hit single.

Marshall Sehorn tried to put the whole Dr John phenomenon
regarding New Orleans a little into perspective when he said,
"I think his new album will probably do more for New Orleans
because Dr John is white, and I'm really saying it like it is,
he is an ofay cat, he's got a lotta soul, he's got the roots of
New Orleans, God bless him, I hope he hits solid gold like a
lot of them. But with people like Earl King, that's all he is
he's a copyist, 'Fess, Earl, every black artist in New Orleans.
It kinda galls me a little bit to see New Orleans coming
through the back door."

Ric Records

Johnny Vincent had set an exciting local precedent with Ace
Records and it was one of his "stone hustling partners," the
late Joe Ruffino, who followed his example and formed Ric
and Ron Records in 1959.

The labels were named after Ruffino's two sons, and headquarters were set up at 630½, Baronne Street, New Orleans.
This particular area was the hub of the music business at the time
and was the home of many of the record companies, publishers
and distributors. Johnny Vincent had a hand in setting up the
labels, "I gave those Mercy Baby tapes to Ruffino to get him
started." But the labels soon assumed their independence, and
as a start Joe Ruffino wanted to get away from the Studio
Band sound. He felt New Orleans records were beginning to
sound the same, as they were, and he was sure there were
enough musicians in New Orleans for him to get by without
using the Studio Band. It was a gamble because by now men
like Lee Allen and Red Tyler were seasoned veterans and
could literally walk in and out of the studio just like that.

Perhaps that was the trouble, and the man who took over the arrangement side was Edgar Blanchard, a veteran guitarist and banjo player.

EDGAR BLANCHARD (2)

"Edgar was very good at arranging but his band was too pop, or considered to be too hip to use in New Orleans," said Mac Rebennack. "His sound was two guitars playing in harmony rather than one guitar playing the bass line and the other playing the chords. He was one of the first cats I heard with the pretty harmony sounds with guitars."

Edgar Blanchard and the Gondoliers had been around for a long time when pianist Lawrence Cotton joined the band in 1959: "I started working with Edgar Blanchard and the Gondoliers, he was a fine guitarist, after leaving Lloyd Lambert. As a matter of fact, he had a fine little band, like this stuff the Coasters were doing, we used to do a thing on 'Hang Down Your Head, Tom Dooley,' man, it would crack you up. I stayed with these guys two or three years. We even went over to Pensacola, we had that one day off on Sunday when we'd come home but we used to work six nights over at Pensacola and Mobile. That's where we stayed with Edgar Blanchard. Sure, I loved Edgar."

Frank Fields also worked with the Gondoliers for a time. "Well, I toured all over the country with them," he said, "playing army camps, navy camps, officers' clubs and that sort of stuff. Then I got tired of the road and came back to Sugar Boy."

"Edgar Blanchard was around a lot," continued Mac Rebennack. "He used to play with his band the Gondoliers, at Natal's Lounge towards St. Bernard Parish, out across the Industrial Canal. Edgar was more in touch than most with the music of the kids by playing at black and white clubs. He'd work in soul clubs around Mobile, Alabama and stuff, and come back and work in white clubs in New Orleans. His band could play anything from cocktail music to hard R & B. Edgar's band would back up visiting blues artists like Gatemouth Brown who would then play fiddle with the band behind singers like Annie Laurie."

He is not well represented on record. After he had recorded for Don Robey's Peacock label way back in 1949, he cut two good instrumentals for Specialty in 1956 including "Mr Bumps" with Roy Montrell on second guitar which was dedicated to the A & R man, Bumps Blackwell. He had two more releases on Ric which showed his hard R & B style, the instrumentals "Let's Get It" and "Knocked Out", and his cocktail style on "Lonesome Guitar." The flip of "Knocked Out" was the very bouncy and catchy "You Call Everybody Darling," with Blanchard on banjo and Gerri Hall in the vocal group.

Blanchard supervised all the early Ric sessions before giving way to ex-Specialty man, Harold Battiste. He died of cirrhosis of the liver in September 1972.

JOHNNY ADAMS

Johnny Adams was a mainstay of the Ric label. His records followed a softer, more middle-of-the-road line than many other New Orleans artists of the time. Adams had a fine, big ballad voice which was suited to this more popular type of material, and when his records with violins were released, Joe Ruffino was heard to exclaim, "Ric records have got class!" Releases like "Come On" and "A Losing Battle" sold well locally but his output was very uneven, as it veered from good R & B to saccharine pop.

When Ric and Ron folded towards the end of 1962, Adams recorded for the Watch label with Wardell Quezergue as producer and it was clear that he was developing an impressive soulful style. He made a comeback in 1969 when he had three minor hits with Shelby Singleton's SSS International label and an excellent album, "Heart And Soul", which included three original Ric recordings.

EDDIE BO

Another important Ric artist was Eddie Bo. It is doubtful if many artists anywhere have had their records released on as many labels as he has. But unlike many of his contemporaries of the 1950's, he has managed to keep abreast of the continual changes in popular music trends over the years, and so he has recorded blues, R & B, rock 'n' roll, soul, freak-out music, novelties, speciality dance records, even instrumentals.

"Bo was never a great piano player," said Mac Rebennack, "he was more in the be-bop tradition and is a more hip singer than the average New Orleans singer. He varies from that real New Orleans style into a jazz style. He sings in the flatted 5th that horn player Charlie Parker used, and the jazz influence comes out in his singing and playing as well. Eddie Bo used to give new talent a start in his band but in the last few years he has been using the old professionals. He always used to give musicians a start, like Milton 'Half A Head' Batiste, trumpet, John Boudreaux, drums, bass players like Eustace Gillum and Otis Devraney. Eddie Bo kept a good band and put on good shows; he had a cat in his band called 'El Bo' who had a little comedy act and would do a little dancin' with Eddie Bo. He has always had a good reputation around New Orleans in the tradition that Tommy Ridgley, Sugar Boy and Danny White had for a good show."

Eddie Bo's records have been uneven. His best early records were "I'm Wise" for Apollo and the pounding rocker "Oh Oh" with Paul Gayten for Chess. Some of his most rewarding work is found in his sessions for Ric between 1959 and 1962. An early Ric release, "Tell It Like It Is," an original colloquialism in 1960, with the old 2/4 time parade beat, was a fair-sized hit which spent most of the summer months "bubbling under" the Top 100 charts. "Warm Daddy" was a poor follow-up. A lazy and catchy riff was set up but nothing built on from there, and it faded out without reaching any sort of climax. "It Must Be Love" was better with a nice Fats Domino bass line and the now obligatory string section, but best of all was "Check Mr Popeye," which stirred up a lot of action and was leased to Swan Records, of Philadelphia, in 1962, for national distribution.

Throughout the sixties and into the seventies, Eddie Bo has tended to concentrate on supervising recording sessions as well as making his own records and the occasional personal appearance. He has been a strict New Orleans man, content to live and work in the Crescent City, and this is why he's not better known elsewhere.

LENNY CAPELLO

Lenny Capello, a white boy, went along with Joe Ruffino when the split with Johnny Vincent was made. His style was not particularly original and his records didn't really sell. For all that, "Tootles" and "Cotton Candy" were solid rockers in the Larry Williams groove, and later, "90 Pound Weakling," amusingly built around the Charles Atlas "kicking sand" incident, owed a lot to the Clowns and the Coasters.

AL JOHNSON

Better were the two records by Al Johnson who had recorded for Aladdin in 1956 and played at clubs like the Cadillac on Poland Avenue. "Lena" was a jumping rocker based around the "jangly" banjo of Edgar Blanchard. The next release, "Carnival Time," was terrific, and the happy, carefree mood of Mardi Gras was caught in this gay frolic by Johnson and the band as he sang,

> "*It's Carnival Time, whoa, it's Carnival Time.*
> *Oh well, it's Carnival Time, everybody's having fun.*"

The record still goes on sale at every Mardi Gras.

TOMMY RIDGLEY (3)

When Tommy Ridgley joined Ric in 1960 the label had already built up a small but talented roster of local artists. By now, he was firmly established at the Auditorium as resident bandleader, but he was not happy with his time at Ric.

"Now I tell you what was wrong with Ric," he said. "Ric was small, he didn't want to venture out, Mr Ruffino. In fact I had 'Let's Try And Talk It Over,' 'In The Same Old Way,' that was another big one, then 'I Love You Yes I Do,' that was an old tune by Ivory Joe Hunter. I did quite a few for Ric but none of them were hits. I sit and listen to them sometimes and wonder why they didn't hit. 'Should I Ever Love Again,' that was a real bluesy thing. Now you know what, on that particular record, I always said that, the calibre of musicians that Ric had at that time, I never had no say, but I never did like them, especially on that particular record. I know Harold Battiste had something to do with that, he's in California right now, a pretty big fellow, well he was arranger and he had something to do with that. It was all right but we threw it together; if we had took time on that record, I could have had a record on that tune. But they always say mine and Chuck Willis's style is so alike, and so that's why they called me the 'New King of Stroll,' not because the Stroll was the thing. I tried to get Mr Ruffino to lease 'In The Same Old Way' to a bigger company, well I know it ought to be a big record, and my record just wasn't selling, but he wouldn't. That was just part of the business."

Tommy continued to cut records during the 1960's but none ever came to much. However, he and his band are much respected and he still gets some of the best jobs going in the area. In 1973 he started producing and one of his first efforts in this role, Rose Davis's "Sittin' And Drinking," the old Christine Kittrell song, was a local New Orleans hit.

JOE JONES

Through their four-year lifespan Ric had only one sizeable hit, and that was the redoubtable Joe Jones and his famous "You Talk Too Much," which got to No. 3 in the Hot 100 in the fall of 1960. The song was a minor-keyed effort which sold more on its novelty value and fine band arrangement by Harold Battiste, rather than on Jones's rather laboured vocals. The backing side, "I Love You Still," was a real beauty though. The entire band, every man jack of them, excelled themselves on this deceptively simple blues ballad; there was so much going on, so many different cross-rhythms so delicately played and yet everything moulded into one glorious whole. But it was "You Talk Too Much" which grabbed all the attention going.

"Joe recorded that song, 'You Talk Too Much,' three times before it was a hit," said Clarence Ford, who played baritone sax on the Ric session. Yes, Joe had been around for a long time, and had cut his first record for Capitol way back in 1954 before recording for Herald in 1957 and Roulette in 1958. Ford's story is given substance by a news-piece which appeared in "Cash Box" in the May 28, 1960 edition: "Catalino Aguda

Jr. of the Flame Record Co. announces that the diskery's prexy, John F. English, has signed Joe Jones and his Band to a wax pact and that his debut disk is tabbed 'You Talk Too Much.' Joe and crew'll do the side in the up-coming flick, 'The Dead One'."

In any case, Ric got their version on the market in August 1960. Producer Harold Battiste takes up the story: "I started working local gigs with Joe Jones again and there was a guy called Reggie Hall, a pianist, who had written a song called 'You Talk Too Much'. Reggie gave the song to Joe and Joe recorded it. Now Joe is and was a fine business brain, he had the knack of getting everything together and the people together, so Joe started singing the song in his show for a couple of months before the record got issued. In the meantime, I got in with Joe Ruffino at Ric Records who first issued the record. The record started selling and Ruffino gave us promotion money to go out on the road and promote it. Prior to this record, Joe Ruffino's policy had been to issue the record just in the South and he would make enough money to make it worthwhile. And it had worked for Eddie Bo and some others. He knew he wouldn't be paying anybody so he was satisfied. Anyway, he gave us $600 and we got into Joe's station wagon and travelled all over the South at first, then up through Memphis to Chicago and Detroit and over to New York. And we hit every radio station there was, black, white, hillbilly . . . whatever. Anything that had an antenna, we hit!

"That was just around the time that Castro was being televised for his marathon speeches so I figured that we should send a copy of 'You Talk Too Much' to Castro just for publicity and sure enough, we got an answer from an official under Castro. Anyway, we got this reply just as we got to Chicago, where '*Jet*' magazine was, and we took the story to them. So we got a little story in their magazine.

"Anyway, when we hit New York, we had the No. 1 record— but we had run out of money. So we went to see Lloyd Price who we knew from New Orleans and he helped us. This was at the time that Roulette came on the scene. They wanted the record and they wanted Joe Jones. Anyway, Roulette wound up with the record and it hit No. 1 around the country."

Just why did Roulette want the record so badly? The answer came in the *"Cash Box"* story (October 15, 1960), or that was the official version anyway:

"Prexies Morris Levy and Joe Ruffino of Roulette Records and Ric Records respectively, reached an amicable decision concerning the rights to the current chart smash, 'You Talk Too Much.' It was decided that Roulette purchase sole rights to the Joe Jones hit. Henceforth, and effective immediately, Roulette will manu-facture, distribute and sell the former Ric release on the Roulette label. Roulette pressings have already begun and deliveries effected. Kahl Music is the publisher.

"'Talk' was purchased from Ric by Roulette after the discovery that a prior recording of the same tune by Joe Jones was in the Roulette file. Jones had previously recorded for Roulette. In the best interests of both companies, and to avoid the snarls and inconvenience of long drawn-out litigation, the all-encompassing Roulette purchase of the record was agreed upon and consum-mated, an announcement said.

"'Talk' is currently one of the hottest smash hits, and is twenty-one on this week's Top 100. Music publishing rights, held by Ron Publishing Company, a wholly owned subsidiary of Ric Records, has now been transferred in its entirety to its original owners, Kahl Music, Inc., and Ben Ghazzi Publishing Corpn."

Nevertheless the incident was a bitter blow for Joe Ruffino, even though he did not have the necessary resources to cater for a national smash hit. He tried out an answer record, "I Don't Talk Too Much," by Martha Nelson, with the same band but it didn't sell.

Meanwhile, Joe Jones's follow-up record on Roulette, "One Big Mouth," was too obviously based on the hit record and flopped badly. The engaging "California Sun" crept into the charts, and a good album was released which contained old and new material. Jones then went into producing and manage-ment in New York and in 1964 had some success with New Orleans artists, Alvin "Shine" Robinson and the Dixie Cups, but it did not last. "Joe had a big mouth—just like his song," said Mac Rebennack. "He talked his way into deals, and talked his way out just as quick. He had big ideas, and although

Joe got his feet in the door, he had no talent to stay there. It was always people like Harold Battiste, Wardell Quezergue and Melvin Lastie who did the work for him."

Ron Records

Ron Records followed the same R & B policy as its sister label, Ric, and relied entirely on New Orleans artists, some important ones too.

Professor Longhair cut his celebrated recording of "Go To The Mardi Gras" for Ron in 1959, and it is this particular version which is still played at Mardi Gras time. The lyrics embody the festive carnival atmosphere of "Fat Tuesday,"

"*When you go to New Orleans, you ought to go see the Mardi Gras,* (× 2)
When you go see the Mardi Gras somebody will tell you what the Carnival is for.

"*Get your ticket in your hand, you want to go to New Orleans,* (× 2)
You know when you get to New Orleans, somebody will show you the Zulu King.

"*You will see the Zulu King on St Bernard and Dumaine,* (× 2)
And if you stay right there, I'm sure you will see the Zulu Queen."

As an advertisement for the Mardi Gras, it's quite beautiful and this is why it is still played on the radio every half-hour in season. Longhair made just the one session for Ron, and another good single, "Cuttin' Out," was released which had typical Longhair piano changes and furious drum work from John Boudreaux.

Longhair's ex-tenor man, Robert Parker, had his first solo release at this time with the enthusiastic two-part instrumental, "All Nite Long." Disc jockey Larry McKinley produced this session and Eddie Bo, who played piano, put in all the interesting breaks. Parker has a long history as a session man and his time as a solo artist was to come in the mid-1960's when he had a hit with "Barefootin'."

IRMA THOMAS

Another Ron artist who later hit the big time was Irma Thomas, and she is now rated as one of the major soul artists to come out of the 1960's. She was discovered by Tommy Ridgley.

"We were working in this club called the Pimloco and Irma, she was a waitress in there," said Tommy. "I had met her once before and she told me she could sing but I never did get a chance to hear her. But anyway, she came up this night, she said, 'Well, if you say so, I'll go up on the bandstand,' and she sure did outdo Miss LaVell. I don't know if you're familiar with Miss LaVell but she was the biggest girl singer. And Irma came on stage and did a couple of these tunes, and I'll show you how spontaneous it was. We listened to her on the weekend, on the Monday I took her down to Joe Ruffino because I was recording for him, I played, she sang the song. The next day we went back, we had a tune for her, 'You Can Have My Husband, Don't Mess With My Man,' and before the week was out she had recorded. That's how much they thought about Irma, right quick. In fact she played her first professional job with me and I think she made $2, because we went to a club, it was a Monday night."

Irma Thomas really made her reputation when she recorded two beautiful ballads, "It's Raining" and "Ruler Of My Heart," which were produced by Allen Toussaint for Minit Records. Her best record, though, was the soulful "Wish Someone Would Care," which was cut on the West Coast for the revamped Imperial label in 1964. It was just one of those perfect records. Another famous record from this period was "Time Is On My Side," which was picked up by the Rolling Stones.

She has not scaled these peaks since, but she is still a favourite in New Orleans, and when she came back to Uncle Sam's Club on St Charles in recent times she broke all the attendance records.

Other good recordings on Ron included Martha Carter's

beautiful rendition of "I'm Through Crying," which deserved better than it got, tenor player James Rivers had an excellent two-part instrumental, "The Blue Eagle," which had traces of the old Jimmy Reed "walking" rhythms, former Imperial star Bobby Mitchell came up with the nice "Send Me Your Picture," and Eddie Lang had a solid "Easy Rockin'." The Party Boys had a gas of a record, "We Got A Party," which was a throwback to Huey Smith's Clowns. None of these records sold particularly well.

The Ric and Ron labels finally folded in late 1962 after Joe Ruffino died. They had many good records, some great ones, but not enough hits.

The Popeye and other New Orleans Dances

New Orleans music is primarily music to enjoy yourself by, to be happy, to dance to, and the locals did just that. Dance records proliferated everywhere in the early 1960's, inspired by the worldwide popularity of the Twist. The Popeye dance, which was based around the legendary cartoon character, was all the rage in New Orleans in 1962. "Everybody tried to capitalise on it," said Mac Rebennack, "because it was such a different dance to the Hully Gully and the Second Line." Eddie Bo's record, "Check Mr Popeye," caught the insinuous feel of the dance as he sang, "*You'd better check your spinach, Mr Popeye, 'cos Olive's in the danger zone.*" On the flip, "Now Let's Popeye," he told us what the Popeye dance was all about,

> "*Now, you put your right hand on your forehead,*
> *And your left behind your back,*
> *Slide a one and a two . . .*
> *C'mon, let's Popeye, children. . . .*"

Next to Huey Smith's "Pop-Eye," Eddie Bo's "Check Mr Popeye" was the biggest Popeye record and even managed to break out in Northern cities like Pittsburgh.

The Popeye eclipsed the Twist in New Orleans, although the veteran George "Blazer Boy" Stevenson had one of the best twist records anywhere with "New Orleans Twist" on Imperial. The first verse hinted at the competitive element between the two dances,

> *"Well down in New Orleans they're doing the Fly,*
> *And they got a new dance called the Popeye,*
> *Where the bands are playing the people insist,*
> *That they play the music so they can do the Twist."*

In passing, it must be said that the King of The Twist Chubby Checker, was greatly influenced by Fats Domino and the inspiration even went as far as giving birth to Checker's name.

Other popular dances in New Orleans at this time were the Mashed Potato, the Shimmy and the Hully Gully. Some of New Orleans' own dance creations over the years have included the Second Line, the Mess Around, the Barefoot, the Twitch, the Sissy and more recently the Rubber Band.

Chris Kenner summed it all up quite beautifully in "Land Of 1,000 Dances" in 1963.

Minit Records

If there was one label which could be said to represent the change in direction of New Orleans R & B then it must be Minit Records. The new sound was lighter, more melodic and wistful, and if anything funkier than ever. In New Orleans it was called "The Carnival Sound."

Minit Records was the idea of Joe Banashak, who ran A-1 Record Distributors Inc. which distributed every independent label that mattered in the New Orleans area. "I was fed up with making hits for other people," said Banashak, whose most notable feat was to break the incredibly bad "Paper In My Shoes" by Boozoo Chavis, a cajun artist.

Joe Banashak had gained experience in the cut-throat distributing game in Houston, and set up A-1 with the help of Art Rupe. Minit was formed in 1959.

BOOGIE JAKE

The first record on Minit was a down-and-out blues record by Boogie Jake called "Bad Luck And Trouble" which was recorded in Baton Rouge. After showing signs of breaking in the South, it was leased to Chess for national distribution and just got lost. Chess said the Northern dee-jays would not play the record because they found Boogie Jake's name offensive. As a result Jake's real name, Matthew Jacobs, was used on the next release on Minit but it did nothing. Good though they were, Boogie Jake's records had little connection with the New Orleans sounds to come on the Minit label.

ALLEN TOUSSAINT (2)

The man responsible for dishing out the delectable sounds was Allen Toussaint, whose production work in New Orleans throughout the 1960's was to be equal in stature to that of Dave Bartholomew in the 1950's. Besides producing, he writes, plays piano and performs in his own right—he has not been called a genius for nothing.

"How did I get in production? Well, with Joe Banashak here in town," said Allen Toussaint. "He was starting a record company which came on to be Minit Records. He and Larry

McKinley were starting this company, and they were audition-
ing at the studio. And I had been home working with different
singers and everything everyday, and a couple of auditions
were for guys who had come to the house. And we just run
over the tunes, I went to the auditions to play, accompanying
piano for a couple of singers. And through that night I ended
up playing behind anybody else who wanted to audition, since
I was right there anyway. Harold Battiste was supposed to be
the music man for that situation, however he couldn't make
it then and he was already involved in a lot of things, with
Specialty Records and all. And they asked me that night if I
would fill in until Battiste would have the time to come on
back and I went on, began making music with Minit Records,
you know Banashak and Larry McKinley. And I guess that
was how I got into production. We had a few, I guess, 'Ooh
Poo Pah Doo' was about the first big one and after that
comes 'Hello My Lover' and 'T'Aint It The Truth' and
'Mother-In-Law' and things like that. Chris Kenner and his
era.

"My hero was Professor Longhair—Roy Byrd—I liked very
much Professor Longhair, Lloyd Glenn, Albert Ammons and
of course Ray Charles. I didn't study music formally on the
piano. I got my first professional engagement at about 13 or
14, a small band called the Flamingos with Little Snook. That
was the first band I played in. We did that for a few years,
high school dances and things like that on to, I guess, the
Dew Drop.

"I guess the first time I went into the studio was with probably
Dave Bartholomew. Prior to that I went in with Billy Tate,
well we were getting ready to go in, and in the meantime I
was working at the Dew Drop and Dave needed someone to
come in and do tracks with Fats Domino. And Dave had
heard me at the Dew Drop and he had recognised that I had
played like a whole lot of other people, so when it was time
to play Fats Domino you just played like Fats Domino. It was
really a trip, a pleasant one. It happened when Fats was in
Australia or something like that, and he really needed the
tracks down immediately and they'd send the tracks somewhere else and have them done. Which was really heavy in

those days because everything was usually done live, but they were hip enough to do that then. So I went in to play a couple of Fats Domino tunes, 'Young Schoolgirl,' I guess that was the first time I went into the studio.

"Then there was Ace, I didn't do an awful lot of his things but I must have done quite a bit. But normally I would work the studio whoever was recording that day."

Allen Toussaint's first recording session on his own was for RCA Victor. "I'll show you how a guy can happen," said Cosimo Matassa. "Two guys, Murray Sporn and Danny Kesler, came to New Orleans producing things, they had a connection with RCA, also Columbia to release things they produced, and they came to town looking for talent. So they ran an ad. in the paper, 'Talent auditions at the recording studio.' Never again will I do a thing like that! They were lined up around the studio for three days, you know, morning to night. It was just a deluge of people, you know, they came out of the woodwork at you. Well, out of that one of the few things that really happened, one of the things that was recorded, he originally came just to play piano, that was Allen Toussaint."

Red Tyler continues this story: "There must have been hundreds of people there, for days we were in the studio, you know, because you never knew what might come out of this. And we were doing this and Cosimo was in there putting people on tape. Literally hundreds. People in line, waiting, 'I have this tune,' you know. And as the people would come in we'd make up songs, make backgrounds for them, so I think they were quite impressed with what we were doing more with Allen Toussaint. So they said, 'Man, like we're wasting time with all these people, how about a session on this guy.' Allen Toussaint. Well, when they said this to Allen he called me up on the telephone and said, 'Red, look, they want me to do an album, man.' I said, 'An album, a whole album, that's twelve sides.' He said, 'So have you any tunes?' and I said I have a few ideas. So he said, 'We'll make up the songs,' and this is actually what we did. We were in the studio cold, and started making up songs, so fast in fact until we didn't have titles for the songs. And when the tapes were taken to New York we had no idea what those songs were going to be titled.

It just so happens that this tune 'Java' was given a title up in New York. Now in the song 'Java' you'll find the songwriters are Allen Toussaint, Alvin Tyler and Joe Friday. I didn't know who the hell Joe Friday was! He was the guy who titled the tune .... And really it didn't make any difference because the album was titled 'The Wild Sounds Of New Orleans' featuring Allen Toussaint (then called Al Tousan). It never did anything but then Al Hirt came along and recorded 'Java' and it was a big hit. I got big royalties and I can say it's the only time that I have been properly compensated for anything I have written."

"Most of those deals that Danny Kesler set up were real lame," said Mac Rebennack. "Joe Banashak really rescued Allen from that oblivion he was sitting in and gave him the opportunity to start grabbing some of the New Orleans talent like Irma Thomas and Aaron Neville. He was a storehouse full of songs, and all he needed was some artists to go and project his material, and Joe Banashak was the source to get the material out. Every artist who came along to audition for Joe had a bunch of songs from Allen Toussaint who had had ready material all along but was unable to move because of the lame contract.

"Toussaint generally would write the A and B sides for the artists, do the arrangements, cover the whole thing. He was that sort of creative talent. A genius? I was too close to Allen over the years to look at him objectively but he's always been the cat who has one side of a genius like taking melodies you always hear, and incorporate commercials from TV, jingles from advertisements and use these things in songs that people can remember and will make a hit. He always had the talent of using these things in productions. He must have done very well financially as opposed to most New Orleans artists or producers or songwriters. I think Allen through the talent on Minit Records helped keep the New Orleans scene alive and through to now has kept it more alive than anybody."

"My songs, I get inspiration from many, many places," said Allen Toussaint," sometimes from nowhere. Some songs come, there is not one message that applies to me like some, but sometimes a song comes right on through you and you don't have anything to do with it. All you do is put the penmanship to it, that you can't account for at all. You can sit down at the piano and doodle around and sometimes you find something drifting on. To explain writing songs, oh . . ., I'd have to write a song to explain it."

JESSIE HILL

The first production hit for Allen Toussaint and Minit was with Jessie Hill's "Ooh Poo Pah Doo," a two-parter which climbed to No. 28 on "*Billboard*" during the early summer of 1960. The sound was of raw, unpolished excitement, Hill a wild man from the jungle as he shouted and screamed the lyrics based on the catch-phrase, "there's a great disturbance in my mind." Part 1 was the side which sold to a public whose appetite for these crude call-and-response sounds had been whetted by the success of Ray Charles's "What'd I Say" a few months earlier. Part 2 was even better. Led by the strident, wide-ranging tenor of David Lastie and Toussaint's strong low-down piano, the combo took off on a classic, raunchy, down-in-the-alley blues instrumental with Hill giving occasional, almost besotted shouts of encouragement.

"I wrote a song called 'Ooh Poo Pah Doo'," said Jessie Hill, "and I wanted to send it to this cat named Joe Ruffino. I went in there and said, 'Look here, I need some money, man.' You know he really had the best artists you want in New Orleans. I have two versions of all the songs I ever write, you know, and I was gonna sell him a 'Ooh Poo Pah Doo' version for 35 dollars, understand? So he wouldn't buy it. I was hustling and saying I got to get myself together, I need some money. Now Joe Banashak always treated me like I was his son, you know. He always never liked me to be bummin' for nothin' even before I was recording with him. So me and him got together, and I went and recorded it. Five days later Ruffino took to beating his desk, man, saying, 'Look at that, I done lost that for 35 dollars.' So they cut the record, and man, I never had any money in my life, and they give $2,000 in advance, man, I just thought I had all the world. It scared me so bad then, though. I had nobody around me to talk to me with any kind of knowledge or anything about anything."

Although the rhythmic "Whip It On Me" briefly touched the charts, Jessie Hill has never had another hit record. His Minit records are by far the best, including the marvellously drunken "I Got Mine" where the tempo is so relaxed it almost dries up until Hill manages to cry out, "Play it for me, Allen Toussaint!", "Oogzey Moo" with all the Longhair changes from Toussaint, the uptempo "Sweet Jelly Roll" and finally—it just had to be—"Can't Get Enough (of that Ooh Poo Pah Doo)".

He moved out to the West Coast in the mid-1960's and joined the clan of New Orleans exiles led by Mac Rebennack and Harold Battiste and cut an album for Blue Thumb in 1970.

ERNIE K-DOE

With the label gaining momentum Joe Banashak was finding, as others had before him, that he just had not the resources to distribute the label himself on a national level, and he made a deal with Lew Chudd for Imperial to handle the distribution side. The partnership got off to a good start when "Mother-In-Law" by Ernie K-Doe made No. 1 on the national charts in the early summer of 1961.

"Mother-In-Law" was a sensational novelty record which just had to be a chart topper. By the title alone, the record had a head start; in an age when marriage was almost a lifetime institution, "mother-in-law" was the oldest music-hall joke going—everybody knew it. It was a catchy song as well, with the nasal vocal of K-Doe contrasting with the golden rich tones of Benny Spellman's voice repeating the title phrase, and Allen Toussaint's piano to the fore.

Ernest Kador had been around New Orleans for some time before "Mother-In-Law" and had started out as a member of the Blue Diamonds vocal group early in the 1950's and recorded with them for Savoy. His first solo record was "Do Baby Do" for Specialty in 1956 followed by an unproductive session for Herald in 1957. However, he had been playing the main clubs in New Orleans like the Dew Drop Inn, the Club Tijuana and the Sho-Bar on Bourbon Street, and it was from these places that he acquired the know-how for his quite electrifying stage act. He is a magnificent entertainer and showman.

"Hello My Lover" was a small regional hit on Minit before "Mother-In-Law" came out, and then came a series of minor hits with "Te-Ta-Te-Ta-Ta," "I Cried My Last Tear," "A Certain Girl" and "Popeye Joe". Rather like Jessie Hill, Ernie K-Doe has been unable to shake off the effects of his massive hit, and subsequent recordings for Duke and Janus have not meant anything. But he is still an active club performer in New Orleans.

BENNY SPELLMAN

Benny Spellman, the bass voice on "Mother-In-Law," had a small hit on Minit with a pop tune, "Lipstick Traces," which hovered around the No. 80 spot on *"Billboard"* for six weeks in 1962. Spellman had been with Huey Smith and the Clowns before this, and later made good records for Watch and Alon. An Alon master, "The Word Game," was leased to Atlantic in 1965 and a little after he had "Sinner Girl" on the Sansu label. He now works as a salesman for a beer company.

THE SHOWMEN

At the end of 1961, the Showmen became one of the few New Orleans vocal groups to make any impact on the charts when "It Will Stand," their fine tribute to rock 'n' roll, went to No. 61 on *"Billboard."* They came originally from the East Coast, and their lead vocalist, Norman Johnson, later found fame as lead singer of the hit Detroit group, Chairmen of the Board.

ALLEN TOUSSAINT'S PRODUCTIONS

The Toussaint Sound was also faithfully reproduced in a string of good records by Aaron Neville, Eskew Reeder, Irma Thomas, Allen Orange and Diamond Joe. Local hits were enjoyed by Aaron Neville with "Over You," Eskew Reeder with "Green Door" and Irma Thomas with "It's Raining" and "Ruler Of My Heart."

"With Minit, we were never consciously trying to do an R & B record," said Allen Toussaint. "It just happened, there was a tune that went like this, and on the same day, three hours later, we'd do tunes that went like that. And sometimes on the same session, we'd do two tunes on one artist and two on another, split sessions. The same day we did 'Ooh Poo Pah Doo,' that was Part 1 and 2, so that was one thing, and on the same three hours, the next part of that session was things that finally had four violins, a bassoon, an oboe, and there was Allen Orange singing 'When You're Lonely Send For Me,' almost a Robert Goulet type, the same musicians other than they had strings.

"There wasn't a reason that I'm gonna make novelty records, it just so happened that most of the hits were novelties. A whole lot of them weren't, a whole lot of flops weren't, they were very serious, very hearty and all that. My favourite, I sorta like 'Mother-In-Law' but I hear it different from what people hear. I hear something theoretical, what it was supposed to be and how it actually shaped up musically, and what was to go into it. The one that actually produces something always hears it different from other people."

The End of Minit Records

"As far as those heydays at Minit they sorta tapered off," continued Allen Toussaint, "I went into the Army in January 1963 and so far as from my end, the production sorta stopped, as far as me doing it and at the pace we had been doing it. Even when I'd come home on weekends sometime and get something going, we'd go into the studio, but we didn't have the momentum or exhilaration as before. I think it really started slowing off tremendously then.

"Well, Minit was also sold to Lew Chudd, prior to that, Lew Chudd was handling it and it was actually sold. I don't really know all of what was happening because I wasn't into the business at all, I just wanted to make music.

"The Army slowed it down. When I came back out Minit was still in operation, and as a matter of fact I did a couple of things on Irma Thomas after I came out. But there wasn't that enthusiasm of Minit Records that was there before, by that time Liberty Records had bought Imperial which owned Minit, it wasn't, we just didn't have the same type of enthusiasm for some reason."

Instant Records, 1961–63

Joe Banashak was not too happy with the Minit and Imperial deal, although Lew Chudd must have been delighted at the constant flow of hits. Towards the end of Minit before it was finally sold to Imperial, it did seem that Banashak had little involvement with the label's affairs and it was left to Allen Toussaint to fulfil the contractual obligations from the small, reliable roster of artists. In the meantime, Joe Banashak had helped in forming Instant Records.

"Along with Minit Records, Joe Banashak started another company called Instant Records," said Allen Toussaint, "what was the same as Valiant Records with Larry McKinley and Irving Smith, which Larry McKinley ended up dropping out one way or another, not because of no bad scene, he just got out, and Irving Smith and Joe Banashak were into that, and of course me doing what I was doing in the same capacity as for Minit."

"Companies are tighter with their money now," said Al Reed, "but Irving Smith is a wealthy man and he didn't give a damn how much a session would cost to get it right. But then again their most successful sessions on Instant Records were their cheapest sessions, now how do you like that?"

CHRIS KENNER

Chris Kenner gave the new company a great start with the dance record, "I Like It Like That," which after a slow start suddenly took off to become a No. 2 hit on *"Billboard"* and earn an award as the "Best Rock 'n' Roll Record of 1961."

" 'I Like It Like That' was a slang gimmick," said Chris Kenner. "It was a good title and I tried to put a story to it. I worked on it a little while and got it together, you know. We didn't think it would be a hit record. To tell you the truth, we thought it was pretty nice but we didn't think it would be no big thing. I had put it on tape for about two years before I recorded it. I had it on tape at Allen Toussaint's house and one day Joe Banashak stopped by at Allen's house and Allen played him some old tapes and he had this particular song and Banashak liked it. He asked Allen to find the guy, he said he knows where he's at, and Allen came and got me and we talked to Joe Banashak and he recorded it.

"I still won the top tune for the 'Best Writer of the Year,' even though I didn't get to No. 1, I still won the citation. At the Waldorf Astoria, New York. They put my picture in the projector and then they be playing my song and you'll be walking down the aisle. And you get to the stage and the guy hands you a big long thing with a blue ribbon tied to it, you know. Then you get your picture taken and then the orchestra plays waltzes, and they serve drinks. You know, it's a big thing.

"I had a lot of tours with the hit records, with Universal Attractions, they kept us pretty busy. The only days we had off were the ones we took off ourselves, you know, I couldn't make all the gigs they used to book for me. I played package tours with Jackie Wilson, Roy Hamilton, LaVern Baker, the Coasters, Gladys Knight and the Pips. After the Apollo, then the Howard Uptown, and then working all the theatres, I worked with all the big names. Then after that I cooled off for one-and-a-half years and I came back with 'Land of 1,000 Dances' and I got real hot again."

From Kenner, Louisiana, a suburb town of New Orleans, Chris Kenner started out singing with a spiritual group, the Harmonising Four. He recorded first in 1957 for Baton Records, a New York label who made a flying visit to New Orleans. "It was just one of those get-together things, it didn't sell," he said. Then he was signed by Imperial who cut his own tune, "Sick And Tired," which was a later hit for Fats Domino in 1958. He made a boisterous rock 'n' roll number, "Don't Make No Noise," shortly after for Wallace Davenport's Pontchartrain label which was leased much later to Lloyd Price's Prigan label in 1961 and released to cash in on his hit record.

"Something You Got," his next on Instant, was a tremendous New Orleans hit even if it didn't make the national charts. It was a great record to do the Popeye dance to. "The other Popeye records didn't make it with the kids compared to this," said Mac Rebennack.

The next big hit was "Land of 1,000 Dances" which climbed to No. 77 in 1963 and should have gone higher. "It actually came from a spiritual," said Chris, "the name of the spiritual was 'Children Go Where I Send You' and I turned it around. It was inspired by the dance tunes going around." Using his best preaching gospel style, with tantalising support from Allen Toussaint on piano, the band and vocal chorus, Kenner told his listeners that they've got to know how to "*Pony, Mashed Potato, Alligator, Twist, Ya Ya, Sweet Pea, Watusi, Fly, Hand Jive, Slop, Chicken and the Bop, Fish, Slow Twist, Tango and Popeye.*" Not quite a thousand dances but it was enough, and he clinched it when he finally told everybody "*to go across the tracks to a place called I Like It Like That where the name of the band is the Twistolettes.*" "I'm still drawing royalties on that," he said, "Tom Jones, Major Lance, Cannibal & the Headhunters, Wilson Pickett and Fats Domino all recorded that."

"Land of 1,000 Dances" was Chris Kenner's last big hit. He continued to record for Instant until 1969 and in the later years his records had a considerably updated soul sound, with arrangements by Eddie Bo and Sax Kari. "Wind The Clock" and "All Night Rambler" were two of the best songs to come out of New Orleans at this time. Chris's main problem now is that he is recognised in New Orleans more as a songwriter than an artist, and he's working hard to correct that impression. But it may take time.

"Chris Kenner was one of the most heaviest songwriters down there," said Mac Rebennack. "He came up out of the true church tradition, singing in his father's church. He has passed down the real tradition of New Orleans music which you can hear in 'Something You Got,' 'Land of 1,000 Dances' and 'I Like It Like That'—these are all traditional New Orleans type songs. I don't think there was anybody writing better songs from 'Sick And Tired' to 'Something You Got' in the gospel tradition, and his writing influenced Allen Toussaint."

The Instant label did not have any more national hits but they enjoyed local successes in 1962 with the haunting ballad, "All

These Things" by Art Neville, and the more rhythmic "I'm Gonna Put Some Hurt On You" by Raymond Lewis. Records also appeared in the catalogue during 1962 and 1963 by Joe (Mr G) August, Allan Collay, Al Reed, Chick Carbo and James Rivers.

The Minit/Instant Studio Musicians

Allen Toussaint apart, much credit for the success of Minit and Instant Records must go to the backing musicians.

"We had a very good studio band at the time," said Allen Toussaint. "Good is a matter of opinion, but I loved them myself. Everyone was really happy about what was being done, everybody was involved. Like, when a guy was playing, when he had a 20-or 30-bar rest, like he was still involved at the time. It wasn't like, man, watching the clock, 'What time is it?', there was really a lot of enthusiasm and everybody was very happy."

NAT PERRILLIAT

The distinctive tenor sound came from the late Nat Perrilliat. He had a jazz background which showed in his pure vibrato singing saxophone style that was moulded closely on the work of Fathead Newman, Eddie Harris and King Curtis. In the early 1950's he started playing in the reed sections of the bands of Professor Longhair, Smiley Lewis and Shirley & Lee, before working in clubs with modern jazz groups, usually with pianist Ellis Marsailis, clarinetist Alvin Batiste and drummer James Black. In 1967 he came to England with Fats Domino's band.

"Nat Perrilliat was a fabulous person," said Allen Toussaint. "Once he got into the studio, he stayed, you know as far as I was concerned. I wouldn't budge without Nat into the studio and I didn't have to because he was there. He really was a good man."

He died of a brain haemorrhage at the early age of 35 in 1972.

ROY MONTRELL

Roy Montrell, with his immaculate timing and drive, was used as the Minit rhythm guitarist. Montrell had been around for some time and had started with Roy Milton's band after his discharge from the Army in 1951. On his marriage he returned to New Orleans and formed a trio called the Little Hawketts with Lawrence Gate, bass, and Victor Leonards, drums, which worked at the Mardi Gras Lounge, next to the Famous Door Club on Bourbon Street. After a spell touring with Lloyd Price's band, he returned again to New Orleans and did session work for Specialty and Ace besides forming another band for weekend work with Nat Perrilliat, tenor, Curtis Mitchell, bass, and Edward Blackwell, drums.

As a member of Allen Toussaint's house band and later the A.F.O. Combo, Roy Montrell was more or less a resident session guitarist in New Orleans between 1960 and 1962. In 1962 he took over from Walter Nelson as guitarist with Fats Domino and is now the leader of Domino's band. Montrell has had just two record releases in his own name, "Ooh Wow" for Specialty in 1956 and "Mudd" for Minit in 1960.

Allen Toussaint also used Deacon John and George Davis as guitarists on recording sessions.

PETER "CHUCK" BADIE

The string bassist was Chuck Badie who set up a close working partnership with drummer John Boudreaux, and it was this pair that appeared on most Minit sessions. Chuck has played in an extraordinary number of bands, and he will name them all for you if you care to ask—Roy Brown, Paul Gayten, Dave Bartholomew, Fats Domino, Lloyd Price, Charles Brown, Big Joe Turner, Lionel Hampton, Sam Cooke, Hank Crawford, Dizzy Gillespie, Zoot Sims and the A.F.O. Executives. "He's a very enthusiastic person," said Gerri Hall, "he feels what the artist wants and he plays what the artist wants to hear. He is very good at shouting out the changes."

Other musicians used by Allen Toussaint included David Lastie, tenor, Clarence Ford, baritone, Red Tyler, tenor and baritone, Melvin Lastie, cornet, Richard Payne, bass, and James Black, drums. With these men, Toussaint was able to get away from the ensemble riffing sounds of Dave Bartholomew and also the Studio Band, mainly by allowing each instrumentalist a far freer role—at any moment the tenor would stutter through, the trumpet punchily interject, or the baritone moan a deep, bridging phrase. His own brilliant piano and the second line funk of the regular rhythm section of Chuck Badie and ex-Longhair drummer John Boudreaux provided the solid base.

It was from the members of this studio group that the A.F.O. Combo was formed.

A.F.O.

Now that the local record scene was in the hands of local companies, it seemed that every New Orleans musician's wish had been answered. A pipe dream of long standing had come true, but it soon evaporated again, in a mood of bitterness and disgust. Rightly or wrongly, much of the initial blame for the mess which the New Orleans music scene became was laid on the shoulders of an organisation masterminded by Harold Battiste called A.F.O.—"All For One."

It was hard to fault the logic behind Battiste's plan: "It was the black people who were reckoned to be good musicians, yet they weren't the ones who made the money. Lee Allen is an example—he played the saxophone on all the New Orleans sessions, Fats Domino and everyone. At that time, the musicians' scale was $42 a session. Now if Lee worked at worst fifty-two sessions a year he could get around $2,600 for a year which is not much when you consider that those records would sell millions of copies. So I said that instead of him taking the $42, why can't he say, 'Don't pay me anything but give me say 1 per cent on anything I play.' He would have been much better off that way. But it wasn't that easy because the Union demands that he gets a certain salary. My theory then was that musicians who play on the session should own the session."

So Battiste set about forming his own corporation, and, seeking musicians he knew well, picked Alvin "Red" Tyler, saxophone, Allen Toussaint, piano, Chuck Badie, bass, John

Boudreaux, drums, and Roy Montrell, guitar. "And there was Melvin Lastie, cornet, who was an official for the Union—now we needed him to make it official," continued Battiste. "So, we would pay out the cheques to each other so that the Union could take its 2 per cent—which is all they were really interested in anyway—then we would reimburse the money into the corporation to buy another share of stock in the corporation."

Two artists, Prince La La and Barbara George, were signed and recorded at Cosimo's Studio in June 1961 in a split session. It was at this point in time that a big black angel in the form of Juggy Murray appeared on the scene. He had been looking for an A & R man for his Sue record company and whilst in Los Angeles he had come across Sonny Bono who told him to get in touch with Harold Battiste. As a result, Murray became interested in the A.F.O. project and put up the front money to distribute the label under Sue's network.

Prince La La's record, sung in Ray Charles fashion, was a moderate seller. His real name was Lawrence Nelson and he was the guitar playing brother of Walter "Papoose" Nelson. "She Put The Hurt On Me" was due to be recorded by Barbara George but she was a poor singer and couldn't get it right, so it was decided that La La do the song. He died naturally shortly after his second A.F.O. record was released.

Barbara George's "I Know" was a monster No. 3 hit. It was a simple, catchy tune based on "Just A Closer Walk With Thee," and her untrained voice gave it added charm. The backing likewise was devoid of any unnecessary embellishment, with Marcel Richardson, taking over from Allen Toussaint, providing the rock-solid piano background. But it was Melvin Lastie's tuneful cornet solo which really sold the record.

Any thoughts that Harold Battiste had of A.F.O. becoming a black RCA Victor, thanks to Barbara George, were soon shattered when Juggy Murray took exception to him supervising Lee Dorsey's "Ya Ya" session for Bobby Robinson, a rival competitor, whilst "I Know" was still hot. "That was the beginning of some bad things between Juggy and us, and also between Bobby and us," said Battiste. "Now I really like Bobby but money was a problem, the most we ever saw out of Bobby was, I think, $600 for the 'Ya Ya' thing."

The "bad things" with Murray came to a head when he started buying her "a Cadillac, her clothes, the whole works." He never told her she was paying for these out of her own royalties, and eventually he persuaded her to buy up her A.F.O. contract and sign for Sue. Despite the protestations of Battiste and Lastie, first to Murray and then to her, the transfer went through. "It was no use," said Battiste, "fatherly advice is no good when you're fighting Cadillacs and money."

Barbara George's follow-up to "I Know," "You Talk About Love" and the flip, "Whip O Will" were two good chunks of New Orleans R & B, and climbed to No. 46 in spring 1962. It was the last thing she did for A.F.O. and after she went to Sue, nothing. Harold Battiste was right when he said he was the only person who knew how to record her.

After singles by the Blenders, a five-piece group, and the A.F.O. Studio Combo, Sue stopped distributing the A.F.O. label. "I really felt hurt by the Juggy situation," said Battiste. "I changed the colour of our labels (from orange to yellow) and then I realised that the world was not just black and white but it was a world for business people or not." Battiste and the A.F.O. Band tried to pick up the threads and signed a young pianist named Willie Tee, whose "Always Accused" was a pretty impressive debut record. Albums were released by the A.F.O. Combo called "A Compendium" featuring Tami Lynn, and a modern jazz album called "Monkey Puzzle" with Nat Perrilliat, tenor, Ellis Marsailis, piano, and drummer James Black. They also formed a subsidiary label, At Last, with singles by Eddie Bo, Red Tyler and Melvin Lastie. But the company could not find another "I Know," and it was almost as if everyone was letting their jazz backgrounds override the need for simple, commercial material. Another problem, the age-old one, was the lack of good distribution and nothing ever got past Memphis.

"The company was very successful," said Red Tyler, "until I think the venture was to go out to California. We ran into problems. Basically, they had so many musicians out there until they had rules which said you had to be out there for six months or a year before you could work regular. So actually you couldn't work out there regular as a group and some of the guys got fed up with that fact. Chuck Badie, the bass player, he came home and what had happened was that Sam Cooke said, 'I hate to see you guys break up, I'm going to have each of you guys on a $100 retainer a week.' And we had a place up there where we used to rehearse with his artists, we used to call 'The Soul Station.' In fact, Sonny & Cher, the first time they tried anything, we rehearsed right there. I stayed up there a year, it didn't really happen for me. I didn't particularly care for the town so I came home, and I've been playing jazz since." Melvin Lastie was summoned to play with Joe Jones's band at the World's Fair in New York, "so only me, the drummer John Boudreaux, and Tami were left," said Battiste.

Why, then, did A.F.O. take part of the blame for the start of the break-up of a once thriving record scene? "It was a clique of musicians and they were doing all the sessions," said Marshall Sehorn. "They had a production company and they all had an in with the Union. But see, then A.F.O. got greedy, the other musicians kicked out but they couldn't do anything about it. The manufacturers said, 'Hey, everything's starting to sound the same, we want something else.' So people stopped coming, not all of a sudden, but they stopped."

The monopoly of the A.F.O. Band, which was exaggerated because New Orleans still only had the one studio, had left bad feelings and this is a pity because they were partly responsible for adding considerable freshness to the old New Orleans sounds of the 1950's. Their music is their real legacy.

Chess Records, 1960–61

The feverish recording activity in New Orleans in the early 1960's was inspired by the local companies and a few outside labels became interested again, including Chess Records.

CLARENCE "FROGMAN" HENRY (2)

Chess took up Frogman Henry's contract again at the instigation of executive Paul Gayten and had a massive hit first time out with "I Don't Know Why I Love You, But I Do," which climbed to No. 4 in the spring of 1961. It was a good, catchy tune written by Bobby Charles and Paul Gayten, and was given a straight treatment by Henry in contrast to his novelty efforts on "Ain't Got No Home" and others back in 1957.

"In 1960 Chess came down again with one of his A & R men," said Clarence Henry, "and Paul was with them at the time too and we went on into Cosimo's Studio with Allen Toussaint, Big Boy Myles, Justin Adams and other New Orleans musicians and we came about the song 'But I Do.' We had written this song years before, he and I, and in 1960 we were looking for songs when they came down and we happened to come up with this song that we had sketched out before. Nat Perrilliat, he was on the sax intro. to 'But I Do,' he really did something to the song. And it turned out to be a big record that put us on top again and I did a lot of tours around the country. From there we went into Chicago, we used session musicians and I didn't know any of them, but we did fly Allen Toussaint up from New Orleans especially for the session. I was ready to do 'I'm A Fool To Care' when Joe Barry came out with that one, and that knocked me out so I was looking for another one. So we came up with 'You Always Hurt The One You Love' and that was a pretty big seller. And we had 'On Bended Knees,' that was pretty good and we started to get a little slack in between but things have been good through my career.

"When things were slack I was still doing the local clubs, I have been on the Strip, we call it the Strip, Bourbon Street in the French Quarter for fourteen years and it took fourteen years and I've finally got out of the Quarters. Well, everything is out here in the Parish, Jefferson Parish, and a lot of clubs are building up now.

"We do a variety of music, we don't cater to one style of songs, we do dixieland, pop, the classics, you know. We don't do opera though, the only thing we do is soap opera. Really Fats Domino and myself are the only ones doing the old-time music, the other guys went to the sock-it-to-me, this acidelic rock, or something. We stick with the oldies but goodies. We do a little up-tempo, a little modern thing we push in once in a while, but we do the things the people like. We're all right with the younger crowd but mostly the older crowd, so we won't change."

After Chess, Frogman Henry recorded for Huey Meaux's Parrot label, then Dial Records, and an album for Roulette in 1969 called "Clarence 'Frogman' Henry" with the sub-title "Is alive and well living in New Orleans and still doin' his thing." With a bunch of excellent New Orleans sidemen and old songs like "Since I Met You Baby," "Red Sails In The Sunset" and "But I Do" it had all the right ingredients for success but it didn't quite make it.

Clarence Henry can be seen almost any evening in New Orleans with his first-class little band, and his happy, free-wheeling music does not deserve to be ignored in the rush to place accolades on more fashionable people.

Fire/Fury Records, 1960–62

Bobby Robinson, the head of Fire and Fury Records who operated from New York, did not make his first sortie into New Orleans until the early 1960's and this was done at the suggestion of his promotion man, Marshall Sehorn.

BOBBY MARCHAN

The first New Orleans artist recorded was Bobby Marchan, the former lead singer with Huey Smith's Clowns. Nothing happened to his first record "Snoopin' And Accusin' " with the Tick Tocks but Marchan's version of Big Jay McNeely's old song "There Is Something On Your Mind" went to No. 31

'You Talk Too Much'. PHOTOGRAPH BY BILL GREENSMITH

Ric and Ron advertisement, 'Cash Box', 1960. PHOTOGRAPH BY
BILL GREENSMITH

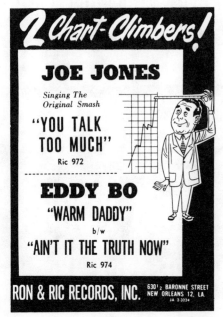

Chris Kenner, 1973. PHOTOGRAPH
BY JOHN BROVEN

'I Like It Like That'. PHOTOGRAPH
BY BILL GREENSMITH

Instant advertisement, 'Billboard', 1961. PHOTOGRAPH BY BILL GREENSMITH

Barbara George, 1961. PHOTOGRAPH
COURTESY BLUES UNLIMITED

Joe Banashak, 1970. PHOTOGRAPH
BY JOHN BROVEN

Duke advertisement, 'Cash Box', 1960.
PHOTOGRAPH BY BILL GREENSMITH

Earl King, 1973. PHOTOGRAPH BY JOHN BROVEN

Ford 'Snooks' Eaglin, 1972. PHOTOGRAPH BY
CHRIS STRACHWITZ

'Hello My Lover'.
PHOTOGRAPH BY BILL GREENSMITH

'I Know'.
PHOTOGRAPH BY BILL GREENSMITH

BILLBOARD MUSIC WEEK HOT 100

FOR WEEK ENDING JUNE 4

#			TITLE — Artist, Label & Number	wks
1	5	18	TRAVELIN' MAN — Ricky Nelson, Imperial 5741	6
2	3	12	DADDY'S HOME — Shep and the Limelites, Hull 740	10
3	7	16	RUNNING SCARED — Roy Orbison, Monument 438	8
4	6	9	MAMA SAID — Shirelles, Scepter 1217	7
5	1	2	MOTHER-IN-LAW — Ernie K-Doe, Minit 623	
6	2	1	RUNAWAY — Del Shannon, Big Top 3067	13
7	8	11	BREAKIN' IN A BRAND NEW BROKEN HEART — Connie Francis, MGM 12995	5
8	4	3	ONE HUNDRED POUNDS OF CLAY — Gene McDaniels, Liberty 55308	11
9	17	43	I FEEL SO BAD — Elvis Presley, RCA Victor 7880	3
10	16	22	31 TRAGEDY — Fleetwoods, Dolton 40	7
11	15	23	34 LITTLE DEVIL — Neil Sedaka, RCA Victor 7874	5
12	18	26	29 HELLO WALLS — Faron Young, Capitol 4533	6
13	28	41	75 STAND BY ME — Ben E. King, Atco 6194	3
14	31	54	74 MOODY RIVER — Pat Boone, Dot 16209	3
15	38	51	62 RAINDROPS — Dee Clark, Vee Jay 383	4
16	9	15	27 HELLO MARY LOU — Ricky Nelson, Imperial 5741	7
17	10	4	4 I'VE TOLD EVERY LITTLE STAR — Linda Scott, Canadian American 123	12
18	13	12	9 PORTRAIT OF MY LOVE — Steve Lawrence, United Artists 291	12
19	22	24	26 GIRL OF MY BEST FRIEND — Ral Donner, Gone 5102	7
20	35	59	BARBARA ANN — Regents, Gee 1065	3
21	25	31	36 THAT OLD BLACK MAGIC — Bobby Rydell, Cameo 190	7
22	11	6	6 YOU CAN DEPEND ON ME — Brenda Lee, Decca 31231	9
23	19	18	15 TONIGHT I FELL IN LOVE — Tokens, Warwick 615	10
24	33	35	43 LULLABY OF LOVE — Frank Gari, Crusade 1021	5
25	8	7	6 YOU ALWAYS HURT THE ONE YOU LOVE — Clarence Henry, Argo 5388	
26	12	7	5 BLUE MOON — Marcels, Colpix 186	13
27	21	20	22 JUST FOR OLD TIME'S SAKE — McGuire Sisters, Coral 62249	12
28	14	10	7 TAKE GOOD CARE OF HER — Adam Wade, Coed 546	11
29	34	36	48 TRIANGLE — Janie Grant, Caprice 104	6
30	36	48	51 PEANUT BUTTER — Marathons, Arvee 5027	5
31	20	19	23 BONANZA — Al Caiola, United Artists 302	8
32	56	77	THE WRITING ON THE WALL — Adam Wade, Coed 550	3
33	46	57	60 THOSE OLDIES BUT GOODIES — Little Caesar and the Romans, Del-Fi 4158	4
34	44	55	66 TOSSIN' AND TURNIN' — Bobby Lewis, Beltone 1002	5
35	45	52	57 I'M A FOOL TO CARE — Joe Barry, Smash 1702	7
36	39	42	56 WHAT A SURPRISE — Johnny Maestro, Coed 552	6
37	41	44	46 EXODUS — Eddie Harris, Vee Jay 378	8
38	57	68	76 LITTLE EGYPT — Coasters, Atco 6192	6
39	24	21	11 BUT I DO — Clarence Frogman Henry, Argo 5378	15
40	65	72	78 HALFWAY TO PARADISE — Tony Orlando, Epic 9441	5
41	43	58	95 RAMA LAMA DING DONG — Edsels, Twin 700	5
42	71	90	BOLL WEEVIL SONG — Brook Benton, Mercury 71820	3
43	63	81	EVERY BEAT OF MY HEART — Pips, Vee Jay 386	3
44	59	63	61 BILBAO SONG — Andy Williams, Cadence 1398	6
45	52	61	79 NEVER ON SUNDAY — Don Costa, United Artists 234	19
46	32	27	24 (DANCE THE) MESS AROUND — Chubby Checker, Parkway 822	8
47	27	14	16 FLAMING STAR — Elvis Presley, RCA Victor LPC 128 (33 compact)	7
48	37	32	36 SOME KIND OF WONDERFUL — Drifters, Atlantic 2096	11
49	53	53	55 GLORY OF LOVE — Roommates, Valmor 008	8
50	55	65	86 YOU'D BETTER COME HOME — Russell Byrd, Wand 107	4
51	60	74	83 IN MY HEART — Time Tones, Times Square 421	4
52	54	62	67 BUZZ BUZZ A-DIDDLE-IT — Freddy Cannon, Swan 4071	5
53	58	75	85 COUNT EVERY STAR — Donnie and the Dreamers, Whale '00	4
54	64	79	82 BETTER TELL HIM NO — Starlets, Pam 1003	3
55	62	67	77 WAYWARD WIND — Gogi Grant, Era 3066	4
56	26	13	8 ONE MINT JULEP — Ray Charles, Impulse 200	13
57	67	83	EVERY BEAT OF MY HEART — Gladys Knight, Fury 1050	3
58	66	73	84 BIG BIG WORLD — Johnny Burnette, Liberty 55318	5
59	61	64	68 THAT'S THE WAY WITH LOVE — Floria Steffan, Big Jim 324	6
60	30	28	21 BUMBLE BOOGIE — B. Bumble and the Stingers, Rendezvous 140	10
61	29	25	25 FUNNY — Maxine Brown, Nomar 106	10
62	68	71	81 A LOVE OF MY OWN — Carla Thomas, Atlantic 2101	3
63	23	17	10 ON THE REBOUND — Floyd Cramer, RCA Victor 7840	13
64	73	94	IT KEEPS RAININ' — Fats Domino, Imperial 5753	3
65	99		QUARTER TO THREE — U.S. Bonds, Le Grand 1008	2
66	70	70	73 THREE HEARTS IN A TANGLE — Roy Drusky, Decca 31193	5
67			DANCE ON LITTLE GIRL — Paul Anka, ABC-Paramount 10220	1
68	81		TELL ME WHY — Belmonts, Sabrina 500	2
69	77	85	I DON'T MIND — James Brown, King 5466	4
70	82		ANNA — Jorgen Ingmann, Atco 6195	2
71			YELLOW BIRD — Arthur Lyman, Hi Fi 5024	1
72	42	45	50 TOUCHABLES IN BROOKLYN — Dickie Goodman, Mark X 8010	8
73	74	78	SPRING FEVER — Little Willie John, King 5503	3
74	76	87	MISS FINE — New Yorkers, Wall 547	3
75	83		MILORD — Teresa Brewer, Coral 62249	2
76	80	88	100 SON-IN-LAW — Louise Brown, Witch 1	5
77			HOW MANY TEARS — Bobby Vee, Liberty 55325	1
78	99		HEART AND SOUL — Cleftones, Gee 1064	2
79	84	86	97 SON-IN-LAW — Blossoms, Challenge 9109	4
80			MY KIND OF GIRL — Matt Monro, Warwick 636	1
81	92		RONNIE — Marcy Jo, Robbee 110	2
82	97	93	NOBODY CARES — Jeanette (Baby) Washington, Neptune 122	5
83			JIMMY MARTINEZ — Marty Robbins, Columbia 42008	1
84	86	98	BROTHER-IN-LAW (He's a Moocher) — Paul Peek, Fairlane 703	3
85	100		DRIVING WHEEL — Little Junior Parker, Duke 335	2
86			I LIKE IT LIKE THAT — Chris Kenner, Instant 3229	1
87			RAININ' IN MY HEART — Slim Harpo, Excello 2194	1
88	96		I FALL TO PIECES — Patsy Cline, Decca 31205	2
89			WHO ELSE BUT YOU — Frankie Avalon, Chancellor 1077	1
90			SUMMERTIME — Marcels, Colpix 196	1
91	94		LONESOME WHISTLE BLUES — Freddie King, Federal 12415	2
92	95	99	THE GIRL'S A DEVIL — Dukays, Nat 4003	3
93			BIG BOSS MAN — Jimmy Reed, Vee Jay 380	1
94			TEMPTATION — Everly Brothers, Warner Bros. 5220	1
95			SACRED — Castells, Era 3048	1
96			TONIGHT (COULD BE THE NIGHT) — Velvets, Monument 4010	1
97	100		HERE'S MY CONFESSION — Wyatt (Earp) McPherson, Spire 1006	2
98			RING OF FIRE — Duane Eddy, Jamie 1187	1
99	94		JURA (I SWEAR I LOVE YOU) — Les Paul and Mary Ford, Columbia 41994	4
100			A LITTLE FEELING — Jack Scott, Capitol 4554	1

BUBBLING UNDER THE HOT 100

1. RESPECTABLE — Chants, MGM 13006
2. I CAN'T DO IT BY MYSELF — Anita Bryant, Carlton 547
3. WATCH YOUR STEP — Bobby Parker, V-Tone 223
4. BRING BACK YOUR HEART — Del-Vikings, ABC-Paramount 10208
5. FOOL THAT I AM — Etta James, Argo 5390
6. BOOK OF LOVE — Bobby Rare, Fraternity 878
7. DREAM — Etta James, Argo 5390
8. LET'S GO AGAIN — Sonny Fulton, Big Daddy 103
9. CHARLIE WASN'T THERE — Barbara Evans, Famous 1003
10. LONELY CROWD — Teddy Vann, Columbia 41994
11. REBEL JOHNNY YUMA — Johnny Cash, Columbia 41995
12. BLUE TOMORROW — Billy Vaughn, Dot 16230
13. YOU CAN'T SIT DOWN — Philip Upchurch Combo, Boyd 3398
14. HOLD BACK THE TEARS — Delacardos, United Artists 310
15. RICARDO — Ralph Marterie, United Artists 315
16. EXODUS — Edith Piaf, Capitol 4564
17. MONDAY TO SUNDAY — Alan Dale, Sinclair 1003
18. CAN'T HELP LOVIN' THAT GIRL OF MINE — Skip and Flip, R.S.V.P. 111
19. I SHOULD — Strong-A-Longs, Warwick 634
20. CUPID — Sam Cooke, RCA Victor 7883

HOT 100 — A TO Z

'Billboard' Hot 100, June 4, 1961. PHOTOGRAPH BY BILL GREENSMITH

in the summer of 1960 and sold 800,000 copies. It was Part 2 of the song which grabbed all the attention with Marchan talking through half the side in best Joe Tex preaching style.

"Bobby Marchan was playing in St Louis, and he told Bobby Robinson to meet him there," said Marshall Sehorn. "Bobby was in Chicago for the Armada convention. And Bobby went and cut Bobby Marchan 'There Is Something On Your Mind.' They were going to go in and just cut a demo tape but as you know it was practically talking all the way, so they just went on and did the rest of it. Bobby Robinson went on and paid for the session, only to find out when he got back to New York that Bobby Marchan had sold the session to two different companies, and had recorded for two different companies. But the mere fact that we cut a union session made it our session, but it was a bad scene.

"Johnny Vincent sued us and so did Leonard Chess. Chess claimed it was his session because he paid for it, but it wasn't his session because he wasn't under contract to him and it was non-union. And Johnny Vincent, let me just say this. The lawsuit with Johnny Vincent could have been avoided. You know, give a man his dues, and credit is due to him. Johnny, we was in Atlantic City that spring at a normal kind of convention, and Johnny came by me. He said to Bobby, 'You know, I have Bobby Marchan under contract, why don't you take me downstairs and buy me a suit and cigar, and we'll let it go at that,' because Johnny loved a big cigar, 'And buy me a drink and cigar and we'll call it quits.' I wouldn't say it was a racial thing, because you can blame anything on racial if you want to, you can say anything. I just think it was a mere fact of Bobby's pride saying, 'I ain't worried about you,' that kind of thing. He said, 'O.K., if you don't come through, I'm gonna sue you.' 'Ha, ha, ha.' A month later Bobby was in a lawsuit."

Eventually Fire had to put up a bond of $12,900 to sidestep an injunction to prevent the record being issued. Bobby Marchan continued to record for Fire after this but never got into the charts again, although he deserved to with "Booty Green," a fine dance record which was cut in New Orleans with Allen Toussaint.

G

His later records have been made outside New Orleans and most are good and lively soul music. If by now his roots are tenuous, Bobby Marchan's contribution to New Orleans will always be seen in his great work with Huey Smith and the Clowns.

LEE DORSEY (1)

Bobby Robinson had much better luck with Lee Dorsey, another New Orleans singer, and there were no contractual problems this time, either. Dorsey is a bouncy, diminutive little character and his bubbling personality overflowed onto his records leaving a trail of good vibrations in his wake. And he sold records, too. His first record on Fury, "Ya Ya," became a No. 7 hit in 1961 and hit over a million in sales.

Dorsey's singing talents were first spotted by a talent scout, Reynauld Richard, who became his manager. His debut recording session was with Instant and Joe Banashak leased the tapes to Ace and ABC Paramount who both issued singles. Marshall Sehorn takes up the story:

"I was down South on a promotion trip, and that was how I first became involved with or know who Allen Toussaint was at the time, travelling into New Orleans. I had a record by, it sounded like Ray Charles on the ABC Paramount label. At that time Ray Charles had an instrumental out called 'One Mint Julep,' and then I heard this local thing by the name of Lee Dorsey called 'Lottie Mo.' Well, not now, but at the time his sound was a whole lot to me like Ray Charles, and it was Allen's piano playing because of the way he was leaving out certain things. But I really thought they had cut him under another name, Ray Charles. That's when I found out that he was here in this town, working with an auto wrecking firm. It was Lee Dorsey.

"So Joe Banashak, who had leased the record to ABC Paramount, who was our distributor at the time, we talked, and I got back to New York and I played the record for Bobby and he said, 'Man, he could be something else.' So we called Pearl Woods who was a friend of ours and did a lot of writing for Bobby at one time, she was working at ABC Paramount. And she said, 'Yeah, we don't even have a contract on him.' I said, 'What do you mean?' 'Well, his contract with a producer in New Orleans ran out, and he won't re-sign with him and he won't sign with us.' "

Bobby Robinson continues: "I called a promoter I knew in New Orleans (I had used his band for Elmore James). I asked if he knew Lee Dorsey and he said, 'Yeah, he lives right down the block.' I asked him to go right now and bring him to the phone, and in about ten minutes Lee was on the phone. He didn't know what was going on. I asked him about the record on ABC and if he was under contract. He told me, 'The guy I did it for sold it to ABC and my contract with him is up.' I asked him if he would like to record for me and when he said all right I told him I would see him next week.

"I flew down to a convention in Miami, and from the convention I went to New Orleans. Lee lived in the 9th Ward which was nearly out of New Orleans way up the Mississippi River. He had a little wooden farmhouse with a porch on it, a real slum. There was one of these country swings on the porch. We were sitting in the living-room talking and I asked him if he had any material. I had only two days before I had to get back to New York, and he didn't have anything. While we were sitting there talking there were some kids on the porch swing who were clapping hands and singing 'Sittin' on the la la, yeah yeah' over and over. I asked him what it was the kids were singing and he said it was just some little thing. We called them in and they were giggling and bashful when I asked them to sing it again. It was such a catchy little thing.

"So, now he's got no material, and I've got no material, but this thing was staying on my mind. I said, 'Let's go uptown,' and we jumped in my rented car and went to a place called the Miller Bar. We sat down and had a few beers and I got a pencil and paper from the barmaid. I was trying to come up with something, but that little melody stayed in my mind. So I said, 'Let's see if we can kick it around and do something with that "Sitting on la la" thing. We can't say "Sittin' on la la" because that sounds like you're sitting on your ass. So let's say something a little different. Suppose we say, "Sitting here la la," "La la" doesn't have to be anything. *"Sittin' here la la, waitin' for my ya ya."* '

"He said, 'Who's ya ya?' and I said 'Ya ya could be your girl friend. Now, the fact that you're sitting here waiting means that she didn't show yet, you're a little worried,' I continued, *'It may sound funny but I don't believe she's coming.'* So we started tapping the beat out and singing what I had so far. He said, 'Yeah, I like that.' We had another beer and I went on, 'The fact that you're sitting waiting and she didn't show means you're a little anxious and you wish she would hurry up.' So tapping out the beat, I said, *'Baby hurry, don't make me worry.'* In fifteen minutes we had it and I knew it was a hit. I said, 'This is the craziest thing I've ever heard, a simple stupid thing, but it's got to be a hit.'

"The next morning we went to see Allen Toussaint, who was the arranger that had 'Ooh Poo Pah Doo' and a few other things. He had a tape recorder and a couple of mikes by his piano. He said, 'I can't write the arrangement, but you sing it and I'll play the piano along with you. You can take it to a friend of mine who can put it together.' He was under exclusive contract to a label and he couldn't do it. I was disappointed because I wanted to use him. Anyway, Lee and I sang duet into the mike because he couldn't remember the words.

"I took the tape to Harold Battiste and he wrote out the chord changes for the band. Then we went right into the studio. The band was cookin' and I knew it was a hit. We cut three or four other things, but I told the engineer, 'Wrap the hit very carefully.' I came back to New York and the record busted wide open."

Following this hit record, Lee went on the road playing the Five Four Ballroom in Los Angeles with Joe Turner and Chuck Berry, in Oakland, California with Lowell Fulson and the Longhorn Club in Dallas with T-Bone Walker.

The next record, "Do-Re-Mi," was based on the same simple, catchy formula and if anything was a smoother production than "Ya Ya." The 400,000 sales were not as good as "Ya Ya," but enough to secure No. 27 spot on *"Billboard"* in the first weeks of 1962.

His other Fury records did not make the charts nationally, but like the two hits they were all good "Carnival Sound" records, as was the Fury album. By 1963 the Bobby Robinson group of labels was in financial trouble, but Lee Dorsey and also Marshall Sehorn were to come back with a vengeance a little later on.

Mercury Records, 1960–62

Mercury Records could be classified as a major independent record company, and their involvement with New Orleans was only passing. Most of the sessions held were under the direction of Shelby Singleton, in liaison with record man Huey Meaux, and they concentrated more on the white Louisiana artists like Joe Barry, Rod Bernard and Jivin' Gene. It was these artists who founded a scene all to themselves, South Louisiana Rock 'n' Roll or Louisiana Swamp Pop as it's now called, which was based on the New Orleans R & B idiom.

"The New Orleans Sound wasn't only based on horns and rhythm," said Cosimo Matassa, "there's a kind of attitude to lyrics too. You find a related thing in the white guys that came out of South Louisiana, the Cajun guys, they all had the same attitude about lyrics. I doubt if they heard each other a lot but all these bands that were in and out of New Orleans played across Southern Louisiana back and forth amongst those little country towns and dances a great deal, and all the guys from the country came to New Orleans a fair amount and heard bands here; not just New Orleans, Southern Louisiana, over the Gulf Coast and like that, Lake Charles, Beaumont, there was a fair amount of interplay. They had that attitude about the lyric and the way they'd say words. There were a lot of records, when they first hit the street, you didn't know if it was black or white, they both sounded the same. Jivin' Gene and Joe Barry, that's a case in point."

Huey Meaux continued to support New Orleans after Mercury had lost interest and cut the early Barbara Lynn hits for Jamie at Cosimo's, besides holding sessions for his own Tribe label.

Duke/Peacock Records, 1960–63

Don Robey, the influential head of Duke and Peacock, had been aware of the talent in New Orleans ever since he had booked artists from the Crescent City through his Buffalo Booking Agency in the late 1940's and early 1950's. In 1960 he had a hit record with "Gonzo" by James Booker.

JAMES BOOKER

"Don Robey came to New Orleans looking for an A & R man in 1959," said James Booker. "I had stopped playing music and went to Southern University and he hit on me. He offered me good money but I wouldn't take the job. So I took him to Edward Frank and anyway he hired Frank.

"Remember Dee Clark? He came through here with Phil Upchurch's group and he needed an organ player and he hired me during my last month at University. My mother covered for me—said I had a breakdown—so I was able to miss a few weeks and take exams the following semester."

The Dee Clark band broke up in Houston after financial disagreements and Dee pawned his organ to Robey, who seeing Booker asked him to stick around and play on a few dates with Bobby Bland, Junior Parker and other Duke artists.

"Don Robey liked the way I played," said Booker, "and told me to record 'Gonzo.' It was called that after Edward Frank and myself had seen a movie together called 'The Pusher.' The drug pusher in the film's name was 'Gonzo'."

"Gonzo," an organ instrumental, became a national hit at No. 43 in 1960. It was really quite an ordinary record but its success was no more than Booker, who had previously recorded for Imperial and Ace, deserved.

"Although I played the piano," continued Booker, "I introduced the organ to Bourbon Street, to the French Quarter. I was the first organist there. Well, I had one job and a man that owned four clubs on Bourbon Street wanted an organ in each one. I was the only organ player in town. There weren't many youngsters out there then, in the middle 1950's. The old timers were really running it, guys from the 20's on up, everybody who was acknowledged as being a monster. They were older cats, not younger ones like now. Wynonie Harris, look how old he was, Roy Brown, all those guys made it in their 30's. They didn't make it when they were teenagers. There were always a few exceptions, teenage prodigies like Little

Esther but Dinah Washington, she wasn't no spring chicken.
It wasn't like today, we got the Jackson Five and all this. Now
Little Willie John, he was real great."

"Booker was a kid genius," said Mac Rebennack. "He'd
been around the studio since he was a small child but he would
never stick around New Orleans long enough to be considered
as resident studio pianist. His mother played organ in church
and he graduated at Southern University. He had the advantage
of studying music and he was influenced by Longhair, Art
Tatum, Lloyd Glenn and Huey Smith. He played such a
variety of music, from 'Malaguena' to Beethoven, his music
was much heavier and more aware than even Allen Toussaint.
He was so far ahead of his time, that's why he's called a genius."

"I used to hang around with guys like Benny Spellman, and
of course Allen Toussaint and Little 'Gonzo' Booker," said
Al Reed. "I think Booker is one of the finest organists in the
whole world. Because anytime a guy can go up and tell Bill
Doggett how to play the organ, well, man, that's chesty. But
then you tell a man he can't play organ and then you go up
there, man, and smoke, you know, well, you know you're good.
And that's what James Booker was like. Many people haven't
heard of James 'Gonzo' Booker but he's one of the finest
organists in the world. Yes, he plays great piano but he plays
a much better organ than he does piano."

None of Booker's follow-ups did anything, and in between
times he also did a lot of session work in New Orleans with
Dave Bartholomew and Imperial.

Don Robey did bring some of his star artists like Bobby Bland
and Junior Parker to record in New Orleans in the early 1960's,
but, with Bland especially, he still preferred the famous brassy
Duke sound to the New Orleans beat.

Imperial Records, 1960–63

Old favourites Fats Domino, Smiley Lewis, the Spiders, and
his own Band were all recorded by Dave Bartholomew for

Imperial in 1960. But newcomers to the label, Earl King, Frankie Ford, Ford Eaglin and Huey Smith stirred up just as much action. In general, Bartholomew was using fuller band backings than before but his productions lost nothing through this.

EARL KING (2)

Earl King's series of records for Imperial between 1960 and 1962 must rank as some of the best items in the Imperial catalogue at this time. His first Imperial record, "Come On," was a two-parter inspired by "Let The Good Times Roll" and "Bon Ton Roulet."

"That Imperial situation," said Earl King, "I met George Davis and he and I were talking and I was just about to cut 'Come On,' the first session I did for Imperial. On that session we did a version of 'The Things That I Used To Do' and George is pretty well responsible for me continuing to play a certain mode that I was working on. I was playing something on guitar and would say, 'Man, I don't like that,' and George would say, 'Man, you leave that in.' And the little passages I was playing I left them in and so the recording came out. Well, all the people wanted the guitar players to play that little interlude I was playing. That was in 1960 and Jimi Hendrix picked this particular song up after Al Robinson had did it. Hendrix did almost the exact version except for the improvisation. I took note on that because I did that in 1960 and he did it in 1969. Well, anyway, George was another person that played a part with me and really wanted me to maintain my thing."

"Earl King is a better orientated production than say Fats would be," said Cosimo Matassa. "He would have a lot of ideas. I think Earl's strength would be in coming up with little figures that fit. You need the lyrics that he thought up. A couple of really good things he did were that real marriage of a good little piece of lyric and a little figure to go with it. Probably the best known was 'Trick Bag,' but he had other things with those little guitar figures that were fantastically appropriate."

A larger band was brought in for the next session and it was the well-disciplined and tight arrangements of Earl and Wardell Quezergue that caught the full emotional quality of Earl's vocals on "Mama And Papa," "You Better Know," "We Are Just Friends" and "You're More To Me Than Gold." The addition of a bigger horn section and a superb James Booker on piano made this a session to remember. With such a large unit a good rhythm section was needed to keep things hot, and the bass work of George Davis and the incredible funk drumming of Robert French did just this.

Earl King remembers this session clearly: "One thing I didn't like about Dave Bartholomew was you could never perfect anything with Dave. You did something and you didn't like how it sounds, you say, maybe, 'I'd like to try another take,' and then Dave would say 'That's good enough, you don't need all that.' Like the one I was talking about, 'Mama And Papa,' I wasn't satisfied with the projection on the tune and I said, 'Look, I want to do this over,' this was at Cos' three-track at Gov. Nicholls. 'I'd like to do it over,' and Dave said, 'Uh, uh, Earl, what you trying to do, you don't need all that. That's it, let's go to the next tune.' The trouble was that he's been doing it with Fats for years, simple stuff, 'You don't need all that, man,' he'd say. On 'You're More To Me Than Gold' one of the mikes failed and to finish the session all of us crowded around a single mike."

"Trick Bag" and "Always A First Time" were real killers, and the record proved to be his best seller for Imperial. It would be hard to find a better example of the New Orleans funk of the early 1960's than is found on "Trick Bag." With King using an open-chorded guitar sound with those intricate figures and Robert French playing so many different accents and beats on his drums, Earl sings out his hurt feelings, about his wrongdoing woman,

> *"I saw her kissing Willie across the fence, I heard her tellin' Willie*
> *I don't have no sense,*
> *The way you've been acting is such a drag, you done put me in a*
> *trick bag."*

Poor Earl can't win as she goes running back to Dad who interjects in best Coasters' style,

> *"She's my daughter, and I'm her pa,*
> *You ain't nothin' but a son-in-law."*

Earl King's a loser on a winning record. " 'Trick Bag' means hanging you off, ripping off, duped," said Earl.

"Always A First Time" is a real treat. Earl King shows how he can put across the full meaning of a song as he sings,

> *"What good it profits me to be King of the Throne,*
> *And have all the riches a man can own,*
> *And yet be in this world so all alone."*

The band set up a myriad of cross-rhythms and must have left the session feeling well pleased with themselves.

After the Imperial days, Earl King's own recording career has been distinctly low-keyed with isolated releases on Amy, Hot Line, Wand, Kansu and a lot of unissued sides for Motown. However, he has continued to play a leading role in the New Orleans record scene as a songwriter and producer. His importance to New Orleans should not be under-rated even if he has tended to fight shy of publicity. Allen Toussaint's genius has managed to break that barrier and likewise Earl King's turn will come.

FRANKIE FORD (2)

The minor success of Frankie Ford's "You Talk Too Much" and "Seventeen" was justification enough for signing him from Ace. Indeed, Fats apart, he was the only other Imperial New Orleans artist to break into the national charts at this time. But his call-up to the U.S. Army was a block to any further aspirations that he or Imperial may have had.

FORD "SNOOKS" EAGLIN

Imperial's Ford Eaglin is better known as Snooks Eaglin, the blind guitarist who has acquired a world-wide reputation in the blues field. In its way his Imperial work was just as wide and varied as his folk-blues recordings with Harry Oster. From the New Orleans R & B sound with his brilliant version of Wee Willie Wayne's "Travellin' Mood," Fats Domino's "Goin' To The River," the Spiders' "I'm Slippin' In," Dave

Bartholomew's "Would You," Johnny Fuller's "Don't Slam That Door," the Ray Charles-styled blues of "By The River" and "See See Rider" through to the lilting ballads of George Davis's "Reality" and Jesse Belvin's "Guess Who." Other people's songs, many different styles, all given a personal interpretation. Snooks hadn't changed one bit.

"He was doing pretty good in England," said Dave Bartholomew, "but we could never get the break on him as an R & B artist."

"Snooks came up through the church rather than playing blues," said Mac Rebennack. "When he first went on the road he would sit down with just his guitar and play all the Ray Charles records; he played 'Drown In My Own Tears' playing the piano part, the horn part and the bass part just by himself on the guitar. He learnt these kinds of things first by playing in church. Secondly he played with Allen Toussaint's band before Allen was a studio musician and who was very proficient at playing Ray Charles music. Snooks was always very good and he could play in the old tradition of playing the melody, the chords and the bass on the guitar like Chet Atkins but in the blues tradition. He could play all the musical parts of things like 'High Society' and dixieland songs like 'All By Myself.' Snooks turned into being one of the stronger blues cats."

Snooks has remained out of the limelight during the 1960's and has lived with his wife in the small town of St Rose, just playing occasional dates. He made a reappearance at the New Orleans Heritage Festival in 1972 and since then has played gigs with Professor Longhair as supporting guitarist. Snooks Eaglin wouldn't want to be called a bluesman but it is there that his reputation remains.

WEE WILLIE WAYNE

In 1962 Imperial re-released James Wayne's recording of "Travellin' Mood" which had been cut originally in 1956. It had a lazy rhythmic swamp beat and was one of his best records. Imperial was sufficiently impressed to release an album which was a compilation of his work recorded in New Orleans dating from 1951. "Wee Willie Wayne ranks among the top handful of rhythm and blues singers who have come out of New Orleans" wrote the intrepid Imperial sleeve-note writer, but in truth Wayne's style was much more Texas than New Orleans.

The End of Imperial Records

Recording activity under Dave Bartholomew remained at a high level in 1962. Fats Domino, Bobby Mitchell, Dave Bartholomew, Earl King, Ford Eaglin, with new signings Blazer Boy, Robert Parker, Wardell & the Sultans, Slim Harpo and Shirley & Lee were all recorded; Bernadine Washington had a good local record with "He's Mine."

And then in 1963 everything ended when Lew Chudd sold his companies to Liberty Records. As ever, Lew Chudd's timing was exquisite. He had started at the right moment in 1947 and had now got out when things were becoming distinctly sticky for independent labels in 1963.

"I just think he got out of business a little too early," said Dave Bartholomew with understandable regret, "but he got what he wanted because we had some very successful years. Imperial promoted records well, and was a very, very fine company. Lew Chudd was on fire, by this I mean he was a terrific worker. He could sell more records in the world than anybody else if he wanted to."

Dave Bartholomew received several offers for recording work but they all meant him leaving New Orleans and he didn't want to do that. "Besides I had been in the studios long enough," he says now. So he went into semi-retirement, just playing with his band because he enjoyed it, and living off the royalties of all his successful songs.

Fats Domino's contract was taken up by ABC Paramount and the rest of the artists and musicians were left to fend for themselves. They had lost a vital outlet, and the sale of Imperial marked the final withdrawal of the outside independent companies from New Orleans.

PART IV

The End of an Era
The Start of Another . . .
1963-73

Fats Domino (4)

Meantime, Fats Domino was still performing and recording quite prolifically. His popularity had found a steady level after the heady heights in the heyday of rock 'n' roll. Harrison Verrett had noticed a slight drop as early as 1960 when he recalled that during a week's engagement at the Apollo Theatre, Harlem, Fats only had two good nights whereas Jackie Wilson played to capacity audiences during his stay.

However, ABC Paramount could not have been very happy at the returns on their investment in Fats after they had signed him in 1963, and the sales of his records certainly dipped. Perhaps the main fault lay in the ultra commercial attitudes of his new company, and as with their other major black artists, Lloyd Price, Ray Charles and B. B. King, they did not hesitate to use large orchestral backings, banks of violins, heavenly choirs, the works in fact. Bill Justis and Felton Jarvis were brought in as producers and the sessions were held at Nashville. The only trouble was that these lavish productions were becoming outdated in 1963; simplicity, which had been the keynote of Dave Bartholomew's success with Fats, was not on the ABC Paramount agenda. Fats and the Nashville Sound didn't really hit it off.

In the circumstances, it is easy to dismiss Fats Domino's recorded output for ABC Paramount. Certainly there was a lot of very ordinary material which did not suit his very personal style one little bit, but amongst the dross there were still many delights to savour. Songs like "Monkey Business," "Heartbreak Hill," "The Girl I'm Gonna Marry," "Reelin' And Rockin' " and instrumentals, "Fats On Fire" and "Fats Shuffle" all had the chicken gumbo flavour of New Orleans—they can be rated along with his better Imperial material. "Red Sails In The Sunset" and "There Goes My Heart Again" were the pick of the over-produced material and were his two best sellers for ABC. The album market was building up in the States by this time and four reasonable albums were put on the market.

In 1965, Fats was contracted to Mercury Records who like ABC Paramount had not been adverse to signing star names. Of their rock 'n' roll stars, Jerry Lee Lewis had modest success,

Chuck Berry was a disaster, and Fats Domino a little better. Mercury's approach was on the same high-powered commercial level of ABC Paramount and Domino's singles did nothing. The company redeemed themselves, however, when they recorded his show live at the Flamingo Hotel, Las Vegas, in June 1965. The selections and style were strictly in the good old Imperial groove, with "Please Don't Leave Me" and "So Long" standing out for the raw excitement they generated. It was one of those rare occasions when a band is properly caught in tip-top form, they were really good. It was a comforting and reassuring release.

Fats' stay with Mercury ended abruptly in a minor mystery when an interesting sounding album, "Southland U.S.A.," and a single, "I Walk The Lonely Nights," were withheld from general release at the eleventh hour, after promotional copies had been sent out. The Mercury well had suddenly run dry.

By the end of 1965, Fats Domino was an established part of the lucrative Las Vegas scene, and judging by the genuine response on the live album, he was a welcome newcomer for the jet-setting gamblers, playboys and socialites. He was also known to play the odd table or two. In 1967, the late Brian Epstein, manager of the Beatles, put up enough money to lure him away to a more sober London where he played a week-long engagement at the Saville Theatre in the West End.

Fats Domino and his Band had actually been to Europe once before, in 1962, when they appeared at the 3rd Jazz Festival in Antibes and Juan-les-Pins in the south of France. They were not liked. The review in *"Jazz Hot,"* the French jazz magazine, began, "Fats Domino porte une montre de 4,800 dollars. Il ne sait pas qui est Thelonius Monk." It was a cool opening but it was altogether too much when the music started to boogie out. "Au zoo!" and "Le Domino Circus" cried the audience, according to the report. Fats must have been great.

When Fats played in England in 1967 the response was exactly the reverse, so much so that the concerts are widely considered to be the best by any visiting American R & B artist and band.

In a *"Blues Unlimited"* review of the shows, the author wrote:

"Legends are built with comparative ease in the anonymity of the recording studio, and how easily such myths are destroyed in the harsh reality of 'in person' performances. If a legend was to be destroyed at the first of the three shows I was to see, what shattered remnants would be left at the end of the last performance on Saturday?

"The curtain rose on a darkened stage. The band swung into a noisy and boisterous trumpet led intro. and through the smog-like gloom the spotlight caught the Fat Man himself. Fears that Domino wouldn't survive the battery of sound were quickly allayed when, without a break, he went into the beautiful 'Blueberry Hill.' This was the moment of truth for we knew then that this was going to be one of the finest live blues shows any of us had ever witnessed. The Saville immediately seemed to be the right place for such a performance.

"Domino's piano and vocal artistry were just as his records had predicted, the band a compulsive blend who conjured up memories of those golden days with Imperial. The rest of the programme consolidated the splendid start. The goodies were there *en masse*, 'Blue Monday,' 'I'm Ready,' 'Ain't That A Shame,' 'When My Dreamboat Comes Home,' 'Walking To New Orleans,' 'My Blue Heaven,' 'I Want To Walk You Home,' 'Red Sails In The Sunset,' 'My Girl Josephine.' In all 20 songs were performed and if there was a highlight it had to be 'Every Night About This Time.' Truly vintage Domino!

"The first performance on the Saturday followed on similar lines, although there was only a 60 per cent capacity audience, and the immediate tension was thereby lessened. It was still fine stuff and new numbers introduced to this set were 'I'm Walkin',' 'I'm Gonna Be A Wheel Someday,' 'Sick And Tired,' 'Let The Four Winds Blow,' and a near classic rendition of 'The Fat Man.'

"The second performance was something else! With the Saville packed to capacity, we could sense the electric atmosphere as we took our seats. Domino and the Band took the bit between the teeth, and after the ever popular 'Blueberry Hill' and 'The Fat Man,' Fats hit the jackpot with a superb five-minute piano solo on 'Ain't That Just Like A Woman.' Herb Hardesty turned the clock back years when he took an extended solo on 'All By Myself,' cavorting from one end of the stage to the other, playing on his back . . . shades of the good old days of rock 'n' roll! A few more numbers and so it ended with the usual 'When

The Saints Go Marching In' with Fats bumping the piano off stage."

It was a rave review but time has not allowed personal opinions to alter. Fats had justified himself in the best way possible—by getting on stage and being really great. As Clarence Ford, a member of that band, said, "It was the best band around at that time."

It was also in 1967 that Fats Domino and Dave Bartholomew got together once more and reputedly owned the Broadmoor record company, which was named after a district in the middle of New Orleans. Two singles were released by Fats but the age-old problem of distribution managed to nullify the inbuilt sales value of his name on the label. The entire Fats' Broadmoor sessions were bought up later by Reprise and when these recordings were released in album form they were seen to be below par. It was a tepid affair without much enthusiasm from the participants; "Lawdy Miss Clawdy" was the only song performed in the old Fats style and it was the only number which scored.

When Fats was signed by Reprise Records in 1968, he was given a star-studded backing group for his sessions which included King Curtis, tenor, James Booker, piano, Chuck Rainey, bass, and Earl Palmer, drums. There was still a tendency to over-produce, but there was a spark and drive which had been largely missing from the ABC and Broadmoor studio recordings. The title of the first album, "Fats Is Back," inferred that he had been away too long, and the opening track reminded listeners what they had been missing as excerpts from his old Imperial hits, complete with scratches, hisses and fake audience, were lumped together before Fats embarked on an engaging selection of R & B which included such good things as "My Old Friend," "I Know," "Honest Papas Love Their Mamas Better" and "One For The High-way." A couple of Beatles songs, "Lady Madonna" and "Lovely Rita," were really no more than fillers, although "Lady Madonna" managed to nudge into the Top 100 in September 1968. But after this bright start, Reprise had no further ideas and Fats was dropped in 1970.

In fact, the new decade began disastrously for Fats when his terrific band was torn apart by a terrible car accident at Natchitoches, Louisiana, in 1970; his bass player, James Davis, was killed and tenor men Clarence Ford and Robert "Buddy" Hagans were so badly injured that they have never played with Fats again. These musicians have never been satisfactorily replaced, and in 1972 Herb Hardesty, the real pillar of the band, became so disillusioned with the new line-up that he quit.

In 1973, Fats Domino was again playing concerts with the regularity that he had done when at the peak of his career. But performing to the white middle-aged "oldies but goodies" crowd, and doing those old hits night after night, it's understandable that a certain edge has gone off his work and a degree of mechanisation has crept in. He managed to squeeze a short European tour into his tight schedule, and if, critically, he was not as well received as in 1967, attendances were high enough to confirm him as the No. 1 Musical Ambassador of New Orleans. Now he needs to get some more records going.

The Small Local Labels

The New Orleans record scene was left in 1963 to the small local labels which had mushroomed in the dark shadows of the larger companies who by now had vacated the city. They did not have the capital, flair or expertise to flourish, and they lost out through lack of exposure.

"When we were successful with A.F.O.," said Red Tyler, "we actually had a meeting with maybe about 25 or 30 of these little record companies, we called them up to our office, and we said you're gonna lose everything you have because we've been in this all our lives, you know, and everybody thought that because we were a success that all you had to do was form your company and you were going to make it. So we tried to say, 'Why don't you go into other parts of entertainment, other fields?' and they said, like, we couldn't tell them what to do. It all came about because of our success, really, because they had no record company that was local prior to to us, and they really came up suddenly, they had quite a few of them. We told them what they were doing was crowding the field and you're gonna lose your shirts. But they said, 'They want to keep us from the money, they want to stop us.' A lot of people came up on a shoestring trying to make it, some were successful."

"All the new artists that were coming up and some of the old artists began recording for the local independents," said Earl King, "it seemed that New Orleans was at a standstill in production, but yet they had more recordings done during the 1960's, I imagine than they did during the 1950's."

Earl King himself was involved in many of these sessions as writer, arranger, and producer, much of the time in collaboration with Wardell Quezergue.

WARDELL QUEZERGUE

Wardell is a bespectacled Creole who keeps himself very much to his family and his music. Along with Allen Toussaint, it was mainly his productions that managed to keep a spark alive in New Orleans music in the 1960's. "Wardell had played with Dave Bartholomew's band as a trumpeter and arranger," said

Mac Rebennack. "He also arranged his own bands, the Sultans and the Royal Dukes of Rhythm. He had a revue with fourteen pieces and four singers and everything. It pretty much went from the traditional stuff, like the band would play big band arrangements of 'Body And Soul' to the latest Top 40 and R & B records. From doing this stuff, Wardell became aware how to arrange good R & B records. A few years before I had played piano with Wardell's band around New Orleans and he had all those union halls locked up for dances and gigs, and union meetings and stuff like that. He would be the house band for all artists visiting New Orleans."

Wardell Quezergue's arrangements tended to be bigger, noisier than Allen Toussaint's. He used a fuller horn and brass section which showed he had learnt a lot from his days with Dave Bartholomew and Fats Domino. Another feature of his work was the modern rhythms he was using, that were whipped along by the technical grace and proficiency of George Davis's guitar work.

Despite his many productions in New Orleans, Wardell achieved only moderate success, but in 1970 and 1971 he acquired more fame than he ever did in the 1960's when he produced two No. 1 national hits, "Groove Me" by King Floyd on Chimneyville and "Mr Big Stuff" by Jean Knight on Stax, both recorded in the Malaco Studios, Jackson, Mississippi.

Frisco Records

Wardell Quezergue's first production assignment had been with Frisco Records, a small label which was owned by the very personable Connie La Rocca and dee-jay, Hal Atkins, and run from offices in North Claiborne. The first release was "Stubborn Old Me" by Al Adams (a pseudonym for Hal Atkins) which had a sound that was reminiscent of the Earl King Imperial sides, and was probably a similar band.

DANNY WHITE

It was a good start which was capitalised upon by Danny White with "Kiss Tomorrow Goodbye," written by Al Reed.

The record sold so well locally in the fall of 1962 that it was taken up by Arlen Records of Philadelphia; it started to break out nationally before internal strife quickly stopped it in its tracks. This tuneful blues ballad is still played in New Orleans today, and everyone still thinks it's potential hit material. After this, Danny White kept trying to emulate this song without success, although it's interesting to note that his later Frisco records were produced in Memphis by the young, upcoming production team of David Porter and Isaac Hayes. Even if he was not known outside New Orleans, Danny White's local reputation was high, and he could always be relied upon to put on a good show with his band, the Cavaliers. "We was doing a lot of Coasters things, 'Why Is Everybody Picking On Me,' 'Get A Job' and things like that," said White's trumpeter, Henry "Hawk" Hawkins, "we had the identical sound because we had a good band and show. I was em-ceeing and doing comedy."

WILLIE WEST

Willie West was the other regular Frisco artist, and his records were good, underplayed R & B. He had recorded a little earlier for Rustone Records of Houma, Louisiana and made "Did You Have Fun" for them, a tuneful South Louisiana ballad which was a moderate seller. West later recorded with Allen Toussaint and was featured vocalist with the Meters group for a time.

Rip Records

Rip Records was formed by Rip Roberts in 1962 and operated from 1863, Duels Street. "His real name is Rippo Roberts," said Deacon John, "he's a local promoter, he used to bring Ray Charles down to New Orleans, he used to be the only guy that could bring Ray Charles down. He had a whole lot of hustle going on the side and the first thing you know he's got a record company. He had success with his first recording, some guy, Reggie Hall, recorded a little thing called 'The Joke.' It sold real good. After that he tried to get a big roster of artists, everybody knew about me, so I was next in line. I'd give anything to get on records then, 'Just sign, here, kid, just sign, sign.' ''

DEACON JOHN

"I Can't Wait" and "When I'm With You" was a particularly good coupling by Deacon John. He sang in the same wistful style of many of the Minit artists, which he had probably picked up when he was doing session work for them, and with tasteful use of violins, the record had much charm.

"The Rip record was my first record as a solo artist," said Deacon John. "It was a terrible production but I think they played it a couple of times on the radio and they said the song wasn't good enough to be played on the air . . . the guy's session was rushed off, man. The musicians came late, and we tried to catch something together and cut down on expenses. Smokey Johnson was on drums, he's still playing, Roy Evans plays guitar, he's in a society band now, William Houston's Society Band, Wardell Quezergue did the arrangements, George French played bass, he's with the Storyville Jazz Band right now. Basically that was it, the rhythm section. They dubbed the strings on later, they didn't have enough time to put the strings on and they didn't want to pay overtime. . . . It was a real cheap session, like the musicians cost 50 bucks and the studio cost about 25 dollars."

"Deacon John" Moore with his band, the Ivories, became a popular attraction in New Orleans in the 1960's, although he cut only one more record, "Many Rivers To Cross," which was released by Bell.

Rip Records also arranged a distribution deal with Chess and records by Reggie Hall (Joe Jones's old pianist) with "The Joke" and Eddie Bo with "You're The Only One" were released nationally. One of the rarer records on Rip is Professor Longhair's "Whole Lotta Twistin' " which is a thematic variation of his ever-present stage song, "Whole Lotta Lovin'."

Watch Records

Watch Records was formed in 1963 by Joe Assunto, who ran
the One Stop Record Shop at 330, South Rampart Street, and
Henry Hildebrand, who owned All South Distributors, the
main rivals to A-1 Distributors, from 630, Baronne Street. "Joe
Assunto was a really beautiful person," said Mac Rebennack.
"He would give Professor Longhair a job at his record shop
when he was out of work, and at the time of Watch Records,
musicians like Longhair, Johnny Adams, and Earl King used
to hang out at the record shop, and a piano and tape recorder
was put in there."

Wardell Quezergue was again in charge of productions
which included "Slow Down" by Benny Spellman, "Part Of
Me" by Johnny Adams and the famous Indian Mardi Gras
rhythms of Professor Longhair's "Big Chief" with Earl King
on vocals.

The label was later distributed by London Records, but
despite this mark of respectability, Watch and it's sister label,
Johen could not come up with the required hits.

The Dark Ages

In 1964, New Orleans was a depressed area musically. Like the rest of the American record industry, it was in the process of recovering from the onslaught of the Beatles who had caused the biggest upheaval since Elvis Presley; the death of President Kennedy was also hanging over everybody like a dark cloud.

"With my band, the Ivories, we kept changing musicians," said Deacon John. "And I got caught in the . . ., right after the Twist went over then came the Beatles, and that was when the whole music scene changed, not only New Orleans. The whole rock music scene changed, the guys started getting big amplifiers, they didn't want no horn players, all the music that was recorded reflected this. Everybody was growing their hair long, before that everybody was wearing crew-cuts, loafers and ivy league. Then all of a sudden these guys came along with their long hair and looking like sissies, and big boots, and big mountains of equipment, they got managers and producers, so all groups started thinking like that. In order to survive I had to change the whole thing around. It was kinda hard for me because I wasn't white."

In other words, the existing order had been overturned and one of the casualties was rhythm and blues. The music was now called Soul, and although Tamla/Motown was exploiting this far more sophisticated form of R & B and using some of the New Orleans rhythm patterns in doing it, it took a little while for New Orleans to get in the soul groove itself.

New Orleans in New York

ALVIN ROBINSON

Although recorded in New York, Alvin Robinson kept the old New Orleans sounds in the charts with Chris Kenner's song, "Something You Got," which reached No. 52 on *"Billboard"* in 1964.

After his Imperial recordings in 1960, Robinson was signed by Joe Jones who was now concentrating on artist management in New York. A record deal was made with Tiger Records owners, Jerry Leiber and Mike Stoller, the famed producers of the Coasters vocal group.

Alvin Robinson, a huge man of 255 pounds whose nickname was "Shine," went with Leiber and Stoller when they disbanded Tiger Records and formed Red Bird Records with George Goldner, the former chief of Gee, Gone and End Records. His first record for Red Bird, "Down Home Girl," was terrific. Leiber and Stoller's production was superb whilst it was clear that Joe Jones had a hand in the arrangements—the piping brass, lowdown piano and second line rhythm were all there. Robinson's voice, showing Ray Charles's influence as ever, was heavily laced with sarcasm as he sang,

"Lord, I swear the perfume you wear was made out of turnip greens,
Every time I kiss you girl, it tastes like pork and beans,
Even though you're wearing them citified hi-heels,
I can tell by your giant steps you've been walking through them cottonfields,
Oooh . . . you're so . . . downhome, girl"

And then,

"I'm gonna take you back to New Orleans, down in Dixieland,
I want to watch you do the Second Line with an umbrella in your hand,
Oooh . . . you're so . . . downhome, girl."

Incredibly it was not a hit, and Leiber and Stoller reckoned it was the best record put out by Red Bird. After this Robinson recorded for Blue Cat, Atco and Joe Jones before moving out to the West Coast and recording for Pulsar and also with Dr John on the "Gumbo" album.

THE DIXIE CUPS

Another Joe Jones act from New Orleans, three high school girls who were known as the Dixie Cups, had a national No. 1 hit with "Chapel of Love" on Red Bird, "a record I hated with a passion," said Mike Leiber. "Chapel Of Love" was pure pop and there was nothing much in the record which hinted at a New Orleans background, although traces could be detected on the flip, "Ain't That Nice," which was penned by Earl King. The Dixie Cups were far from one-hit-wonders and continued to score right through until 1965, the best being "Iko Iko" which was the old Sugar Boy Crawford song, "Jock A Mo," dressed up with a true New Orleans beat.

Nola Records

Back in New Orleans, a new local record company, Nola Records, was formed by producer Wardell Quezergue and Clinton Scott in the latter part of 1964. Immediately they started to put out good records produced by Wardell himself.

SMOKEY JOHNSON

The first Nola record to stir up any action was the two-part instrumental, "It Ain't My Fault," by Wardell's drummer, Joe "Smokey" Johnson. The treatment brought back memories of the old drum hits by Cozy Cole and Sandy Nelson in the late 1950's. In 1965 it was something of a novelty for a drummer to be so extensively featured and any possibility of monotony, a real danger with this sort of record, was avoided by the intriguing rhythm patterns which were set up by Johnson, and the soaring alto of Walter Kimball and the other horns which surged in later. "It Ain't My Fault" was an odd title for an instrumental but the musicians literally brought the title phrase alive by their interpretation. A great record.

WARREN LEE

"Every Hour, Every Day" was an infectious, fast moving song from Warren Lee Taylor, with Wardell and crew in noisy support; the flip, "Key To Your Door," was more lowdown and blue than most New Orleans records. Warren Lee was another good local artist who never got any exposure outside of New Orleans, not even when he later went to record for Allen Toussaint and cutting such fine records as "Star Revue" and "Climb The Ladder" on Deesu.

WILLIE TEE

"Teasin' You" by Willie Tee was an early hit for Nola. The song was written by Earl King after he had seen Huey Smith stood up by a woman outside a club in Bourbon Street. With a catchy, middle-tempo beat distinguished by the punchy horn arrangements of Wardell Quezergue, the song was a natural for Willie Tee who had been around the local scene since the late 1950's playing piano.

"My influences as a singer were local artists like Eddie Bo and Tommy Ridgley," said Willie Tee. "The first band I played with was the Seminoles with my brother Earl Turbinton and Erving Charles, and then Melvin Lastie told me he liked the way I sang and he asked me to record for their company, A.F.O., him and Harold Battiste. Harold Battiste was my music teacher in Junior High School, I played the saxophone terribly, and I recorded for them, never no real thing or hit record. In 1965 I got involved with Wardell Quezergue, they had a company called Nola Records and I did 'Teasin' You'. The tune enabled me to do quite a bit of travelling, the first time I got out of New Orleans, but all of the monies from the record I never got because I was not aware what the business end of it was about."

Willie is a man of high principle who considers himself more of a jazz musician rather than a R & B artist. But he didn't help his own cause by playing modern jazz when he went out on tour, as his brother Earl Turbinton admits: "I think we were a little impracticable, we had a hit rock record out but we opened up playing 'Milestones' for a tune-up or some jazz tune that we wanted to play, and we went through a whole period of really playing supposedly in a rock setting but playing the music we wanted to play, and felt like we were forced to play the other things because we had to survive."

"Thank You John" and "Walkin' Up A One Way Street" were other good records that Willie Tee cut for Nola which were similar to "Teasin' You" but not as successful. However, they have been enough to earn Willie a sizeable reputation in the strange world of soul record collectors.

Earl Turbinton set up a "Jazz Workshop" in the French Quarter in 1967 which flourished for a while and now both he and Willie are striving to explore the world of music together, to create something for themselves and New Orleans. They have the talent to do it.

Dover Records

At this point in time, Nola was having chronic distribution problems, the constant scourge of small labels in New
Orleans. The Smokey Johnson and Warren Lee records were
leased to Vee-Jay, Willie Tee's to Atlantic and an instrumental by drummer June Gardner to Blue Rock, a Mercury
subsidiary.

Cosimo Matassa was acutely aware of these problems and
attempted to resolve them when he set up Dover Records.
The philosophy was quite simple. "The idea was, that nobody
ever did, was to set up a New Orleans record company,"
said Cosimo, "that would either produce things on its own or
properly compensate other producers. For instance, we started
Dover and we automatically gave producers 10 per cent when
4 or 5 per cent was routine. In fact, everybody was signed up
as producers, got a 10 per cent, then I could afford to give
the artists 4 or 5 per cent and still make money and pay his
overheads. That was the concept of the thing." In effect, the
idea was for Dover to provide an all-round package for the
small labels which covered the entire processes of making and
selling records.

Al Reed formed his own label, Axe Records, at this time
and he described how he came to be tied up with Dover: "I
got some money together and thought, 'What the hell, I
might as well produce records on myself,' because others were
producing me as they wanted and not as I wanted. So I got
me a few hundred dollars and went into Cosimo's studio. I
rented the place and hired my musicians, and I went in to do
a session called 'White Lightnin','" it was a Jimmy Reed-type
blues. And on the flip was 'I'll Cut You If You Stand There,
Shoot You If You Run.' Cosimo was over at the session and
asked me what I was going to do with it:

"I said, 'I'm gonna lease, what do you think I'm gonna do
with it?'

"He said, 'No sense in you going out of town and lease it
to somebody that you don't even know, you can lease it to
me. At least if anything goes wrong, I'm right here for you to
come to me and talk to me, these other people you'd have to

travel or get your lawyer out of town and sue them for your bread and stuff like that.'

"So I said, 'What do I get out of this?'

"He said, 'Well, you lease to me and I'll pay for this entire session. And I'll give you 8 per cent.'

"I said, '8 per cent, that ain't bad, what else?'

"He said, 'You have an open account here with Dover and you can produce yourself and any of your artists and we'll cover all sessions and all costs, we'll cover everything under that 8 per cent to you.'

"I said, 'You got yourself a deal.'

"So I leased it, I leased to him and I recorded several artists, there was a young man named Larry Breaux who was under contract to the late Elijah Walker and a girl named Yvonne Wise. And of course I did that '99 44/100 Pure Love' which was the best record I did produce with him, it got recognition but it was not really a big record. It was a regional record but it did very well. I don't know how many copies it sold, I never received an accounting, not one on any of the records I ever produced for Cosimo and his Dover Corporation. What happened was it wasn't properly merchandised. The promotion on the records was nil! The promotion on these records I got came from my own, shall we say, outside dealings."

ROBERT PARKER

Dover had instant success with Nola Records when Robert Parker's dance record, "Barefootin'," took off and became a No. 7 hit in the early summer of 1966. Parker had a very relaxed, unhurried singing style which was quite amazingly effective considering that he was only really thought of as a saxophone player in New Orleans until this time. Although the soul beat was coming through, the New Orleans Sound was still clearly apparent on "Barefootin'," and this and later records like "Everybody's Hip Huggin'," "Foxy Mama" and "Holdin' Out" had great charm. On public appearances, though, Parker was content to ape the big soul records of the moment like "Mr Pitiful," "In The Midnight Hour" and "Hold On I'm Comin'."

Parlo Records

Parlo Records was formed by schoolteacher, Warren Parker, with musicians Red Tyler and George Davis. They came into the Dover family right away and had a massive hit first time out by Aaron Neville.

AARON NEVILLE

"Tell It Like It Is" was the song which earned Aaron Neville, Art's brother, a gold record in the early part of 1967. The hit potential of this bluesy ballad was not obvious at first, but after several plays it began to have an hypnotic effect, and besides, its title was perfect in a time of rampant Black Power. George Davis's Fats Domino-like horn arrangement did nothing to harm sales, either.

Aaron Neville's career dated back to the late 1950's and the Hawketts, but he had got his real start when he was recording with Minit. However, his revival was cut short when Parlo fell apart at the seams. "This was the first thing they tried in the producing field and it was a smash," said Art Neville, "but business-wise, nobody was really up on what to do, consequently the thing just folded up on them."

The End of Dover Records

For a while, it had seemed that Dover was fulfilling all the hopes of the small labels in New Orleans but by 1968 it had collapsed in ruin, leaving a whole lot of broken men and as it had a monopoly, a record scene in utter destruction. How did it happen?

"The unfortunate thing was that while I knew about recording in the studio," said Cosimo Matassa, "and I knew where it was everywhere in the record business and knew what it took to get records played and that sort of thing, I didn't know anything about the record business and that was my downfall. I put everything I could beg borrow or steal into a new studio and Dover Records and a record pressing plant, we had everything, we had a New Orleans distributing company. A local wholesaler, distributor type, we had other independent labels besides the things we picked up, and Dover distributed nationally and licensed internationally. And we had some hit records, did a lot of business and I went broke.

"We had trouble with distributors, credit and that sort of thing. And then I got to understand that some of the things an independent record producer would want a record company to do, you couldn't do for him on the same basis that a fatherly well-to-do parent couldn't do everything a teenage son or daughter asked them to do, even if they were able to do it, on the basis that it would be better for them not to do it, or only let them do it if they could carry it off on their own. For instance, probably the people we did most things with were Nola, when Dover folded, the studio and all that got caught up in the bills thing because I made myself personally responsible for everything, and it wasn't possible to pay the bills. One major creditor anyhow, he didn't bother to take Dover or the pressing plant, he just took Cosimo's recording studio. That's what put us out of business. That was the kind of keystone of the whole thing. Shut that down, and boom, everything was gone, there was no way to save anything. I'm old fashioned enough not to claim bankruptcy, so we stretched it out, whatever money we could pay people with we did, it was just down to the bare walls of the building.

"In the case of Nola, when we folded they owed us about $70,000 for studio time, we just turned the studio over to them. Any time they wanted they would ring up and set a date so the consequence was they did a lot of dates, and if they had come up with the money we might not have gone under. And following on from that, they might have been more selective with their things, they might have been better disciplined in their operations, maybe we did them a disservice by giving them a *carte-blanche*. You know, they recorded themselves out of business, the same way we sold ourselves out of business.

"Because if you could get sales, the more records you can sell, fine, I found out the hard way that 'freebies' in that period in the record business, it was common that a distributor would get 300 free records if he bought a thousand. I was dumb enough, I have to use that word advisedly, dumb enough,

One Stop Record Shop with Joe Assunto. PHOTOGRAPH BY JAMES LA ROCCA

Fats Domino at the Saville Theatre, 1967. Left to Right: James Davis, Fats Domino, Clarence Brown, Roy Montrell, Wallace Davenport.
PHOTOGRAPH BY STEVE RICHARDS

Fats Domino's Band, 1967. Left to Right: Clarence Brown, Roy Montrell, Wallace Davenport, Herb Hardesty, Nat Perrilliat, Clarence Ford, Walter Kimball, Robert Hagans. PHOTOGRAPH BY STEVE RICHARDS

Herb Hardesty, 1960. PHOTOGRAPH COURTESY MIKE LEADBITTER

DANNY WHITE FAN CLUB
FRISCO RECORDING STAR

TEAR OFF ALONG
DOTTED LINE

To register as an Official Member
of the
DANNY WHITE FAN CLUB

Please fill out on reverse side and
mail to:

Danny White Fan Club

1140 N. Claiborne Avenue

New Orleans, La.

Danny White Fan Club, 1962. COURTESY JAMES LA ROCCA

Deacon John, 1973. PHOTOGRAPH BY JOHN BROVEN

Alvin Robinson and The Dixie Cups, 1966. PHOTOGRAPH BY STEVE RICHARDS

Willie Tee and Earl Turbinton, 1973. PHOTOGRAPH BY JOHN BROVEN

'*Barefootin*'.' PHOTOGRAPH BY BILL GREENSMITH

'*Tell It Like It Is*'.
PHOTOGRAPH BY BILL GREENSMITH

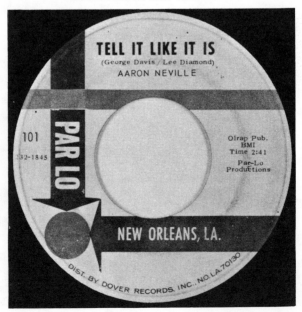

Boogie Bill Webb, 1970. PHOTOGRAPH BY JOHN BROVEN

Polka Dot Slim, 1972. PHOTOGRAPH BY HANS ANDREASSON

Marshall Sehorn, 1973. PHOTOGRAPH
BY JOHN BROVEN

Lee Dorsey, 1966. PHOTOGRAPH
BY STEVE RICHARDS

Sansu Enterprises, Clematis Avenue.
PHOTOGRAPH BY JOHN BROVEN

Allen Toussaint, 1972. PHOTOGRAPH COURTESY SANSU RECORDS

The Meters, 1972. Left to Right: Leo Nocentelli, George Porter, Joseph Modeliste, Art Neville. PHOTOGRAPH COURTESY SANSU RECORDS

George Davis, 1973. PHOTOGRAPH BY JOHN BROVEN

Aaron Neville, 1973. PHOTOGRAPH BY JAMES LA ROCCA

PHOTOGRAPH BY JOHN BROVEN

Home of the Blues concert ticket. COURTESY JAMES LA ROCCA

Infinity Unlimited Presents
Home of the Blues, Part I

- featuring -

Ernie K. Doe	Benny Spellman
Chris Kenner	Robert Parker
Earl King	Aaron Neville

Tommy Ridgley and His Band

ST. BERNARD CIVIC AUDITORIUM

8245 Judge Perez Drive

Friday, July 6, 1973

DOORS OPEN 8:00 P.M. - SHOW 9.00 P.M.

TICKETS $4.00 (advance) $5.00 (at door)

N? 2734

to keep the freebies going even after we had the hit established. You know, 'Tell It Like It Is,' we sold on the books over a million, we had given away on the freebies thing about 400,000. What should have happened was that after we had passed the 150,000 or so, we should have said, 'Well, fellas, the freebies are over, they're 20 cents a piece now, you're gonna pay the bare royalties and cost of manufacturing the disc,' which incidentally is what I think they do these days."

Al Reed, with his Axe label, was acutely aware of the happenings behind the collapse of Dover. "Apparently there were people in his organisation that he delegated certain duties to," he said. "These people were not necessarily qualified to run his business, he allowed his business to be run by others when he should have been running his business himself. These people's names I don't recall because one is a friend of mine, the other, she's not a friend of mine but she knows who she is. When Cos had 'Barefootin' ' and 'Tell It Like It Is,' they knew they needed help to make those records million sellers, in fact 'Tell It Like It Is' did better than two and a half million. There were people ready to help them because they had good records, they made promises to these people, something in return for their assistance. Well, these people called back for them to reciprocate, they could never get in touch with them. They refused to talk, they were out, they would never return calls. They would never correspond with these people. Success doesn't last forever, they forgot that these same people that helped them on the way up, were the only people that could keep them up there. And these same people would also help to bring them down, and they did, they did. Because they met all these same people on the way down, and on their way down, everybody turned their backs, they refused to help them.

"One man in particular, with whom I was closely associated, asked me:

" 'Hey, Al, do you know the cat singing this tune?'

"I said, 'Yeah, I know the cat.'

" 'He a buddy of yours?'

"I said, 'Yeah.'

" 'Is he all right?'

H

" 'Yeah, he's all right, man.'

" 'So I'm gonna play this record because you know the artist.'

"He said, 'Did you see this damn company here, every record they send me, that's where they end up.'

"The trash-can. He refused to play anything with the Dover trademark, because as you know, they handled about 23 or 25 different labels, Axe, Art, Debt, Eight Ball, White Cliffs, oh man, so many. They actually handled that many labels and this was something many people weren't aware of. And every record, every label, that Dover handled that carried the Dover trademark, was thrown in the trash-cans all over the country. It was money wasted to press the records. Because these were the people that helped make them on their way up and the same people killed them, killed them off. They were spending all this money on sessions, and then they went all out on promotion, what good was that? You've already messed up the wrong people, so these people they don't give a damn about you now, man, you have had it.

"A lot of money was put in product, promotion and merchandise, plus he was diversifying most of the money that was coming in, plus he didn't collect on a hell of a lot of records that he had out. This money wasn't coming in, suddenly people were demanding their money, he could pay off them and he couldn't pay off the Government, the Federal or the State. So it was common knowledge that they closed in on him, when the Feds closed in on him they confiscated every damn thing in the building, they tried to get the building. I think they did get the building, they were locking up his house, the building. Most of the contents were picked up at auction by Allen Toussaint and Marshall Sehorn. The masters are in a warehouse in Memphis or something, the Government got them, still have."

Everyone in New Orleans likes Cosimo Matassa, they still do, despite what happened to Dover. He retains an interest in the present Jazz City Studio although his activities in this direction are in a very minor key, especially when one considers that he was more or less responsible for almost everything that had come out of New Orleans until 1968. Cosimo likes to talk about the contribution of others to New Orleans; his own has been huge indeed, and yet all he's got to show is a mass of debts.

Instant Records, 1964 on

Somehow, Joe Banashak did not get involved with Dover, and his Instant label has managed to survive the depressed times of the New Orleans recording scene in the late 1960's. Instant Records has always been a solid source of homespun New Orleans R & B, although they have never found another artist to reproduce hits on the scale of Chris Kenner or a producer of such consistent output as Allen Toussaint.

On his return from the Army in 1965, Allen Toussaint continued his links with Joe Banashak for a while, producing records by Eskew Reeder (formerly known as "Esquerita" in his rock 'n' roll days) with a string-laden "I Done Woke Up," Diamond Joe with a typical piece of Toussaint on "Too Many Pots" and Chris Kenner's "Never Reach Perfection."

ALON RECORDS

Allen Toussaint was involved with Joe Banashak in Alon Records, which was formed by Banashak when Irving Smith dropped out of Instant and that company had to change its spots. "That was Joe Banashak's label, or supposedly Joe Banashak's and mine," said Allen Toussaint, "but Alon wasn't my name modified at all, it was N.O.L.A. reversed."

It was Toussaint's own group, the Stokes, which he had formed whilst in the Army, which gave the label two small instrumental hits with "Whipped Cream," later recorded by Herb Alpert & his Tijuana Brass, and "Young Man, Old Man." Willie Harper was successful shortly before this with "A New Kind Of Love" which was a very attractive tune, and Benny Spellman came up with "The Word Game," Ernie K-Doe's "T'Aint It The Truth" and a Huey Smith-inspired romp, "No Don't Stop." Al Fayard, Skip Easterling and Eldridge Holmes were also recorded by Toussaint but his association with Banashak ended when he formed a new partnership with Marshall Sehorn.

SEVEN B RECORDS

Seven B Records was another local label distributed by Joe Banashak in the mid-1960's. The first release, "Pass The Hatchet" by Roger and the Gypsies, was a 46-bar instrumental which combined the old and new rhythms of New Orleans, a sort of parade beat with soul. It was a good local hit and presaged the later records by the Meters in this style. Long-established Eddie Bo was the main Seven B artist and also producer, but his arrangements did not have a strong overall sound and in musical terms, Seven B's catalogue was one of New Orleans' weaker and less influential labels.

POLKA DOT SLIM

When Allen Toussaint left, Joe Banashak put his label product in the hands of several men, which at least meant a variety of different sounds. One such man was Sax Kari, a man with a lot of experience in the business, and he produced Polka Dot Slim's "Ain't Broke Ain't Hungry" and "A Thing You Gotta Face" in 1964. The record was certainly a departure for Instant and indeed New Orleans because it was one of the dirtiest blues records anywhere in a long time. Polka Dot Slim's vocals and harmonica showed his Mississippi background and the rest of the swamp-blues accompaniment was overdubbed by Kari himself.

Along with guitarist Boogie Bill Webb, the old Imperial artist, and country blues and gospel guitarist Babe Stovall, Polka Dot Slim must represent what must be the last of the rural country bluesmen still playing in New Orleans. Polka Dot Slim is still found playing in small bars at the back of town, whilst Babe Stovall's exhibitions are confined to weekend street singing. Boogie Bill, on the other hand, treats his music as a hobby and has a good job as a longshoreman; his musical performances, which range from material by Tommy Johnson to Chuck Berry, are confined to private parties with friends and visiting blues collectors.

Eddie Bo took over as main producer and arranger for Instant and his productions reflected his modern outlook, with a marked emphasis on the latest funky soul sounds on records by Chris Kenner and Art Neville. Huey Smith was also engaged on the production side and gave the label a couple of small hits with the Hueys and the Pitter Pats. In 1969 he had some heavy and really good soul productions, in his own name with the Bobby Williams Group, and also the old De Luxe star, Larry Darnell.

"The Place (New Orleans)" by The Big Wolfe was an isolated production by Kenny Smith, and a good one too. The Big Wolfe sounds white and his one record captured part of New Orleans' character when he sang,

> *"There's a place I'm gonna tell you about,*
> *Where every night they swing and they shout,*
> *The neon lights shine on Bourbon Street,*
> *And all you can hear is that rock 'n' roll beat,*
> *Where there's red beans, slot machines, and cute*
>   *little girls in tight blue jeans,*
> *New Orleans. . . ."*

SOLID GOLD

In 1969 Joe Banashak issued his very first album on Instant. It had taken him ten years to do it, although he had leased an album of Chris Kenner's early material to Atlantic. The Instant album was called "Solid Gold" and was an anthology of hit records that Banashak had had over the decade on the Instant, Alon and Seven B labels featuring Art Neville, Lee Dorsey, Chris Kenner, Roger and the Gypsies, the Pitter Pats, Aaron Neville, the Stokes, Willie Harper and Raymond Lewis.

The sleeve-notes by Greg Mason, the dee-jay with WNOE, showed a great awareness that New Orleans artists had benefitted very little in terms of financial gain or publicity from "the unique sound that is New Orleans" and with indignity wrote: "It is jarring to hear listed as newcomers, names like Art Neville and Lee Dorsey. It is understandable that a song writer like Allen Toussaint might not be well known, even if Herman's Hermits ('A Certain Girl'), the

Rolling Stones ('Fortune Teller') and numerous other British groups had recorded much of his material. And admittedly Chris Kenner might be a strange name to some, even though his own original versions of 'Land Of 1,000 Dances' and 'I Like It Like That' were giants in R & B circles, before they became giants in the pop world when later redone by Cannibal & the Headhunters and the Dave Clark Five. But to dig these established greats as NEW artists!''

Quite clearly, the age of cover versions had not ended in the mid-1950's but in fairness these were not true covers since they were not competing with the original recordings. And the royalties from these new recordings should have ended in the pockets of the New Orleans writers.

The "Solid Gold" album did not sell too well mainly because it was released just as there was a wholesale change towards stereo recordings, real or rechannelled, and almost overnight mono recordings went out, sadly, like a light. Instant soldiered on and in 1972 the label appeared to recharge its batteries and a steady flow of recordings came from Lee Bates, Sam Alcorn and James "Skip" Easterling who had a magnificent version of Willie Mabon's "I Don't Know."

Noted for his gambling exploits on the local racetracks, Joe Banashak seems to have brought the same "hit or miss" tactics to his little record company. He does not think he will get rich through Instant, but remains some sort of optimist, otherwise he would have given up. But he does consider part of the trouble has been the long distance which separates New Orleans from the central recording axis of Hollywood, Nashville and New York. "If I had my time over again," he said, "I would be willing to start by working in New York for five years with no pay, just so that I could get the necessary experience in the business." Joe Banashak has had his moments in New Orleans but they should have been bigger, for him, his artists, and the music of the city.

Sansu Enterprises

Everyone in New Orleans is looking to Sansu Enterprises, and its partners Allen Toussaint and Marshall Sehorn, to bring the city out of its musical doldrums. Like Instant, it is one of the few survivors from the dark days of the late 1960's which Lawrence Cotton described as "very pitiful, man." But unlike Instant, Sansu is going from strength to strength and is already making its presence felt, not only in New Orleans but in the music industry at large where it matters. Toussaint and Sehorn first got together way back in 1965.

"I went to Allen's house and asked if he would do the arrangements for Lee Dorsey for me," said Marshall Sehorn. "I had a couple of silly songs, not that I was trying to capitalise on 'Ya Ya' or 'Do-Re-Mi' or nothing, I just thought at that particular time 'Shortnin' Bread' could be done up like 'Shotgun' which Junior Walker had out at the time. And 'The Kitty Cat Song' which was a very nice easy novelty. Then I told Allen, I said, 'If there's anything else you feel you want to do, feel free, do three or four songs, what about it?' And he wrote 'Ride Your Pony' and 'Work Work Work.' So we went into the studio and 'Ride Your Pony' came out the 'A' side which was like a mother. So I took it to New York and placed it with Larry Uttal of Bell Records. And Allen's discussion and mine, we more or less let each other know that we would like to venture into a partnership with each other. But nobody said, 'Hey, you want a partnership?' The atmosphere was there, so when the record hit, the record was a big hit and Lee was appearing at the Apollo, I called Allen, and I asked him if he would come up and work with Lee on stage because I felt we needed him. So he said, fine, he wanted to come to New York anyway. So one night after the Apollo, Allen and I was on our way back downtown and I asked at that time what was his plans for the future, what was he gonna do. And he mentioned to me, he said, well, he mentioned once before something about partnership, if it was still open I got eyes for it. So the next day we talked over lunch and talked . . . Paul Marshall of New York was my attorney at the time, so Paul started the paper work. September of 1965 we had a partnership together which we incorporated right away, and started Marsaint Music, a division of Sansu. Later on Marsaint was incorporated along with Rhinelander Music which I'd had for years prior to Marsaint, but I just brought it all in to the fold of Sansu. Allen has been a great inspiration to me, more or less we've come to know each other like a hand in a glove."

"Marshall's a very good promotion man," said Allen Toussaint, "a go-getter, a really fine promotion man, rapport personified all the way, really on the case, which I thought was very good, and in me he recognised the music thing. We had worked together a little before, like Lee Dorsey and Bobby Marchan when Marshall was on Fire and Fury, so he was sort of familiar with what I did and I was sorta familiar with what he did. And also he's an honest man, really heavy, and that saves a whole lot of headaches, even second thoughts and decisions. So we went on into it to form Sansu and form a record company and go all the way as far as we could possibly go."

LEE DORSEY (2)

"Ride Your Pony" started the new partnership off on the right footing, and started a purple patch for Lee Dorsey which lasted through 1966 and included international hits with "Get Out Of My Life Woman," "Working In The Coalmine" and "Holy Cow." It was Dorsey's fresh and happy approach which appealed, and although he was unable to keep up the remarkable chain of hit parade successes his records retained a certain warmth and zest in tunes like "Confusion," "Go-Go Girl" and "Wonder Woman."

By 1970, Lee Dorsey's natural happy singles had fallen out of favour and when his contract was taken up by Polydor, Allen Toussaint tried a "concept" power-to-the-people type album called "Yes We Can." Musically it came off well but it was not picked up by the serious white market at which it was aimed and did not sell. Maybe the message bit had been overdone by then anyway, but perhaps it was not Lee Dorsey's bag in the first place. "Lee Dorsey is a corner-bar type dude," said Al Reed, "you gotta give him corner-bar type music. How the hell you gonna dress up a man in a tuxedo to go to a corner-bar, he's out of place, and that's what they're doing with Lee, he's out of place right now. Because Lee is funky, listen to Lee's voice, he has the twang, he has the nasal sound, you can listen to him and tell this is a ghetto kid, this is a ghetto cat."

BETTY HARRIS

Lee Dorsey's Sansu recordings were released on Amy, a subsidiary of Bell, and it was Betty Harris who had the first hit on the Sansu label, with the soul ballad, "Nearer To You" in August 1967. It was the only hit for her and the label. It must be said that her Sansu records deserved better for sides like "What A Sad Feeling," "Bad Luck," "What'd I Do Wrong," "Trouble With My Lover" and "I'm Evil Tonight" were top quality uptown soul with a strong blues influence. Toussaint's productions were near perfect and his piano was often exceptional even by his own high standards with plenty of "those weird harp-like glissandos."

Betty Harris had scored previously with "Cry To Me" on Jubilee in 1963 and on this record she showed all her assets of control and timing which enabled her to become immersed in every song she performed and prepared her for her artistic peak with Allen Toussaint and Sansu.

The early years for Sansu were bitty and Lee Dorsey apart, success was not easy to come by. Toussaint and Sehorn suffered an early set-back when their Deesu label which had good records by Maurice Williams, Wilbert Harrison, Willie West and Warren Lee went down with Dover Records who distributed the label. Allen Toussaint's hit touch was also eluding him with his Sansu label artists which included Curley Moore, Benny Spellman, Diamond Joe and Al Fayala but he came good with the Meters. He had not sold over thirty million records for nothing.

THE METERS

The Meters comprise of Art Neville, the veteran musician on organ, Leo Nocentelli, guitar, George Porter, bass-guitar, and Joseph "Zigaboo" Modeliste, drums, and they hit it big in 1969 when "Sophisticated Cissy," "Cissy Strut," "Ease Back" and "Look-ka Py Py" were all instrumental hits on the Josie label in the Sly and the Family Stone modern funky soul bag.

"The Meters were a big hit in the late 1960's," said Allen Toussaint, "they were very fresh and well rounded off, and Art Neville, the organ player, has an awful lot to do with it even though the Meters is not an organ player plus some sidemen, the Meters is a group. It was a very fresh approach to some same old same-o, as far as we really know, but it was a fresh approach. The Meters are the highlights of the last three years."

"We started the Nitecap," said Art Neville, "we stayed there about two years and we had the biggest following in the city, the Nitecap is on Louisiana Avenue and Carondolet. It's still one of the hottest spots in the city right now as far as R & B goes. It's jumped around different managers, it was at one time a white club. What happened was this was where we got the music together, we had a thing where we were playing in between a jazz thing because we did a lot of jazz, because most of the cats wanted to play jazz, we thought this was happening. I don't want to take all the credit for it, we did it together, we got together, came up with the funky thing. We've been together almost seven years, the same personnel, you know.

"We left the Nitecap and we wound up in the French Quarter at the Ivanhoe, it was the Ivanhoe piano bar, with shirts and ties, you know, choked up all evening. It really wasn't the Meters then, it was Art Neville and the Neville Sounds. And so after talking to Allen Toussaint and Marshall Sehorn we finally got a chance to record as session men.

"They listened to us, I figure just about a year, every now and then and sit down, they wouldn't say nothing about recording. And so one day when we were still doing background work for them we were doing something in the studio and we decided to try to cut some tracks on the group, we had some dispute over what name we were going to use afterwards, so we came up with the name the Meters. Something everybody, it would be an easy name to remember. We did 'Sophisticated Cissy,' that was the dance going on in New Orleans, then we came up with this thing 'Cissy Strut' and that tune just went up, that did it. And we've been trying to get a hit ever since!

"We were nominated twice by 'Record World,' one year we were the 'No. 1 Most Promising Instrumental Group.' A lot of people were trying to compare us with Booker T. and the MG's at the time, but . . . I know myself, the organ, I always did it like Booker T., so you possibly will hear a little small flavour but I play technically wrong unlike Jimmy Smith, but I'm listening for effect, I'm playing for a certain type of effect. Everything we've done so far, it just co-ordinates together. It's what I would call organised freedom. You got four different ideas but the four different ideas all seem to work together. That what it boils down to, the Meters."

ALLEN TOUSSAINT (3)

Since 1970, Allen Toussaint has wisely concentrated on the booming album market but to date none of them, by Lee Dorsey, Ernie K-Doe or the Meters (whose "Cabbage Alley" album was expected to do better than it did) have clicked in a big way. At the same time he has tried to turn himself into a solo album performer.

He was signed by Scepter Records of New York in June 1970 and a good selling single, "From A Whisper To A Scream," was released on the Tiffany label. A beautiful album, "Toussaint," was put on the market and an engaging selection of vocals and piano instrumentals showed that there was plenty of room for an artist of this calibre. Whilst the New Orleans Sound was not too prominent the music was good enough to defy any artificial barriers created by narrow definitions. You could call it "easy listening soul," perhaps, but it was a great start. Allen Toussaint was not happy, though. "It was cases of undecision, misrepresentation, and nobody else's fault but my own," he said. Certainly the next album on Warner Brothers "Life Love and Faith" was a let-down which came nowhere near the standard of the Scepter release. It's easy to say that Allen Toussaint cannot record himself, that he knows only how to express himself through others. But he is a genius and he will come through in his own right.

"Time is beginning to catch up on Allen," said Marshall

Sehorn. "When I say time, maybe he's catching up with time. I would prefer saying though that Allen is now getting the recognition he's well overdue for. I would say that one of the factors that brought that about was his affiliation with the Band when he did 'Life Is A Carnival' and when he did the horn arrangements for the live albums they cut in New York, 'Rock Of Ages.' Paul Simon, he's now just finished doing cuts for Paul Simon. He's the golden touch of the golden idol, all of a sudden for the hip white set. He's been here all the time, he's been nowhere, people didn't bother to find out he was. We won't go into that, but I would say personally from me, he's the most talented man I've ever known."

Sansu Records, 1973

"I've been trying to put my house in order," continued Marshall Sehorn, "that's why I've never had any hits. The only records we really put out were the Meter records. Now when Jubilee went bankrupt I haven't had a hit with Warner Brothers since I've been with them. I don't think it's because they haven't had hits on the album, I don't think you can say 'Cabbage Alley' is not a hit, if it's released today it's not a hit. After a while you take notice of yourself, try to put your house in order, and you ask yourself is it really me, is it the record company, is it the artist? We haven't put that many records out in the last few years. The singles market there's been very little, the LP market, the only two albums really that's been out has been the Allen Toussaint album and the Meters album on Warner Brothers.

"Allen took off, did the things with the Band and a couple of other things, and I'm glad to see it because, you know, you can become depressed if the things you're doing aren't being heard or maybe it's the direction you're going in. But somebody likes what we're doing, like I made the statement yesterday, we made more money in the last three years without a hit than we did with the three years with a hit. And that's hard to believe but we have. So it's not always what's on top of the 100 that makes a company's success. Catalogue product, publishing catalogue, tunes that they put in LP's and singles, putting together the Rhinelander catalogue with Chappell was a great help. The Marsaint catalogue with Warner Brothers Music was a great help and we just borrowed $350,000 from the Bank to build a studio. We've got all the equipment together, we've got everything now."

New Orleans in the Future

"Well, you can say I'm bragging about it, but I think we're the forerunner of the New Orleans Sound. I think we've picked the wheel up and we're turning it, or we're turning it as fast as getting it. The only thing now, the wheel will probably get out of hand in about two years because I expect every major record company to be here, to be affiliated with some producer, or open some office, kinda like in Memphis and Muscle Shoals. I'm looking for it to be bigger than Muscle Shoals, as big as the Memphis music scene or even bigger." So continued Marshall Sehorn.

"Because first of all, there is a lot of new money coming in the city, not just music money, a lot of new money. You see the reason why New Orleans hasn't got off the ground before is because the loudasses that made all the money out of the business didn't put any back. They built their own houses, they own big cars and played racehorses with it. Never put anything back into it to make it grow. We have, the city, if it wasn't for outside money the new dome stadium wouldn't be built. All these high-rise buildings you see down in New Orleans, that came about since I was here in 1965. And since I moved here the city has taken on a new skyline and it all comes from Texas oil money. And if that be the case then we have, let's say a year from now, if we are successful, I won't say very, with this studio, you know that some oil man isn't gonna let us make all this money. He ain't gonna let me and Allen sit here across town and have no competition, 'cos he's gonna have money to piss up a wild hog's ass. So he's gonna build another, he's gonna get in the record business, like in Memphis, people going into the record business up there, lawyers and doctors put up the money, a lot of the studios built up there come from doctors' and lawyers' money, get rich fast scheme, that's what they thought. To me that's what gonna make New Orleans be a major record centre. If Nashville only had three studios Nashville wouldn't be shit, but the mere fact they have about twenty studios in Nashville, it brought musicians in from all over the world. Nashville musicians, there ain't a person living in Nashville that was born in Nashville that's a musician. He's either from Shreveport, Lubbock (Texas), Dallas (Texas), Houston (Texas), El Paso, Oklahoma or somewhere in California or somewhere in New Jersey or West Virginia.

"New Orleans, we've got a better start than Nashville had when they started. We have the basic roots, all we gotta do is to get these young kids out here in these high schools a chance to explode, give 'em a chance to be seen, someone to hear their material, someone to introduce their songs. It's gotta happen.

"Another thing, what's gonna make this city happen is for us to quit being so damn picky, and when I say we, I feel as if I'm a New Orleanian now, my company's not that way, but the city as a whole has taken this attitude. 'Well, this dude don't know too much about what I'm doing,' nobody wants to help each other here, nobody wants to go out of their way to help anybody either. There was this organisation a while back, everybody argued about what it was gonna do for them, nobody said whatever it's gonna do for me, what is it gonna do for the city. If it didn't mean nothing to them personally, they didn't want no part of it. It's always been that here. 'If you can't put no money in my pocket, to hell with you.' And that's what's been the matter, it's always been the matter around here."

Things are looking brighter again in New Orleans, there are decent studio facilities at last, and the economy of the city is booming. But stubborn attitudes do need changing including those of the local radio stations, and also the club owners.

LOCAL RADIO

"In order for the artists to record again," said Earl King, "it's gotta be put in the people's ear if they do have a product. Because it happens every time here, the King Floyd, the dee-jays here talk about it, it'll flop. Like they start to pick it up after it's bust open in the rural areas. And that happens every trip. Like you can count on it, every local record that takes off, it creates a problem before it can take off around here. The Aaron Neville, 'Tell It Like It Is,' they had a problem but it took off, the dee-jays didn't want to play it, and all this kind of jazz. We get a lot of dee-jays here today that come here just to rip off the producers, writers, artists whatever. They're not concerned with the music or the heritage of New Orleans or anything like that. One thing they never talk about is the dee-jay personality when New Orleans was real hot. We had an image and we had a white market that was broad, we had personalities like Ken Elliott—Jack The Cat, Herb Holiday, Jim Stewart, Poppa Stoppa, we had James 'Okey Dokey' Smith, that was about it on the black side, the rest of the radio stations we didn't need them, that was enough there. But this was the power structure we had, so then it dropped down to just one radio station that would play some local recordings because you would get the Top 40 stations, who said there's no local stuff we can play because we programmed our computer. They'd say, 'We'd be glad to play it,' but they didn't. That's another feature that declined our market, it may not seem like much, but man, it all adds up. So the question of recording some of the local artists again and do they have a chance, well, they have a chance if they can be heard. Everything we do we know it can't be a winner, we understand that, but the things that have materialised around here, we have so much problems at the birth of it, and it makes you wonder and say, 'Man, it happens every time.'

"So that is one of the situations that we are plagued with, I think it all sums up to personalities because this is the cause behind a lot of conflict, 'cos personal hang-ups, people motivated by certain desires and they want to throw their weight around just to be doing something, not knowing they are really hurting the people, the artists involved, and the market in general.

"Let me give you another example, 'Mr Big Stuff' by Jean Knight, they had a little problem with people wanting to play that, they say, "Aw that's another local record, I don't know. I'm afraid to touch it.' If you miss one time you're in trouble because they say I thought the other one you had was good and it didn't happen, it didn't happen so now you're hung up. You walk in there with your artist's record, and you say, 'Well, I got a new one,' and they say, 'Man, I don't know when I'll be able to do you any good, you know, local.' "

THE REVIVAL AND THE CLUB OWNERS

"I think there is going to be a big revival," said Deacon John, "I can feel it coming. A lot of the British groups are trying to get into the New Orleans Sound, like Savoy Brown, they got a R & B sound, Led Zeppelin, they got a few things reminiscent of New Orleans, the Rolling Stones came down here and taped the whole thing. I know what they're gonna do, they're gonna go home and study it, they're gonna have a new album that sounds like New Orleans. They're gonna take all the money and New Orleans is still gonna be here. . . . 'It's a nice place to be', that's what the musicians say who come away. When they leave and they go away, people say, 'He's from New Orleans, woo, man, we've heard all about that shit, you must be terrible, you must be making all kinds of money down there,' and when they come down here and live down here, they split too.

"There are just so many groups that will play for nothing, it's getting a bigger and bigger problem every day. The club owners, he can get a group for under $100 which is under scale, and the new groups coming out sound good, lot of equipment, managers, and they work cheap. And the club owners will say, 'We'll keep this group, damn your Deacon John, he charges too much. He's in the Union (laugh), boy, that Union ought to make some money.' You've a few serious club owners but they're hard to find.

"The only salvation you've got is to get a hit record. If not a hit record, something that will keep you in the limelight long enough so you can make a killing and retire or something. Something like that. You have to keep pushin', keep on tryin'. Maybe one day you'll get a Cadillac, some shit, . . . you get a Cadillac, a road manager who charges you 10 per cent, the agency charges you 20 per cent, the system man charges you another 10 per cent, the Union charges you 3 per cent and 7 per cent for your pension fund, your lawyer charges you 5 per cent, so actually you come out winding up making only about one-third of what you are actually getting. I finally realised this, you've got to have astronomical figures just to come out with something. It almost seems impossible. It just seems you're never gonna get there."

THE YOUNG MUSICIANS

Considering the New Orleans music scene has been dormant more or less since the mid-1960's, it was amazing to find so many established artists and musicians playing at the Louisiana Heritage Festival in April 1973. Men like Professor Longhair, Deacon John, Earl King, the Meters, Ernie K-Doe, Tommy Ridgley, Red Tyler, Willie Tee, James Rivers, Frank Fields, Chuck Badie, Edward Frank, George Davis, George French, Robert French. With talented people like this, and there are so many more, the decline in New Orleans' fortunes is hard to believe; on the other hand, the material is there, ready and waiting, for the imminent revival.

For this revival to sustain its impetus, the young musicians must carry on the musical traditions. Of course, they will all start out with big rosy stars in their eyes. "Man, we'll meet the right people, the man with the big cigar saying 'I'm gonna make you a star'," laughed Deacon John, " 'Buy you a Cadillac, fighting the girls off,' you know it's all dope and pussy, that money, you think, 'Oh man, that's the life.' It's not really like that. Even if you're the Rolling Stones. But I just hope New Orleans will keep producing musicians, if that ever stops it will be dead around here. New Orleans has got this strange mystique about it, the kids come up surrounded by parades, music, all kinds of extravaganza, they got parades, parades, Mardi Gras, it's orientated towards entertainment; there are strong religious roots in New Orleans, the musicians that come up in these surroundings, they've just got to be better. It's not always true though, because they're born, not made. But your environment has a whole lot to do with it, how you're gonna lay it on, you know."

Allen Toussaint delivered a timely warning when he said, "If New Orleans isn't careful there will be no New Orleans music, and if we're not careful on how we look at it now, there might not be. At one time you could really say that New Orleans music, you would really know what you were talking about, but as things grew, like music being a child and getting to be a teenager, it grows up like everything else does, and there is a certain innocence that goes away with it. The young musicians coming up, well, there are always young musicians coming up and filling in spaces where the older guys get out, but I find lately that since the field has been so crowded that the young guys coming up are not even pursuing what New Orleans meant to music. I think they're, like, buying music from elsewhere and accepting what has been endorsed by a whole lot of people, like certain things are born and they grow up in New York. What happens? I find that lately if you refer to New Orleans music I find you have to relate back to 'then' as opposed to 'now.' New Orleans is taking a nap or something, going to sleep a little, which is sort of detrimental. And if this contribution to music by New Orleans is not constantly reinforced at home, it will vanish after a while. But in all the music that I hear there are still the strong origins there, there is still a New Orleans music and we will hear a rejuvenation of it.''

Jumpin', Dancin', Carryin' On

"The only thing I can hope for and I believe will happen," Marshall Sehorn finally said, "is that other people will become aware and as conscious as Allen and myself are of New Orleans music, the sound, there's nothing like it in the world. You can go anywhere you want to, there's no music like New Orleans music, there's no other singers like New Orleans singers, there's no other people like New Orleans people. Nobody else has as good a time as we do, nobody else shakes their ass as much as we do, and that's everybody, everybody from old to young, black and white, Indians, jumpin', dancin', carryin' on and having a good time. And that's what it's all about, that's what this city is all about."

Soon, very soon, everybody will come back, Walking to New Orleans.

New Orleans — 1978 by Tad Jones

By 1978 some predictions we made in 1974 have come to pass, while others have faltered. Who has succeeded or failed is not important. The musical elements which functioned in the social subconscious now operate on a conscious level. As one musician put it, "New Orleans is listening to itself again."

"Cash Box" and *"Billboard"* too often measure success by ratings and sales figures. New Orleans in the last few years has produced few "hits." Allen Toussaint and Marshall Sehorn's Sea-Saint Recording Studio, opened January 1974, has brought much notoriety to the city. Paul McCartney, John Mayall, LaBelle, King Biscuit Boy, and Frankie Miller have all had varying degrees of success with Sea-Saint productions. The studio produced two regional hits by the Meters: "Hey Paka Way" (1974) and "They All Asked For You" (1975). Singer Tony Owens scored with "The Letter That Broke My Heart" (Island) and Robert "Barefootin'" Parker gained moderate exposure with his "Give Me the Country Life." Texas guitarist and vocalist Jon Fouse's composition "Tuesday Morning" brought a bright bouncey New Orleans style Mardi Gras tune to the local airways. The Wild Tchoupitoulas, James Booker, Earl King, and Willie Tee have released LPs in the last year, and even Fats Domino returned to Cosimo's studio on Camp Street to cut a few tracks (not yet released). More New Orleans artists are being recorded today than ever before.

It is radio which gives records the proper exposure, and local stations are generally unresponsive to the needs of local artists. WNOE is the forerunner in helping local musicians by sponsoring weekly broadcasts of live concerts by local bands.

If any music is to survive it must have an involved audience, not one of just listeners. The club revival, with more musicians producing more music than ever before, has sparked this renewed interest. It inspired the return of Earl King and the Rhapsodizers, the city's popular funk rhythm dance group. James Booker and Jessie Hill have returned home from the West Coast. Others performing periodically are Eddie Bo, Bobby Mitchell, and The Dixie Cups. Professor Longhair, nearing sixty, is playing some of the most inspiring piano sets ever.

The trends for music in the city seem more positive than ever. As one drummer put it, "This music ain't nothin' but a party and if the people are right we can play all night."

Appendix

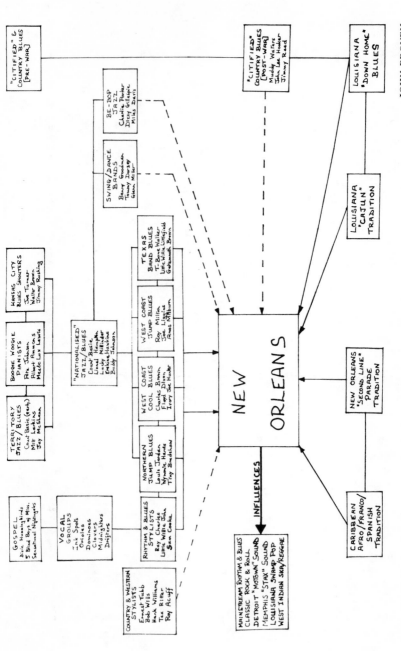

"CITIFIED" & COUNTRY BLUES [PRE-WAR]

"CITIFIED" COUNTRY BLUES [POST-WAR]
Muddy Waters
Little Walter
Jimmy Reed

LOUISIANA "DOWN HOME" BLUES

BE-BOP JAZZ
Charlie Parker
Dizzy Gillespie
Miles Davis

SWING/DANCE BANDS
Benny Goodman
Tommy Dorsey
Glenn Miller

KANSAS CITY BLUES SHOUTERS
Joe Turner
Walter Brown
Jimmy Rushing

BOOGIE WOOGIE PIANISTS
Pete Johnson
Albert Ammons
Meade Lux Lewis

TERRITORY JAZZ/BLUES
Count Basie (early)
Milt Larkin
Jay McShann

"NATIONALISED" JAZZ/BLUES
Count Basie
Lionel Hampton
Lucky Millinder
Erskine Hawkins
Buddy Johnson

TEXAS BAND BLUES
T-Bone Walker
Little Willie Littlefield
Goldsmith Brown

WEST COAST JUMP BLUES
Roy Milton
Joe Liggins
Amos Milburn

WEST COAST COOL BLUES
Charles Brown
Floyd Dixon
Ivory Joe Hunter

NORTHERN JUMP BLUES
Louis Jordan
Wynonie Harris
Tiny Bradshaw

GOSPEL
Dixie Hummingbirds
5 Blind Boys of Miss.
Sensational Nightingales

VOCAL GROUPS
Ink Spots
Orioles
Dominoes
Clovers
Midnighters
Drifters

RHYTHM & BLUES STYLISTS
Ray Charles
Little Willie John
Sam Cooke

COUNTRY & WESTERN STYLISTS
Ernest Tubb
Bob Wills
Hank Williams
Tex Ritter
Roy Acuff

LOUISIANA "CAJUN" TRADITION

NEW ORLEANS

NEW ORLEANS "SECOND LINE" PARADE TRADITION

CARIBBEAN AFRO/FRANCO/ SPANISH TRADITION

INFLUENCES

MAINSTREAM RHYTHM & BLUES
CLASSIC ROCK & ROLL
DETROIT "MOTOWN" SOUND
MEMPHIS "STAX" SOUND
LOUISIANA SWAMP POP
WEST INDIAN SKA/REGGAE

JOHN BROVEN
BOB TRICK

REFERENCES

The following Books, Articles and Magazines were consulted for reference purposes:

BOOKS

Louis Armstrong, *Satchmo*, Prentice Hall, 1954.
Carl Belz, *The Story Of Rock*, Oxford Univ., N.Y., 1969.
Mark T. Carleton, *Politics And Punishment*, Louisiana State Univ., 1971.
Samuel B. Charters, *Jazz New Orleans 1885–1963*, Oak, 1963.
Charlie Gillett, *The Sound Of The City*, Outerbridge & Dienstfrey, 1970.
John Godrich and Robert M. W. Dixon, *Blues And Gospel Records 1902–42*, Storyville, 1969.
John Godrich and Robert M. W. Dixon, *Recording The Blues*, Studio Vista, 1970.
Karl Gert zur Heide, *Deep South Piano*, Studio Vista, 1970.
Tony Heilbut, *The Gospel Sound*, Simon and Schuster, 1970.
Mike Leadbitter and Neil Slaven, *Blues Records 1943–1966*, Hanover, 1968.
Mike Leadbitter (Ed.), *Nothing But The Blues*, Hanover, 1971.
John Lester, *I'll Take New Orleans*, Adams, 1971.
A. J. Liebling, *The Earl Of Louisiana*, Louisiana State Univ., 1970.
Alan Lomax, *Mister Jelly Roll*, Duell, Sloan and Pearce, 1950.
Bill Millar, *The Drifters*, Studio Vista, 1971.
Joseph Murrells, *Daily Mail Book Of Golden Discs*, McWhirter, 1966.
Paul Oliver, *Blues Fell This Morning*, Cassell, 1959.
Paul Oliver, *The Story Of The Blues*, Barrie & Rockliff, 1969.
Frederic Ramsey, Jr., *Been Here And Gone*, Rutgers, 1960.
Lyle Saxon, Edward Dreyer and Robert Tallant, *Gumbo Ya-Ya*, Louisiana Library, 1945/Bonanza.
Tom Stagg and Charlie Crump, *New Orleans, The Revival*, Bashall Eaves, 1973.
Marshall Stearns, *The Story Of Jazz*, Oxford University, 1956.
Robert Tallant, *Voodoo In New Orleans*, Collier, 1962.
Joel Whitburn, *Record Research*, Joel Whitburn, 1970.
Graham Wood, *An A–Z Of Rock And Roll*, Studio Vista, 1971.
Various, *1972 Country Music's Who's Who*, Record World, 1972.
Various, *Rhythm And Blues 1943–68*, BMI, 1969.

ARTICLES

John Abbey, *Behind The Scenes With Harold Battiste*, Blues & Soul, 1971.

John Abbey, *Behind The Scenes With Johnny Vincent*, Blues & Soul, 1971.

John Abbey, *Betty Harris*, Blues & Soul, 1969.

John Abbey and Jonas Bernholm, *Aaron Neville*, Blues & Soul, 1970.

Jonas Bernholm, *Don't Pity Me—The Curley Moore Story*, Shout, 1971.

Jonas Bernholm, *Huey "Piano" Smith*, Shout, 1971.

Robert A. "Bumps" Blackwell, *The Discovery Of Little Richard*, Penniman News, 1968.

Derek Brandon, *Alvin Robinson*, Soul Music Monthly, 1967.

John Broven, *Behind The Sun Again*, Blues Unlimited, 1973.

John Broven, *I Like It Like That (Chris Kenner)*, Melody Maker, 1973.

Brian G. Chambers, *The Return Of Frankie Ford*, Rockpile, 1971.

Timothy Cruse, *Resurrecting New Orleans—The Gulf Coast Originals Never Left Home*, Rolling Stone, 1972.

Tony Cummings, *Lee Dorsey—The Ya Ya Man*, Soul Music Monthly, 1966.

Garry George, *Jessie Hill: The Ooh-Poo Pah Doo Man*, Cash Box, 1972.

Charlie Gillett, *All For One: A Study In Frustration And Black Organisation*, Cream (U.K.), 1971.

Don Heckman, *Five Decades Of R & B*, BMI, 1969.

Lee Hildebrand, *Irma Thomas*, R & B Magazine, 1970.

James La Rocca, *Polka Dot Slim*, Blues Unlimited, 1970.

Steve La Vere, *Papa Lightfoot*, Blues Unlimited, 1969.

Mike Leadbitter and John Broven, *Behind The Sun*, Blues Unlimited, 1970.

Bill Millar, *Robert Parker*, Soul Music Monthly, 1967.

Rick Milne, *Johnny Vincent*, Blues Unlimited, 1969.

Tom Stagg, *Alonzo Stewart, The Baby Of The Band*, Footnote, 1972.

Charles Suhor, *New Jazz In The Cradle*, Downbeat, 1961.

Steve Tracey, *King Of The Blues (Henry Glover)*, Blues Unlimited, 1971.

Art Turco, *Bobby Robinson*, Record Exchanger, 1972.

Mike Vernon, *Clarence Henry*, Soul Music Monthly, 1967.

Mike Vernon, *Here Comes Smiley (Lewis)*, Jazz Monthly, 1967.

Mike Vernon, *The Domino Men*, Jazz Monthly, 1967.

Gil Webre, *I Like To Make Records (Fats Domino)*, Times Picayune, 1958.

Jerry Wexler and Ahmet Ertegun, *The Latest Trend: R & B Disks Are Going Pop*, Cash Box, 1954.

Richard Williams, *The Dr John Story—Talkin' 'Bout New Orleans*, Melody Maker, 1972.

Valerie Wilmer, *Dynamite (James) Rivers*, Melody Maker, 1972.

Writer not known, *Ernie K-Doe At 35, Rock's Old Man*, Figaro, 1972.

Writer not known, *Shy But Allen (Toussaint) Is Real Smooth*, R & B World, 1968.

MAGAZINES

The following magazines have been consulted frequently:

Billboard, 2160, Patterson Street, Cincinnatti, Ohio, 45214, U.S.A.

Blues & Soul, 42, Hanway Street, London W1P 9DE, U.K.

Blues Research, 65, Grand Avenue, Brooklyn, New York, 11205, U.S.A.

Blues Unlimited, 38a, Sackville Road, Bexhill-on-Sea, Sussex, U.K.

Cash Box, 1780, Broadway, New York, 10019, U.S.A.

Footnote, Flat 3, 37 High Street, Cherryhinton, Cambridge, U.K.

Jazz Journal, 27, Willow Vale, London W12 0PA, U.K.

Let It Rock, 4, Mill Street, London, W.1, U.K.

Shout, 46, Slades Drive, Chislehurst, Kent, BR7 6JX, U.K.

Storyville, 63, Orford Road, London E17 9NJ, U.K.

Also:

Jazz Monthly, *R & B Monthly* and *Soul Music Monthly* which, sadly, are published no longer.

OTHER SOURCES

Specialty Label Singles Listing, 1946–64, Terence Courtney and Mike Leadbitter.

The Imperial and Aladdin Files, courtesy of Steve La Vere and Mike Leadbitter.

United States Travel Service brochures.

Aquarius (Mardi Gras), Humphrey Burton, ITA, December 1972.

The Philpott File—Topsville, Bottomsville, Trevor Philpott, BBC-tv, May 1972.

SONG CREDITS

Extracts from the following songs have been quoted in the text and acknowledgment is given for permission to reprint material in this book. Any inadvertent omission will be corrected in future printings if notification is sent to the publisher.

Always A First Time, *E. King*, Travis.
Before I Grow Too Old, *R. Guidry*, *A. Domino*, *D. Bartholomew*, Travis.
Carnival Time, *D. Johnson*, *J. Ruffino*, Ron.
Don't You Just Know It, *H. Smith*, *J. Vincent*, Ace.
Down Home Girl, *J. Leiber*, *A. Butler*, Trio.
Go To The Mardi Gras, *R. Byrd*, *T. Terry*, Ron.
Land Of 1,000 Dances, *C. Kenner*, Tune Kel—Anatole.
New Orleans Twist, *P. King*, *D. Bartholomew*, *W. Quezergue*, Travis.
Now Let's Popeye, *D. Johnson*, Ron.
Sea Cruise, *H. Smith*, Ace.
Single Life, *B. Tate*, *D. Bartholomew*, Commodore.
The Place (New Orleans), *K. Smith*, *C. Pawfeth*, Counterpart.
Trick Bag, *E. King*, Travis.
Walking To New Orleans, *A. Domino*, *D. Barthblomew*, *R. Guidry*, Travis.
Ya Ya, *L. Dorsey*, *B. Robinson*, Fast & Barich.

All publishers are affiliated to BMI.

BIOGRAPHICAL DATA

Everyone listed was born in New Orleans, except where noted. This list has no pretence to completeness.

Justin Adams, 1923.
Lee Allen, *Pittsburgh, Kansas*, July 2, 1926.
Archibald (Leon Gross), September 14, 1912–January 1973.
Dave Bartholomew, *Edgard, La.*, December 24, 1920.
James Black, 1939.
James "Little" Booker, December 17, 1939.
Clarence "Juny Boy" Brown, June 10, 1940.
Roy Brown, September 10, 1925.
Bobby Charles (Robert Guidry), *Abbeville, La.*, 1938.
Erving Charles, Jr., 1941.
Jimmy Clanton, *Baton Rouge, La.*, September 2, 1940.
Cornelius Coleman, July 5, 1929–February 1973.
Cousin Joe (Pleasant Joseph), *Wallace, La.*, December 21, 1907.
Wallace Davenport, June 30, 1925.
Deacon John (Moore), June 21, 1941.
Antoine "Fats" Domino, February 26, 1928.
Lee Dorsey, December 24, 1926.

Jack Dupree, July 4, 1910.
Fird (Ford) "Snooks" Eaglin, January 21, 1936.
Frank Fields, *Plaquemine, La.*, May 2, 1914.
Clarence Ford, December 1929.
Frankie Ford, *Gretna, La.*, August 4, 1940.
Paul Gayten, *Kentwood, La.*, January 29, 1920.
Barbara George, August 16, 1942.
Shirley Goodman, 1938.
Guitar Slim (Eddie Jones), *Greenwood, Miss.*, December 10, 1926–
    1959.
Robert Hagans, *Bogalusa, La.*, December 18, 1922.
Clarence Henry, March 19, 1937.
Ernie K-Doe (Kador), 1936.
Chris Kenner, *Kenner, La.*, December 25, 1929.
Earl King (Silas Johnson), February 6, 1934.
Smiley Lewis (Overton Amos Lemons), *Union, La.* July 5, 1920–
Cosimo Matassa, April 13, 1926.   Oct. 7, 1966.
Roy Montrell, February 27, 1928.
Curley Moore, June 1943.
Aaron Neville, 1941.
Art Neville, 1937.
Robert Parker, October 14, 1930.
Nat Perrilliat, November 29, 1936–1972.
Polka Dot Slim (Monroe Vincent), *Woodsville, Miss.*, December 9,
    1919.
Lloyd Price, March 9, 1934.
Professor Longhair (Roy Byrd), *Bogalusa, La.*, December 19, 1918.
Mac Rebennack (Dr John), 1940.
James Rivers, 1937.
Alvin Robinson, December 22, 1937.
Huey Smith, January 26, 1934.
Willie Tee (Turbinton), February 6, 1944.
Irma Thomas, *Pontachoula, La.*, 1941.
Allen Toussaint, 1938.
Earl Turbinton, September 23, 1941.
Alvin Tyler, December 5, 1925.
Harrison Verrett, *Napoleonville, La.*, February 27, 1909–*c.*1963.

THE MAJOR NEW ORLEANS R & B BANDS

This list of the better known New Orleans R & B bands is given
in the knowledge that the personnels for live performances tended
to be somewhat elastic, and is intended as a guide only.

DAVE BARTHOLOMEW

1946   Dave Bartholomew, *vocal and trumpet*; Meyer Kennedy, *alto*; Clarence Hall, *tenor*; Fred Lane, *piano*; Frank Fields, *bass*; Dave Oxley, *drums*.

1950   Dave Bartholomew, *vocal and trumpet*; Joe Harris, *alto*; Clarence Hall, Alvin "Red" Tyler, Herb Hardesty, *tenors*; Salvador Doucette, *piano*; Ernest McLean, *guitar*; Frank Fields, *bass*; Earl Palmer, *drums*.

1961   Dave Bartholomew, *vocal and trumpet*; Meyer Kennedy, *alto*; Clarence Hall, Warren Payne, *tenors*; James Booker, *piano*; George Davis, *guitar*; George French, *bass-guitar*; Robert French, *drums*.

1973   Dave Bartholomew, *vocal and trumpet*; Warren Payne, *tenor*; Lawrence Cotton, *organ*; Justin Adams, *guitar*; Richard Payne, *bass*; Albert "June" Gardner, *drums*.

EDGAR BLANCHARD & THE GONDOLIERS

1959–60 Edgar Blanchard, *vocal and guitar*; August "Dimes" Dupont, *alto*; Warren Hebrew, *tenor*; Lawrence Cotton, *piano*; Frank Fields, *bass*; Alonzo Stewart, *vocal and drums*.

SUGAR BOY & HIS CANE CUTTERS

1957   James "Sugar Boy" Crawford, *vocal and piano*; Leroy "Batman" Rankin, *tenor*; Edgar "Big Boy" Myles, *trombone*; Billy Tate, *guitar*; Frank Fields, *bass*; Chester Jones, *drums*.

FATS DOMINO

1950   Antoine "Fats" Domino, *vocal and piano*; Wendell Duconge, *alto*; Robert "Buddy" Hagans, *tenor*; Harrison Verrett, *guitar*; Billy Diamond, *bass*; Cornelius "Tenoo" Coleman, *drums*.

1960   Fats Domino, *vocal and piano*; Herb Hardesty, Robert Hagans, Lee Allen, *tenors*; Clarence Ford, *baritone*; Walter "Papoose" Nelson, *guitar*; Jimmie Davies, *bass-guitar*; Cornelius Coleman, *drums*.

1967   Fats Domino, *vocal and piano*; Herb Hardesty, Nat Perrilliat, Robert Hagans, *tenors*; Clarence Ford, Walter Kimball, *baritones*; Wallace Davenport, *trumpet*; Roy Montrell, *guitar*; Jimmie Davis, *bass-guitar*; Clarence "Juny Boy" Brown, *drums*.

1973   Fats Domino, *vocal and piano*; Frederick Kemp, Walter Kimball, Maurice Simon, *tenors*; Roger Lewis, *baritone*; Roy Montrell, *guitar*; Dave Douglas, *guitar and bass-guitar*; Clarence Brown, *drums*.

PAUL GAYTEN

1946   Paul Gayten, *vocal and piano*; Jack Scott, *guitar*; George H. Pryor, *bass*; Robert Green, *drums*.

1954   Paul Gayten, *vocal and piano*; Lee Allen, *tenor*; Jack Willis, *trumpet*; Waldren "Frog" Joseph, *trombone*; Frank Fields, *bass*; Frankie Parker, *drums*.

CLARENCE "FROGMAN" HENRY

1957   Clarence Henry, *vocal and piano*; Eddie Smith, *tenor*; Walter Epps, *guitar*; Eugene Jones, *drums*.

1973   Clarence Henry, *vocal*; Clarence Ford, Charles Burbank, *tenors*; Warren "Jake" Myles, *piano*; Erving Charles, Jr, *bass-guitar*; Nolan Coleman, *drums*.

JOE JONES

1960   Joe Jones, *vocal*; Harold Battiste, *tenor*; Theodore Riley, *trumpet*; Reggie Hall, *piano*; Roy Montrell, *guitar*; Acy Fairman, *bass*; Leo Morris, *drums*.

LLOYD LAMBERT (with Guitar Slim)

1955–58 Lloyd Lambert, *bass*; Joe Tillman, Gus Fontennette, *tenors*; John Girard, *trumpet*; Lawrence Cotton, *piano*; Oscar Moore, *drums*.

PROFESSOR LONGHAIR

1952   Roy "Professor Longhair" Byrd, *vocal and piano*; Robert Parker, *tenor*; Walter Nelson, *guitar*; John Boudreaux, *drums*.

TOMMY RIDGLEY & THE UNTOUCHABLES

1957–65 Tommy Ridgley, *vocal and piano*; Lawrence Marinot, Charles Burbank, *tenors*; Dalton Rousseaux, *trumpet*; Justin Adams, *guitar*; Tommy Shelvin, *bass-guitar*; *unknown drums*.

THE ROYAL DUKES OF RHYTHM

1963–66 James Rivers, Robert Parker, *tenors*; Wardell Quezergue, Emery Thompson, *trumpets*; Edward Frank, *piano*; George

Davis, *guitar*; George French, *bass-guitar*; Joe "Smokey" Johnson, *drums*.

N.B. For special shows, this band sometimes used eleven horns plus shakers.

HUEY SMITH

1954   Huey "Piano" Smith, *piano*; Earl King, *vocal*; Robert "Catman" Caffrey, *tenor*; "Blind" Billy Tate, *vocal and guitar*; Roland Cook, *bass-guitar*; Charles "Hungry" Williams, *drums*.

1958   Huey Smith, *piano*; Robert Parker, Rufus "Nose" Gore, Walter Kimball, *tenors*; James "Little" Booker, *piano and organ*; Raymond Lewis, *bass-guitar*; Jessie Hill, *drums*.

ALVIN "RED" TYLER

1961   Alvin Tyler, *tenor*; Tami Lynn, *vocal*; Emile Vernette, *piano*; Peter "Chuck" Badie, *bass*; Smokey Johnson, *drums*.

1973   Alvin Tyler, *tenor*; Germaine Basile, *vocal*; Edward Frank, *electric piano*; Chuck Badie, *bass*; Cornelius Bass, *drums*.

THE BEST SELLING NEW ORLEANS SINGLES 1946–72

This is a compilation of hit singles by artists from and closely connected with New Orleans. Again, the differential between "*Billboard's*" R & B charts and then the "Hot 100" as from November 1955 should be borne in mind.

Artist	Label	Highest Position	First month of entry
JOHNNY ADAMS			
Release Me	*SSS International 750*	82	December 1968
Reconsider Me	*SSS International 770*	28	June 1969
I Can't Be All Bad	*SSS International 780*	89	October 1969
LEE ALLEN AND HIS BAND			
Walkin' With Mr Lee	*Ember 1027*	54	January 1958
Tic Toc	*Ember 1039*	92	October 1958
ELTON ANDERSON			
Secret Of Love	*Mercury 71542*	88	January 1960
ARCHIBALD			
Stack-A-Lee	*Imperial 5068*	10	June 1950

Artist	Label	Highest Position	First month of entry
JOE BARRY			
I'm A Fool To Care	*Smash 1702*	24	April 1961
Teardrops In My Heart	*Smash 1710*	63	August 1961
EDDIE BO			
Hook And Sling (Part 1)	*Scram 117*	73	August 1969
JAMES BOOKER			
Gonzo	*Peacock 1697*	43	November 1960
ROY BROWN			
† Good Rockin' Tonight	*De Luxe 3093*	‡	June 1948 and April 1949
Long About Midnight	*De Luxe 3154*	‡	October 1948
Rainy Weather Blues	*De Luxe 3189*	‡	January 1949
Rockin' At Midnight	*De Luxe 3212*	‡	March 1949
Please Don't Go	*De Luxe 3226*	‡	September 1949
† Boogie At Midnight	*De Luxe 3300*	3	November 1949
† Hard Luck Blues	*De Luxe 3304*	1	July 1950
† Love Don't Love Nobody	*De Luxe 3306*	2	September 1950
Long About Sundown	*De Luxe 3308*	6	October 1950
Big Town	*De Luxe 3318*	8	August 1951
Bar Room Blues	*De Luxe 3319*	‡	December 1951
Party Doll	*Imperial 5427*	89	April 1957
Let The Four Winds Blow	*Imperial 5439*	38	June 1957
IKE CLANTON			
Down The Aisle	*Ace 583*	91	May 1960
Sugar Plum	*Mercury 71975*	95	August 1962
JIMMY CLANTON			
†*Just A Dream	*Ace 546*	4	July 1958
*A Letter To An Angel	*Ace 551*	25	October 1958
A Part Of Me	*Ace 551*	38	November 1958
My Own True Love	*Ace 567*	33	August 1959
Go, Jimmy, Go	*Ace 575*	5	November 1959
Another Sleepless Night	*Ace 585*	22	May 1960
Come Back	*Ace 600*	63	August 1960
Wait	*Ace 600*	91	October 1960
What Am I Gonna Do	*Ace 607*	50	January 1961
Venus In Blue Jeans	*Ace 8001*	7	August 1962
Darkest Street In Town	*Ace 8005*	77	January 1963

Artist	Label	Highest Position	First month of entry
LARRY DARNELL			
I'll Get Along Somehow	Regal 3236	3	November 1949
†For You, My Love	Regal 3240	1	November 1949
I Love My Baby	Regal 3274	4	August 1950
Oh Babe	Regal 3298	5	November 1950
THE DIXIE CUPS			
*Chapel Of Love	Red Bird 10–001	1	May 1964
People Say	Red Bird 10–006	12	July 1964
You Should Have Seen The Way He Looked At Me	Red Bird 10–012	39	October 1964
Little Bell	Red Bird 10–017	51	December 1964
Iko Iko	Red Bird 10–024	20	April 1965
FATS DOMINO			
†*The Fat Man	Imperial 5058	6	April 1950
†Every Night About This Time	Imperial 5099	5	December 1950
Rockin' Chair	Imperial 5145	9	December 1951
†*Goin' Home	Imperial 5180	1	May 1952
How Long	Imperial 5209	9	December 1952
†*Goin' To The River	Imperial 5231	2	April 1953
†*Please Don't Leave Me	Imperial 5240	5	July 1953
Rosemary	Imperial 5251	10	October 1953
Something's Wrong	Imperial 5262	6	December 1953
You Done Me Wrong	Imperial 5272	10	April 1954
*Thinking Of You	Imperial 5323	‡	February 1955
Don't You Know	Imperial 5340	12	March 1955
†*Ain't That A Shame	Imperial 5348	86	May 1955
†*All By Myself	Imperial 5357	3	September 1955
†Poor Me	Imperial 5369	3	November 1955
†Don't Blame It On Me	Imperial 5375	6	February 1956
†*Bo Weevil	Imperial 5375	35	February 1956
†*I'm In Love Again	Imperial 5386	5	April 1956
My Blue Heaven	Imperial 5386	21	April 1956
When My Dreamboat Comes Home	Imperial 5396	22	July 1956
†So Long	Imperial 5396	44	July 1956
*Blueberry Hill	Imperial 5407	4	September 1956
†*Blue Monday	Imperial 5417	9	December 1956
What's The Reason I'm Not Pleasing You	Imperial 5417	50	January 1957

Artist	Label	Highest Position	First month of entry
†*I'm Walkin'	Imperial 5428	5	February 1957
†Valley Of Tears	Imperial 5442	13	May 1957
*It's You I Love	Imperial 5442	22	May 1957
When I See You	Imperial 5454	36	August 1957
What Will I Tell My Heart	Imperial 5454	64	August 1957
Wait And See	Imperial 5467	27	October 1957
*I Still Love You	Imperial 5467	79	October 1957
The Big Beat	Imperial 5477	36	December 1957
I Want You To Know	Imperial 5477	48	December 1957
Yes My Darling	Imperial 5492	55	March 1958
Sick And Tired	Imperial 5515	30	April 1958
No, No	Imperial 5515	55	April 1958
Little Mary	Imperial 5526	49	June 1958
Young School Girl	Imperial 5537	92	September 1958
*Whole Lotta Loving	Imperial 5553	6	November 1958
Coquette	Imperial 5553	92	November 1958
When The Saints Go Marching In	Imperial 5569	50	February 1959
Telling Lies	Imperial 5569	50	February 1959
I'm Ready	Imperial 5585	16	May 1959
Margie	Imperial 5585	51	May 1959
I'm Gonna Be A Wheel Some Day	Imperial 5606	17	August 1959
I Want To Walk You Home	Imperial 5606	8	August 1959
*Be My Guest	Imperial 5629	8	November 1959
I've Been Around	Imperial 5629	33	November 1959
Country Boy	Imperial 5645	25	February 1960
If You Need Me	Imperial 5645	98	February 1960
Tell Me That You Love Me	Imperial 5660	51	May 1960
Before I Grow Too Old	Imperial 5660	84	May 1960
*Walking To New Orleans	Imperial 5675	6	June 1960
*Don't Come Knockin'	Imperial 5675	21	July 1960
Three Nights A Week	Imperial 5687	15	September 1960
Put Your Arms Around Me Honey	Imperial 5687	58	September 1960
†My Girl Josephine	Imperial 5704	14	October 1960
Natural Born Lover	Imperial 5704	38	November 1960
What A Price	Imperial 5723	22	January 1961
Ain't That Just Like A Woman	Imperial 5723	33	January 1961

I

Artist	Label	*Highest Position*	*First month of Entry*
Shu Rah	*Imperial 5734*	32	March 1961
Fell In Love On Monday	*Imperial 5734*	32	March 1961
It Keeps Rainin'	*Imperial 5753*	23	May 1961
†Let The Four Winds Blow	*Imperial 5764*	15	July 1961
What A Party	*Imperial 5779*	22	October 1961
Rockin' Bicycle	*Imperial 5779*	83	October 1961
I Hear You Knocking	*Imperial 5796*	67	December 1961
Jambalaya	*Imperial 5796*	30	December 1961
You Win Again	*Imperial 5816*	22	February 1962
Ida Jane	*Imperial 5816*	90	March 1962
My Real Name	*Imperial 5833*	59	May 1962
Nothing New (Same Old Thing)	*Imperial 5863*	77	June 1962
Dance With Mr Domino	*Imperial 5863*	98	July 1962
Did You Ever See A Dream Walking	*Imperial 5875*	79	October 1962
There Goes My Heart Again	*ABC 10444*	59	May 1963
Red Sails In The Sunset	*ABC 10484*	35	September 1963
Who Cares	*ABC 10512*	63	January 1964
Lazy Lady	*ABC 10531*	86	February 1964
Sally Was A Good Old Girl	*ABC 10584*	99	September 1964
Heartbreak Hill	*ABC 10596*	99	October 1964
Lady Madonna	*Reprise 0763*	100	September 1968

* N.B. You Said You Loved Me, I Lived My Life (1952), Love Me, Don't Leave Me This Way (1953) were also certified million selling records.

LEE DORSEY

†*Ya Ya	*Fury 1053*	7	September 1961
Do-Re-Mi	*Fury 1056*	27	December 1961
Ride Your Pony	*Amy 927*	28	July 1965
Get Out Of My Life, Woman	*Amy 945*	44	January 1966
Working In The Coal Mine	*Amy 958*	8	July 1966
Holy Cow	*Amy 965*	23	October 1966
My Old Car	*Amy 987*	97	May 1967
Go-Go Girl	*Amy 998*	62	October 1967

Artist	Label	*Highest Position*	*First month of entry*
Everything I Do Gonna Be Funky	*Amy 11055*	95	June 1969
FRANKIE FORD			
*Sea Cruise	*Ace 554*	14	February 1959
Alimony	*Ace 566*	97	August 1959
Time After Time	*Ace 580*	75	January 1960
You Talk Too Much	*Imperial 5686*	87	October 1960
Seventeen	*Imperial 5735*	72	March 1961
PAUL GAYTEN (see also Annie Laurie)			
True	*De Luxe 1063*	‡	October 1947
Goodnight Irene	*Regal 3281*	‡	September 1950
Nervous Boogie	*Argo 5277*	68	November 1957
Windy	*Argo 5300*	78	July 1958
The Hunch	*Anna 1106*	68	November 1959
BARBARA GEORGE			
†I Know	*AFO 302*	3	November 1961
You Talk About Love	*AFO 304*	46	March 1962
Send For Me	*Sue 766*	96	September 1962
GUITAR SLIM			
†*The Things That I Used To Do	*Specialty 482*	1	December 1953
BETTY HARRIS			
Cry To Me	*Jubilee 5456*	23	September 1963
His Kiss	*Jubilee 5465*	89	January 1964
Nearer To You	*Sansu 466*	85	July 1967
CLARENCE (FROGMAN) HENRY			
†Ain't Got No Home	*Argo 5259*	30	December 1956
I Don't Know Why, But I Do	*Argo 5378*	4	February 1961
You Always Hurt The One You Love	*Argo 5388*	12	May 1961
Lonely Street	*Argo 5395*	57	August 1961
On Bended Knees	*Argo 5401*	64	November 1961
A Little Too Much	*Argo 5408*	77	January 1962
JESSIE HILL			
Ooh Poo Pah Doo (Part 1)	*Minit 607*	28	April 1960
Whip It On Me	*Minit 611*	91	July 1960

1*

Artist	Label	Highest Position	First month of entry
JIVIN' GENE			
Breakin' Up Is Hard To Do	*Mercury 71485*	69	September 1959
JOE JONES			
You Talk Too Much	*Roulette 4304*	3	September 1960
California Sun	*Roulette 4344*	89	April 1961
ERNIE K-DOE			
†Mother-In-Law	*Minit 623*	1	April 1961
Te-Ta-Te-Ta-Ta	*Minit 627*	53	July 1961
I Cried My Last Tear	*Minit 634*	69	November 1961
A Certain Girl	*Minit 634*	71	November 1961
Popeye Joe	*Minit 641*	99	February 1962
CHRIS KENNER			
†*I Like It Like That	*Instant 3229*	2	June 1961
†Land of 1,000 Dances	*Instant 3252*	77	June 1963
EARL KING			
Those Lonely, Lonely Nights	*Ace 509*	‡	August 1955
JEWEL KING			
†3 × 7 = 21	*Imperial 5055*	15	March 1950
KING FLOYD			
*Groove Me	*Chimneyville 435*	1	September 1970
Baby Let Me Kiss You	*Chimneyville 437*	29	March 1971
JEAN KNIGHT			
*Mr Big Stuff	*Stax 0088*	2	May 1971
You Think You're Hot Stuff	*Stax 0105*	57	late 1971
ANNIE LAURIE (with Paul Gayten—1)			
Since I Fell For You —1	*De Luxe 3082*	‡	October 1947
Cuttin' Out	*Regal 3235*	‡	December 1949
I'll Never Be Free—1	*Regal 3258*	8	April 1950
It Hurts To Be In Love	*De Luxe 6107*	61	June 1957
SMILEY LEWIS			
Bells Are Ringing	*Imperial 5194*	10	September 1952
†I Hear You Knocking	*Imperial 5356*	‡	March 1955

Artist	Label	Highest Position	First month of entry
LITTLE RICHARD			
†*Tutti Frutti	*Specialty 561*	21	December 1955
†Long Tall Sally	*Specialty 572*	13	March 1956
Slippin' And Slidin'	*Specialty 572*	33	April 1956
Rip It Up	*Specialty 579*	27	June 1956
†Ready Teddy	*Specialty 579*	44	June 1956
The Girl Can't Help It	*Specialty 591*	49	January 1957
Lucille	*Specialty 598*	27	March 1957
Send Me Some Lovin'	*Specialty 598*	54	March 1957
†Jenny, Jenny	*Specialty 606*	14	June 1957
Miss Ann	*Specialty 606*	56	June 1957
Keep A Knockin'	*Specialty 611*	8	September 1957
Good Golly Miss Molly	*Specialty 624*	10	February 1958
Ooh! My Soul	*Specialty 633*	35	May 1958
True, Fine Mama	*Specialty 633*	68	June 1958
Baby Face	*Specialty 645*	41	September 1958
Kansas City	*Specialty 664*	95	May 1959
Bama Lama Bama Loo	*Specialty 692*	82	July 1964
BARBARA LYNN			
†You'll Lose A Good Thing	*Jamie 1220*	8	June 1962
Second Fiddle Girl	*Jamie 1233*	63	September 1962
You're Gonna Need Me	*Jamie 1240*	65	December 1962
Don't Be Cruel	*Jamie 1244*	93	February 1963
(other hit records recorded outside of New Orleans)			
BOBBY MARCHAN			
There's Something On Your Mind	*Fire 1022*	31	June 1960
THE METERS			
Sophisticated Cissy	*Josie 1001*	34	February 1969
Cissy Strut	*Josie 1005*	23	April 1969
Ease Back	*Josie 1008*	61	July 1969
Look-ka Py Py	*Josie 1015*	56	December 1969
AARON NEVILLE			
†*Tell It Like It Is	*Parlo 101*	2	December 1966
She Took You For A Ride	*Parlo 103*	92	March 1967
ROBERT PARKER			
†*Barefootin'	*Nola 721*	7	April 1966
Tip Toe	*Nola 729*	83	January 1967

Artist	Label	Highest Position	First month of entry
LLOYD PRICE			
†*Lawdy Miss Clawdy	*Specialty 428*	1	May 1952
Restless Night	*Specialty 440*	5	October 1952
†Ain't It A Shame	*Specialty 447*	7	February 1953
†Just Because	*ABC 9792*	29	February 1957
Lonely Chair	*KRC 301*	88	September 1957
†*Stagger Lee	*ABC 9972*	1	December 1958
Where Were You (On Our Wedding Day)	*ABC 9997*	23	March 1959
†*Personality	*ABC 10018*	2	May 1959
†*I'm Gonna Get Married	*ABC 10032*	3	August 1959
†Come Into My Heart	*ABC 10062*	20	November 1959
Won't Cha Come Home	*ABC 10062*	43	November 1959
Lady Luck	*ABC 10075*	14	February 1960
Never Let Me Go	*ABC 10075*	82	March 1960
No If's—No And's	*ABC 10102*	40	May 1960
For Love	*ABC 10102*	43	May 1960
Question	*ABC 10123*	19	July 1960
Just Call Me	*ABC 10139*	79	September 1960
You Better Know What You're Doing	*ABC 10162*	90	December 1960
Misty	*Double L 722*	21	October 1963
Billie Baby	*Double L 729*	84	January 1964
PROFESSOR LONGHAIR (as Roy Byrd)			
Bald Head	*Mercury 8175*	5	August 1950
ALVIN ROBINSON			
Something You Got	*Tiger 104*	52	June 1964
SHIRLEY & LEE			
†I'm Gone	*Aladdin 3153*	2	December 1952
†Feel So Good	*Aladdin 3289*	‡	August 1955
†*Let The Good Times Roll	*Aladdin 3325*	27	August 1956
†I Feel Good	*Aladdin 3338*	38	December 1956
I've Been Loved Before	*Warwick 535*	88	July 1960
Let The Good Times Roll	*Warwick 581*	48	September 1960
Well-A, Well-A	*Warwick 664*	77	August 1961
THE SHOWMEN			
It Will Stand	*Minit 632*	61	November 1961
	Imperial 66033	80	and July 1964

Artist	Label	Highest Position	First month of entry
HUEY SMITH AND THE CLOWNS			
*Rocking Pneumonia And The Boogie Woogie Flu	Ace 530	52	August 1957
*Don't You Just Know It	Ace 545	9	March 1958
Don't You Know Yockomo	Ace 553	56	December 1958
Pop-Eye	Ace 649	51	February 1962
BENNY SPELLMAN			
Lipstick Traces	Minit 644	80	May 1962
THE SPIDERS			
†I Didn't Want To Do It	Imperial 5265	3	February 1954
IRMA THOMAS			
†Wish Someone Would Care	Imperial 66013	17	March 1964
Anyone Who Knows What Love Is	Imperial 66041	52	July 1964
Times Have Changed	Imperial 66069	98	November 1964
He's My Guy	Imperial 66080	63	December 1964

* Million selling records.
† BMI Award Winners.
‡ Information not to hand.

Material originally published by *"Billboard"* magazine in their R & B and Hot 100 Charts.

Data assembled from Joel Whitburn's *"Record Research"*, Bill Daniel's *"Dusty Charts"* (*Record Exchanger*) and *"R & B Hits"* (*Golden Memories*).

Information regarding million selling records obtained from Joseph Murrells's *"Daily Mail Book Of Golden Discs."*

ALBUM DISCOGRAPHY

New Orleans was basically a singles market and these records have been fully described in the text. The list which follows is comprised of the more important albums, most of which are compilations of singles releases anyway. Regrettably a lot of the albums are deleted and hard to find. (U.K. catalogue numbers are listed in *italics*.)

JOHNNY ADAMS, *"Heart & Soul,"* SSS International 5.

His early R & B and later soul sides placed together in one good album.

JIMMY BEASLEY, *"Twist With . . .,"* Crown LP 5247.
An excellent Fats Domino-type set of the 1950's.

ROY BROWN, *"Hard Luck Blues,"* King KS 1130.
The early, influential De Luxe and King sides.

BOBBY CHARLES, Bearsville BR 2104.
An uneven recent album, which has its moments and received heavy critical acclaim.

FATS DOMINO
The Fats Domino Story Vol. 1-6, United Artists (1977 release).
Rare Dominos Vols. 1 & 2, Liberty LBL 83174; United Artists UAS 29152.
Domino '65 (Live At Las Vegas), Mercury 20070 MCL; *Philips 6336 217.*
Fats is Back, Reprise RS 6304; *Valiant VS 107.*
The list of Fats Domino albums is daunting. The Imperials, all of them, are the true mouthpiece of New Orleans R & B. The ABC and Reprise sets fall slightly short but the Mercury "live" album captures the band in supreme form.

LEE DORSEY
The Best of . . ., Sue ILP 924.
The Best of . . ., Regal Starline, SRS 5023.
Yes We Can, Polydor 244042; *Polydor 2489 006.*
The early Fury sides make up most of the Sue release, and the Amy sides form the basis of the Regal Starline budget album. Both have more musical merit than often credited with. "Yes We Can" is a more serious, concept-type record.

DR JOHN
Gris Gris, Atco 234; *Atlantic 588 147.*
Gumbo, Atco SD 7006; *Atlantic K 40384.*
In the Right Place, Atco 7018; *Atlantic K 50017.*
These three albums really comprise the chief works of the Dr John phenomenon to date.

JACK DUPREE, *Blues From the Gutter,* Atlantic 8019; *London LTZ-K 15171.*
A classic album recorded in New York but with the New Orleans roots still showing strongly through.

SNOOKS EAGLIN
That's All Right, Bluesville BVLP 1046
Blues From New Orleans Vol. I, Folkways FA 2476; *Storyville SLP 119.*
> Snooks dressed up in his famed folk-blues outfit, although his R & B still remains in the vaults.

GUITAR SLIM, *The Things That I Used to Do,* Specialty SPS 2120.
> Apart from his first New Orleans sessions, Guitar Slim never captured his true self on record again, and it shows.

BETTY HARRIS, *Soul Perfection, Action ACLP 6007.*
> Betty Harris as singer and Allen Toussaint as producer seem to bring out the best of each other on this brilliant set of Sansu recordings.

CLARENCE (FROGMAN) HENRY
You Always Hurt The One You Love, Argo LP 4009; *Pye Int. NPL 28017.*
Is Alive and Well, Roulette SR 42039.
> Two good representative albums of Frogman's output.

JOE JONES, *You Talk Too Much,* Roulette R 25143.
> Typical New Orleans music of the late 1950's and early 1960's with Domino-like vocals and incomparable band support.

ERNIE K-DOE, Minit LP 24002.
> His early Minit sides and including his biggest hits from "Mother-In-Law" on down.

CHRIS KENNER, *Land of 1,000 Dances* Atlantic 8117; *Atlantic 587 008.*
> His early Instant singles and all the hits. Great.

SMILEY LEWIS
I Hear You Knocking, Imperial LP 9141.
Shame Shame Shame, Liberty LBS 83308.
> A major New Orleans artist and these albums tell you why.

LITTLE RICHARD, *Grooviest 17 Original Hits,* Specialty SPS 2113.
> All his important rock 'n ' roll hits which show just how much the New Orleans Sound contributed to his success.

THE METERS
Look-ka Py Py, Josie 4011.
Cabbage Alley, Reprise MS 2076; *K 44242.*
The updated funky New Orleans soul sound.

AARON NEVILLE
Tell It Like It Is, Parlo I.
Like It Is, Minit LP 40007; *Liberty LBY 3089.*
Nothing else touches the hit single on the Parlo set, whilst the massive hit induced the re-issue of his fine Minit sides.

EARL PALMER, *Drumsville, Liberty LRP 3201.*
An easy listening rework of a few rock 'n' roll hits, just enough of his drumming filters through to show just why he is so highly rated in New Orleans and on the West Coast.

ROBERT PARKER, *Barefootin',* Nola 1001; *Island ILP 942.*
New Orleans R & B joins forces with soul in a appetizing set.

WALTER "FATS" PICHON, *Appearing Nightly at The Old Absinthe House,* Decca DL 8380; *Brunswick LAT 8181.*
Typical night club cocktail music.

LLOYD PRICE
Lloyd Price, Specialty SP 2105; *Sonet SNTF 5007.*
The Best of . . ., Regal Starline SRS 5025.
The Specialty shows how strong his New Orleans roots were, whilst the ABC collection on Regal is better than expected.

PROFESSOR LONGHAIR, *New Orleans Piano,* Atlantic SD 7225; *K 40402.*
The only album of ventage recordings presently available by the legendary master of New Orleans rock 'n' roll.

TOMMY RIDGLEY
The New King of the Stroll, Flyright LP 519
Engaging selection of his early sixties Ric recordings.

SHIRLEY & LEE
Legendary Masters (double album) United Artists
UA-LA069-G2
Comprehensive collection of their influential Aladdin recordings. Strong stuff.

HUEY SMITH & THE CLOWNS
Huey "Piano" Smith And The Clowns, Sue ILP 917.
Havin' A Good Time, Ace LP 1004.
For Dancing, Ace LP 1015.
'Twas The Night Before Christmas, Ace LP 1027.
Rock & Roll Revival!, Ace 2021.
　　Simply essential (if you can get them).

ALLEN TOUSSAINT
Wild Sounds of New Orleans, RCA Victor LPM 1767.
Toussaint, Tiffany 014; *Wand 14.*
Life Love and Faith, Reprise MS 2062.
　　The instrumental RCA album included the later million selling hit, *"Java"* (by Al Hirt). *"Toussaint"* is a very fine but the more recent album on Reprise does not really do justice to the man's undoubted talents.

WEE WILLIE WAYNE, *Travellin' Mood,* Imperial LP 9144.
　　Relaxed city blues with strong Texas influence dating from the early 1950's.

ANTHOLOGIES
New Orleans Bounce Vol. 1-New Orleans R & B, Liberty (Japan) LLS-70076 (Dave Bartholomew, Jewel King, Bobby Mitchell, Hawks, Roy Brown, Sugar Boy Crawford, Chris Kenner, Al Robinson, Boogie Jake.)

New Orleans Bounce Vol. 2-New Orleans Guitarists, Liberty (Japan) LLS-70077
(Earl King, Smiley Lewis, Billy Tate, Jesse Allen.)

New Orleans Bounce Vol. 3-New Orleans Boogie & Blues, Liberty (Japan) LLS-70078
(Archibald, Tommy Ridgley.)

New Orleans Bounce Vol. 4-New Orleans Soul of Ages, Liberty (Japan) LLS 70080.
(Irma Thomas, Del Royals, Ernie K-Doe, Eskew Reeder, Diamond Joe, the Showmen.)
Superb collections of great and rare material from Imperial and Minit.

Dr. John and His New Orleans Congregation, Ace 2020.
(Big Boy Myles, Mac Rebennack, Ronnie Baron, Roland Stone, Joe Tex, Earl King, Bobby Marchan, Lee Dorsey). Mixed but entertaining selection for the Ace/Vin/Rex catalogues.

Solid Gold, Instant LP 71000
>(Art Neville, Lee Dorsey, Chris Kenner, Roger & the Gypsies, the Pitter Pats, Aaron Neville, the Stokes, Willie Harper, Raymond Lewis.)
>The best sellers from Joe Banashak's group of labels, Instant, Alon and Seven B.

New Orleans, Sonet SNTF 5021.
>(includes Lloyd Price, Guitar Slim, Art Neville, Jerry Byrne, Ernie K-Doe, Roy Montrell, Lil Millet, Earl King.)
>Very representative album of Specialty's excursions to New Orleans.

INDEX OF NAMES

P denotes photograph(s).